Christmas

Taste of Home
BOOKS

RDA ENTHUSIAST BRANDS, LLC
MILWAUKEE, WI

Contents

GET SOCIAL WITH US!

f LIKE US
facebook.com/tasteofhome

P PIN US
pinterest.com/taste_of_home

O FOLLOW US
@tasteofhome

t TWEET US
twitter.com/tasteofhome

To find a recipe
tasteofhome.com
To submit a recipe
tasteofhome.com/submit
**To find out about other
Taste of Home products**
shop.tasteofhome.com

Taste of Home

© 2022 RDA Enthusiast Brands, LLC.
1610 N. 2nd St., Suite 102, Milwaukee WI
53212-3906

International Standard Book Number:
D 978-1-62145-750-3
U 978-1-62145-751-0
International Standard Serial Number:
1948-8386
Component Number:
D 119600104H
U 119600106H

Executive Editor: Mark Hagen
Senior Art Director: Raeann Thompson
Editor: Hazel Wheaton
Art Director: Maggie Conners
Designer: Arielle Anttonen
Deputy Editor, Copy Desk: Dulcie Shoener

Cover:
Photographer: Dan Roberts
Food Stylist: Josh Rink
Set Stylist: Melissa Franco

Pictured on front cover:
Cranberry Cake Roll, p. 56

Pictured on back cover:
Beef Wellington with Madeira Sauce,
p. 47; Chocolate-Dipped Cranberry
Cookies, p. 201; Buttery Herb Christmas
Tree, p. 136

Holly illustration:
Shutterstock/Leigh Prather

Printed in U.S.A.
1 3 5 7 9 10 8 6 4 2

Bring your loved ones together with Taste of Home Christmas

1. TAPAS & WINE
Your holiday cocktail party will become a masterpiece with a spread of dishes rich in Spanish and Mediterranean flavors.

2. HOLIDAY BASH ON A BUDGET
Make the most of budget-friendly ingredients to throw a pull-out-the-stops holiday dinner party even if you're watching your dollars.

3. HOLIDAY FEASTS
At the center of the holiday celebration is a magnificent meal that will create wonderful memories. Here are three menus built around classic entrees—Beef Wellington, turkey and pork loin—plus a la carte extras to help you set your own unforgettable table.

4. NEW SPINS ON HOLIDAY SIDES
Bring new life to traditional seasonal favorites like green bean casserole, cranberry sauce, mashed potatoes and more.

5. HOLIDAY DESSERT HACKS & HOW TO'S
This collection of recipes comes with sweet bites of advice, clever kitchen tricks and photos to help you pull off stunning desserts.

6. SNOWED IN: ROMANTIC CHRISTMAS FOR TWO
Yes, a holiday shared between just two people can be every bit as special as a feast. This year, enjoy a delicious and memorable small-scale meal perfect for two.

7. SEASONAL GET-TOGETHERS
Here are the perfect menus to go with three parties: a kid-friendly bash, an adults-only brunch, and a casual gathering with seasonal comfort food for the whole family.

8. GRANDMAS'S FAVORITE CHRISTMAS RECIPES
These mouthwatering recipes have a classic, old-fashioned appeal that proves they belong right on Grandma's big dining table!

9. ROLLS, BISCUITS & MORE
Festive baked goods—sweet and savory, quick breads and double-rise yeast breads—will complete your menu in style.

10. CHRISTMAS LIGHTS
Eating healthy doesn't mean sacrificing taste, especially during the holidays. Look here for a temptingly delicious lineup of special-occasion recipes that are so full of flavor, no one will realize they're eating light!

11. DIPPED & DRIZZLED COOKIES
Christmas cookies are divine, but those that are dipped or drizzled are twice as fine! Each of these recipes takes an already scrumptious cookie and adds a special finishing touch.

12. BARKS, BRITTLES & CANDIES
These tempting sweets make the perfect holiday gifts for co-workers, neighbors and friends—whether around the corner or miles away.

13. CRUNCH TIME GIFTS
Despite careful planning, you may need a last-minute gift, and need it fast. Don't panic—all these crunchy, tasty treats can be made in your kitchen in an afternoon!

14. HOLIDAY PLANNER
This handy guide will help you keep your preparations for your holiday celebrations on track, preserve your special memories of the season—and help you plan for next year!

TAPAS & WINE

Make your holiday party a masterpiece with a spread of dishes rich with Spanish and Mediterranean flavors. Tapas are traditionally served as small plates, so your guests can try them all!

ONION BRIE APPETIZERS

Guests will think you spent hours preparing these cute appetizers, but they're really easy to assemble. The tasty combination of Brie, caramelized onions and caraway is terrific.

—Carole Resnick, Cleveland, OH

PREP: 25 min. + chilling • **BAKE:** 15 min.
MAKES: 1½ dozen

- 2 medium onions, thinly sliced
- 3 Tbsp. butter
- 2 Tbsp. brown sugar
- ½ tsp. white wine vinegar
- 1 sheet frozen puff pastry, thawed
- 4 oz. Brie cheese, rind removed, softened
- 1 to 2 tsp. caraway seeds
- 1 large egg
- 2 tsp. water

1. In a large skillet, cook the onions, butter, brown sugar and vinegar over medium-low heat until onions are golden brown, stirring frequently. Remove with a slotted spoon; cool to room temperature.

2. On a lightly floured surface, roll the puff pastry into an 11x8-in. rectangle. Cut Brie into thin slices; distribute evenly over pastry. Cover with the onions; sprinkle with caraway seeds.

3. Roll up 1 long side to the middle of the dough; roll up the other side so the 2 rolls meet in the center. Using a serrated knife, cut crosswise into ½-in. slices. Place on parchment-lined baking sheets; flatten to ¼-in. thickness. Refrigerate for 15 minutes.

4. In a small bowl, beat egg and water; brush over slices. Bake at 375° until puffed and golden brown, 12-14 minutes. Serve warm.

1 APPETIZER: *121 cal., 8g fat (3g sat. fat), 23mg chol., 109mg sod., 11g carb. (3g sugars, 1g fiber), 3g pro.*

MARINATED OLIVES

These olives are nice to have for get-togethers because they're simple to make and they add a little zest to the buffet table offerings.
—Marguerite Shaeffer, Sewell, NJ

PREP: 10 min. + marinating • **MAKES:** 4 cups

- 2 cups large pimiento-stuffed olives, drained
- 1 cup pitted kalamata olives, drained
- 1 cup pitted medium ripe olives, drained
- ¼ cup olive oil
- 2 Tbsp. lemon juice
- 1 Tbsp. minced fresh thyme or 1 tsp. dried thyme
- 2 tsp. minced fresh rosemary or ½ tsp. dried rosemary, crushed
- 2 tsp. grated lemon zest
- 4 garlic cloves, slivered
  Pepper to taste

Place olives in a bowl. Combine the remaining ingredients; pour over olives and stir. Cover and refrigerate for 1-2 days before serving, stirring several times each day. Serve with a slotted spoon. Olives may be refrigerated for up to 2 weeks.
¼ CUP: 98 cal., 10g fat (1g sat. fat), 0 chol., 572mg sod., 3g carb. (0 sugars, 0 fiber), 0 pro.

RISOTTO BALLS (ARANCINI)

My Italian grandma made these for me. I still ask for them when I visit her, and so do my children. They freeze well, too.
—Gretchen Whelan, San Francisco, CA

PREP: 35 min. • **BAKE:** 25 min. • **MAKES:** about 3 dozen

- 1½ cups water
- 1 cup uncooked arborio rice
- 1 tsp. salt
- 2 large eggs, lightly beaten
- ⅔ cup sun-dried tomato pesto
- 2 cups panko bread crumbs, divided
  Marinara sauce, warmed

1. Preheat oven to 375°. In a large saucepan, combine water, rice and salt; bring to a boil. Reduce heat; simmer, covered, until liquid is absorbed and the rice is tender, 18-20 minutes. Let stand, covered, 10 minutes. Transfer to a large bowl; cool slightly. Add eggs and pesto; stir in 1 cup bread crumbs.
2. Place remaining 1 cup bread crumbs in a shallow bowl. Shape rice mixture into 1¼-in. balls. Roll in crumbs, patting to help coating adhere. Place on greased 15x10x1-in. baking pans. Bake until golden brown, 25-30 minutes. Serve with marinara sauce.
1 APPETIZER: 42 cal., 1g fat (0 sat. fat), 10mg chol., 125mg sod., 7g carb. (1g sugars, 0 fiber), 1g pro.
DIABETIC EXCHANGES: ½ starch.

GOAT CHEESE SPREAD IN ROASTED PEPPER CUPS

I had a similar dish in a restaurant in Seattle, and I just had to try making it. This is the result, and it's fantastic! I've taken it to work for parties and my boss once commented, "It's so good, it must be illegal!"
—Jenny Rodriquez, Pasco, WA

- -

PREP: 25 min. • **BAKE:** 40 min.
MAKES: 8 servings

- 4 medium sweet orange or red peppers
- 3 Tbsp. olive oil, divided
- 1 medium onion, finely chopped
- 4 garlic cloves, minced
- 1 pkg. (8 oz.) cream cheese, softened
- 8 oz. fresh goat cheese, softened
- 1 cup grated Parmesan cheese
- 2 to 3 medium tomatoes, seeded and finely chopped
- 2 Tbsp. minced fresh cilantro
- 1 Tbsp. minced fresh parsley
- ½ tsp. hot pepper sauce
- ⅛ tsp. salt
- ⅛ tsp. pepper

HERBED GARLIC TOASTS
- ½ cup butter, softened
- 1 Tbsp. minced fresh parsley
- 2 garlic cloves, minced
- 24 slices French bread baguette (¼ in. thick)

1. Remove tops and seeds from peppers; rub peppers with 1 Tbsp. oil. Place in an ungreased 8-in. square baking dish. Bake, uncovered, at 350° for 15-20 minutes. Remove from oven; turn peppers upside down in baking dish to drain.
2. In a small skillet, saute onion in the remaining 2 Tbsp. oil until tender. Add garlic; cook 1 minute longer. Transfer to a large bowl. Stir in the cheeses, tomatoes, cilantro, parsley, pepper sauce, salt and pepper. Spoon into pepper cups.
3. Return peppers to baking dish, and return baking dish to oven. Bake, uncovered, at 350° until heated through, 25-30 minutes.
4. Meanwhile, for the garlic toasts, in a small bowl, combine the butter, parsley and garlic; spread over baguette slices. Place on an ungreased baking sheet. Bake until lightly browned, 25-30 minutes. Serve with cheese spread.

½ **CUP SPREAD WITH 3 TOASTS:** *445 cal., 35g fat (19g sat. fat), 89mg chol., 583mg sod., 23g carb. (5g sugars, 3g fiber), 12g pro.*

ZESTY MEDITERRANEAN POTATO SALAD

Light, fresh and just a touch spicy, this salad is perfect for a get-together with friends and family. The flavors have a wonderful Mediterranean feel you can pull together any time of year.
—Terri Crandall, Gardnerville, NV

- -

PREP: 25 min. • **COOK:** 15 min. + chilling
MAKES: 8 servings

- 4 large Yukon Gold potatoes, peeled and cubed
- 1½ tsp. salt, divided
- ½ cup olive oil
- ¼ cup lemon juice
- ½ tsp. pepper
- ⅛ tsp. crushed red pepper flakes
- 1 medium sweet red pepper, finely chopped
- ½ small red onion, finely chopped
- ⅓ cup Greek olives, pitted and chopped
- 4 bacon strips, cooked and crumbled
- ½ cup crumbled feta cheese
- ¼ cup loosely packed basil leaves, torn

1. Place potatoes in a large saucepan; add water to cover. Add 1 tsp. salt. Bring to a boil. Reduce heat; cook, uncovered, until tender, 8-10 minutes. Drain and place in a large bowl.
2. In a small bowl, whisk olive oil, lemon juice, remaining ½ tsp. salt, pepper and red pepper flakes until blended. Spoon over the potato mixture; toss to coat. Refrigerate salad, covered, until chilled, about 1 hour.
3. Just before serving, add sweet red pepper, onion, olives and bacon to potatoes. Sprinkle with feta and basil.

¾ **CUP:** *341 cal., 18g fat (3g sat. fat), 8mg chol., 685mg sod., 40g carb. (4g sugars, 3g fiber), 6g pro.*

PROSCIUTTO-WRAPPED ASPARAGUS WITH RASPBERRY SAUCE

Grilling the prosciutto with the asparagus gives this appetizer a salty crunch that's perfect for dipping into a sweet glaze. When a delicious appetizer is this easy to prepare, you owe it to yourself to try it!
—Noelle Myers, Grand Forks, ND

TAKES: 30 min. • **MAKES:** 16 appetizers

⅓ lb. thinly sliced prosciutto or deli ham
16 fresh asparagus spears, trimmed
½ cup seedless raspberry jam
2 Tbsp. balsamic vinegar

1. Cut prosciutto slices in half. Wrap a prosciutto slice around each asparagus spear; secure ends with toothpicks.
2. Heat oiled grill pan or large skillet over medium-high heat. Grill asparagus until the prosciutto is crisp, turning once, 6-8 minutes. Discard toothpicks.
3. In a small microwave-safe bowl, combine jam and vinegar; microwave on high for 15-20 seconds or until jam is melted. Serve with asparagus.
1 ASPARAGUS SPEAR WITH 1½ TSP. SAUCE: *50 cal., 1g fat (0 sat. fat), 8mg chol., 184mg sod., 7g carb. (7g sugars, 0 fiber), 3g pro.*
DIABETIC EXCHANGES: *½ starch.*

ROASTED EGGPLANT SPREAD

Black pepper and garlic perk up this out-of-the-ordinary spread that hits the spot on a crisp cracker or toasted bread slice.
—Barbara McCalley, Allison Park, PA

PREP: 20 min. • **BAKE:** 45 min. • **MAKES:** 2 cups

3 Tbsp. olive oil
3 garlic cloves, minced
½ tsp. salt
½ tsp. pepper
2 large sweet red peppers, cut into 1-in. pieces
1 medium eggplant, cut into 1-in. pieces
1 medium red onion, cut into 1-in. pieces
1 Tbsp. tomato paste
    Toasted baguette slices or assorted crackers

1. Preheat oven to 400°. Mix first 4 ingredients. Place vegetables in a large bowl; toss with oil mixture. Transfer to a 15x10x1-in. baking pan coated with cooking spray. Roast vegetables until softened and lightly browned, 45-50 minutes, stirring once.
2. Transfer to a food processor; cool slightly. Add tomato paste; pulse just until blended (mixture should be chunky). Transfer to a bowl; cool completely. Serve with baguette slices or crackers.
¼ CUP SPREAD: *84 cal., 5g fat (1g sat. fat), 0 chol., 153mg sod., 9g carb. (5g sugars, 3g fiber), 1g pro.*
DIABETIC EXCHANGES: *1 vegetable, 1 fat.*

PICKLED SHRIMP WITH BASIL

Red wine vinegar plus the freshness of citrus and basil perk up marinated shrimp with hardly any prep. Serve over greens if you'd like a salad.
—James Schend, Pleasant Prairie, WI

- -

PREP: 15 min. + marinating
MAKES: 20 servings

½ cup red wine vinegar
½ cup olive oil
2 tsp. seafood seasoning
2 tsp. stone-ground mustard
1 garlic clove, minced
2 lbs. peeled and deveined cooked shrimp (31-40 per lb.)
1 medium lemon, thinly sliced
1 medium lime, thinly sliced
½ medium red onion, thinly sliced
¼ cup thinly sliced fresh basil
2 Tbsp. capers, drained
¼ cup minced fresh basil
½ tsp. kosher salt
¼ tsp. coarsely ground pepper

1. In a large bowl, whisk the first 5 ingredients. Add shrimp, lemon, lime, onion, sliced basil and capers; toss gently to coat. Refrigerate, covered, for up to 8 hours, stirring occasionally.
2. Just before serving, stir minced basil, salt and pepper into shrimp mixture. Serve with a slotted spoon.
½ CUP: 64 cal., 2g fat (0 sat. fat), 69mg chol., 111mg sod., 1g carb. (0 sugars, 0 fiber), 9g pro.
DIABETIC EXCHANGES: *1 lean meat, ½ fat.*

HAM CROQUETTES WITH MUSTARD SAUCE

These crispy croquettes are good for parties, but whenever I have any leftover ham, I'll set it aside for a batch. I shape them early in the day, then simply fry them when I'm ready to serve.
—Kathy Vincek, Toms River, NJ

- -

PREP: 35 min. + chilling
COOK: 5 min./batch • **MAKES:** 1 dozen

2 cups finely chopped fully cooked ham
1 Tbsp. finely chopped onion

1 tsp. minced fresh parsley
¼ cup butter, cubed
¼ cup all-purpose flour
¼ tsp. salt
⅛ tsp. pepper
1 cup 2% milk
1 large egg
2 Tbsp. water
¾ cup dry bread crumbs
Oil for deep-fat frying
SAUCE
1½ tsp. butter
1½ tsp. all-purpose flour
¼ tsp. salt
Dash pepper
½ cup milk
4½ tsp. yellow mustard

1. In a small bowl, combine the ham, onion and parsley; set aside.
2. In a small saucepan, melt butter. Stir in the flour, salt and pepper until smooth; gradually add milk. Bring to a boil; cook and stir for 1 minute or until thickened. Stir into the ham mixture.

3. Spread into an 8-in. square baking dish; cover and refrigerate for at least 2 hours.
4. In a shallow bowl, combine egg and water. Place bread crumbs in a separate shallow bowl. Shape ham mixture into 12 balls (mixture will be soft); roll each ball in egg mixture, then in bread crumbs. Cover and refrigerate 2 hours longer.
5. In an electric skillet or deep fryer, heat oil to 375°. Fry croquettes, a few at a time, for 2-3 minutes or until golden brown, turning once. Drain on paper towels.
6. Meanwhile, in a small saucepan, melt butter. Stir in the flour, salt and pepper until smooth; gradually add milk. Bring to a boil; cook and stir for 2 minutes or until thickened. Stir in mustard. Serve with croquettes.
1 CROQUETTE WITH 2 TSP. SAUCE: 188 cal., 14g fat (5g sat. fat), 44mg chol., 503mg sod., 8g carb. (2g sugars, 0 fiber), 7g pro.

SANGRIA FOR ALL!

Offer your guests the perfect refreshing drink, whether they prefer red, white or rosé!

SALTY DOG SANGRIA
—*Becky Hardin, St. Peters, MO*

PREP: 30 min. + chilling
MAKES: 16 servings (3 qt.)

- 1 cup sugar
- 1 cup water
- 2 bottles (750 ml each) rosé wine
- 2 cups ruby red grapefruit juice
- 1 can (12 oz.) ginger ale
- 1 cup ruby red grapefruit-flavored vodka
  Grapefruit slices
  Coarse sea salt and grated grapefruit zest

1. In a small saucepan, bring sugar and water to a boil. Reduce heat; simmer 10 minutes. Cool completely. Transfer to a large pitcher. Stir in the wine, juice, ginger ale, vodka and grapefruit slices. Refrigerate at least 2 hours.
2. Using water, moisten the rims of 16 wine glasses. Mix salt and grapefruit zest on a plate; hold each glass upside down and dip rim into salt mixture. Set aside. Discard remaining salt mixture on plate. Serve sangria in prepared glasses over ice.
¾ **CUP:** *186 cal., 0 fat (0 sat. fat), 0 chol., 2mg sod., 24g carb. (15g sugars, 0 fiber), 0 pro.*

MARGARITA SANGRIA
—*Andrea Rivera, Westbury, NY*

PREP: 15 min. + chilling
MAKES: 8 servings (about 1½ qt.)

- 1 bottle (750 ml) white wine
- 1 can (12 oz.) lemon-lime soda
- 1 medium lemon, sliced
- 1 cup Anejo tequila
- ½ cup seedless red grapes, halved
- ½ cup mixed fresh berries
- ¼ cup agave nectar or honey
- 3 Tbsp. lemon juice

In a large pitcher or punch bowl, combine all of the ingredients. Refrigerate until cold, at least 2 hours. Serve over ice.
¾ **CUP:** *204 cal., 0 fat (0 sat. fat), 0 chol., 10mg sod., 19g carb. (16g sugars, 1g fiber), 0 pro.*

TOPSY-TURVY SANGRIA
—*Tracy Field, Bremerton, WA*

TAKES: 10 min.
MAKES: 10 servings (about 2 qt.)

- 1 bottle (750 ml) merlot
- 1 cup sugar
- 1 cup orange liqueur
- ½ to 1 cup brandy
- 3 cups cold lemon-lime soda
- 1 cup sliced fresh strawberries
- 1 medium orange, sliced
- 1 medium lemon, sliced
- 1 medium peach, sliced
  Ice cubes

In a pitcher, stir the first 4 ingredients until sugar is dissolved. Stir in soda and fruit. Serve over ice.
¾ **CUP:** *292 cal., 0 fat (0 sat. fat), 0 chol., 11mg sod., 42g carb. (39g sugars, 0 fiber), 0 pro.*

> ### Did you know?
> Sangria takes its name from *sangre*, the Spanish word for "blood," as it was originally made with red wine. Sangria now is made with a variety of wines, including white and rose, as its base.

PISTACHIO-TURKEY MEATBALLS IN ORANGE SAUCE

Pistachios and a bright, spicy orange sauce flavored with honey and basil make these mini meatballs a real party favorite.
—Jeanne Holt, St. Paul, MN

PREP: 25 min. • **BAKE:** 20 min.
MAKES: 4½ dozen

- ⅔ cup chopped pistachios
- 2 green onions, finely chopped
- ¼ cup dry bread crumbs
- 1 large egg, lightly beaten
- 1 tsp. grated orange zest
- ½ tsp. salt
- ⅛ tsp. pepper
- 1 lb. ground turkey
- 1 Italian sausage link (4 oz.), casing removed

SAUCE
- 3 Tbsp. butter
- 1 Tbsp. olive oil
- ¼ cup finely chopped sweet red pepper
- ⅛ tsp. crushed red pepper flakes
- 2 Tbsp. white wine
- 4 tsp. cornstarch
- 1 cup orange juice
- ½ cup reduced-sodium chicken broth
- 1 Tbsp. honey
- ½ tsp. grated orange zest
- 1 Tbsp. minced fresh basil
- 2 Tbsp. chopped pistachios

1. Preheat oven to 375°. In a large bowl, combine the first 7 ingredients. Add turkey and sausage; mix lightly but thoroughly. Shape into 1-in. balls.
2. Place meatballs on greased racks in shallow baking pans. Bake 18-20 minutes or until cooked through.
3. In a large skillet, heat butter and oil over medium heat. Add red pepper and pepper flakes; cook and stir 2-3 minutes or until red pepper is tender. Add wine; cook for 1 minute longer.
4. In a small bowl, whisk cornstarch, orange juice, broth, honey and orange zest until blended. Stir into pan. Bring to a boil; cook and stir 1-2 minutes or until thickened. Stir in basil and meatballs. Sprinkle with pistachios.
1 MEATBALL: *49 cal., 4g fat (1g sat. fat), 12mg chol., 66mg sod., 2g carb. (1g sugars, 0 fiber), 2g pro.*

SPANAKOPITA SPRING ROLLS

I was inspired to turn original spanakopita into a hand-held hors d'oeuvre. I use egg roll wrappers in place of phyllo dough, and now these are the biggest hit among my friends.
—Jade Randall, Las Vegas, NV

PREP: 15 min. • **COOK:** 5 min./batch
MAKES: 14 spring rolls

- 2 pkg. (10 oz. each) frozen chopped spinach, thawed and squeezed dry
- 2 cups crumbled feta cheese
- 4 garlic cloves, minced
- 2 tsp. dill weed
- ¼ tsp. salt
- ¼ tsp. pepper
- 14 refrigerated egg roll wrappers
  Oil for deep-fat frying

1. Mix the first 6 ingredients. With a corner of an egg roll wrapper facing you, place about ⅓ cup filling just below the center of the wrapper. (Cover remaining wrappers with a damp paper towel until ready to use.) Fold bottom corner over filling; moisten remaining wrapper edges with water. Fold side corners toward center over filling. Roll up tightly, pressing at tip to seal. Repeat.
2. In an electric skillet or deep-fat fryer, heat oil to 375°. Fry spring rolls, a few at a time, until golden brown, 3-4 minutes, turning occasionally. Drain on paper towels before serving.
FREEZE OPTION: *Freeze uncooked spring rolls in freezer containers, spacing them so they don't touch and separating the layers with waxed paper. To use, fry frozen spring rolls as directed, increasing time as necessary.*
1 SPRING ROLL: *245 cal., 12g fat (4g sat. fat), 20mg chol., 568mg sod., 22g carb. (0 sugars, 3g fiber), 10g pro.*

MUSHROOM PASTRY TARTS

Putting anything on a puff pastry crust makes for a special treat, but these mushrooms are so good that combining the two creates an unforgettable dish.
—Susan Scarborough, Fernandina Beach, FL

PREP: 50 min. • **BAKE:** 15 min.
MAKES: 1 dozen

- ¼ cup chopped walnuts or hazelnuts
- 3 Tbsp. olive oil, divided
- 2 medium sweet onions, thinly sliced
- 1 garlic clove, minced
- 1 tsp. brown sugar
- ½ tsp. sea salt
- ¼ tsp. coarsely ground pepper
- ⅓ cup dry red wine
- 10 oz. sliced fresh shiitake mushrooms
- ½ lb. sliced baby portobello mushrooms
- 2 tsp. minced fresh thyme, divided
- 1 sheet frozen puff pastry, thawed
- 1 pkg. (4 oz.) fresh goat cheese

1. In a small dry skillet, toast nuts over low heat for 5-7 minutes or until lightly browned, stirring occasionally. Remove and set aside.

2. In a large skillet, heat 2 Tbsp. oil over medium heat. Add onions; cook and stir 6-8 minutes or until softened. Reduce heat to medium-low; cook 20-22 minutes or until onions are deep golden brown, stirring occasionally. Add garlic, brown sugar, salt and pepper; cook 1 minute longer. Transfer to a small bowl.

3. Add wine to pan, stirring to loosen browned bits. Bring to a boil. Cook and stir 1 minute; pour over onions. In same skillet, heat remaining 1 Tbsp. oil over medium-high heat. Add mushrooms and 1 tsp. thyme; cook and stir 8-10 minutes or until liquid is almost absorbed. Stir in onions. Remove from heat; cover and set aside.

4. Preheat oven to 400°. Unfold puff pastry. On a lightly floured surface, roll pastry into a 12-in. square. Cut into two 12x6-in. rectangles. Transfer to baking sheet. Using a sharp knife, score ½ in. from edges of each pastry (do not cut through). Using a fork, poke holes in pastry. Bake 10-12 minutes or until puffed and lightly browned. Remove from oven.

Press down center with a spoon if necessary. Reduce oven setting to 350°.

5. Spoon mushroom mixture over tarts. Sprinkle with walnuts; top with cheese. Sprinkle with remaining thyme. Bake 5 minutes longer or until the cheese is melted. Cut each tart into 6 pieces.

1 PIECE: *199 cal., 12g fat (3g sat.fat), 6mg chol., 193mg sod., 19g carb. (4g sugars, 3g fiber), 4g pro.*

HERBED FETA DIP

Guests can't get enough of this thick, zesty dip that bursts with fresh Mediterranean flavor. The feta cheese and fresh mint complement each other beautifully, creating the perfect sidekick for fresh vegetables or any other dipper you fancy.
—Rebecca Ray, Chicago, IL

TAKES: 25 min. • **MAKES:** 3 cups

- ½ cup packed fresh parsley sprigs
- ½ cup fresh mint leaves
- ½ cup olive oil
- 2 garlic cloves, peeled
- ½ tsp. pepper
- 4 cups (16 oz.) crumbled feta cheese
- 3 Tbsp. lemon juice
  Assorted fresh vegetables

In a food processor, combine the first 5 ingredients; cover and pulse until finely chopped. Add cheese and lemon juice; process until creamy. Serve dip with fresh vegetables.

¼ CUP: *176 cal., 15g fat (5g sat. fat), 20mg chol., 361mg sod., 2g carb. (0 sugars, 1g fiber), 7g pro.*

CREOLE SCALLOP CAKES

This scrumptious appetizer can be prepared ahead of time. You can make both the scallop cakes and the aioli sauce the day before, then cook the cakes just before serving. This not only simplifies last-minute prep, but allows the flavors in the mixture to blend, which makes the dish even more yummy. My family and friends love my specialty scallop cakes.

—Iisha Leftridge-Brooks, Sacramento, CA

- -

PREP: 25 min. + chilling • **COOK:** 5 min./batch
MAKES: 20 scallop cakes (1½ cups aioli)

- 1 large egg, beaten
- ½ cup seasoned bread crumbs
- 2 Tbsp. finely chopped sweet red pepper
- 2 Tbsp. finely chopped leek (white portion only)
- 4 garlic cloves, minced
- 2 Tbsp. honey mustard
- 1 Tbsp. minced fresh thyme
- 1 Tbsp. chopped fennel fronds
- 2 tsp. salt-free lemon-pepper seasoning
- 1½ tsp. Creole seasoning
- 1 lb. sea scallops

COATING

- 1 cup panko bread crumbs
- 4 tsp. dried parsley flakes
- 2 tsp. coarsely ground pepper

SPICY HONEY AIOLI

- 1 cup mayonnaise
- ⅓ cup honey mustard
- 1 Tbsp. lemon juice
- 1 Tbsp. unsweetened apple juice
- 1 tsp. paprika
- 1 tsp. Creole seasoning
- ½ tsp. Cajun seasoning
- ⅓ cup canola oil

1. In a large bowl, combine the first 10 ingredients. Place scallops in a food processor; cover and pulse until just pureed. Fold into the egg mixture.

2. In a shallow bowl, combine the bread crumbs, parsley and pepper. Drop 2 Tbsp. of the scallop mixture into the crumb mixture. Gently coat and shape into a ½-in.-thick patty. Repeat with remaining mixture. Cover and refrigerate at least 30 minutes.

3. Meanwhile, in a small bowl, whisk the mayonnaise, mustard, lemon juice, apple juice and seasonings. Cover and refrigerate until serving.

4. Heat a large cast-iron or other heavy skillet over medium heat. Cook patties in oil in batches until golden brown, 2-3 minutes on each side. Drain on paper towels. Serve with aioli. If desired, top with additional fennel fronds.

1 SCALLOP CAKE WITH 1 TBSP. AIOLI: *169 cal., 14g fat (2g sat. fat), 22mg chol., 291mg sod., 7g carb. (2g sugars, 0 fiber), 5g pro.*

GOUDA TURKEY FRITTATA

This cheesy, filling egg skillet can be served at breakfast, for dinner, or cut in smaller slices and served as part of a small-plate spread. The hearty frittata is a great way to use up turkey leftovers.
—Nella Parker, Hersey, MI

PREP: 30 min. • **BROIL:** 5 min. • **MAKES:** 6 servings

- 1   cup diced zucchini
- 2   shallots, finely chopped
- 1   Tbsp. olive oil
- 1   Tbsp. butter
- 4   large eggs
- 2   Tbsp. water
- 1   cup finely chopped cooked turkey
- 1½ tsp. minced fresh tarragon
- ¼   tsp. salt
- ¼   tsp. pepper
- ½   cup shredded Gouda cheese

1. Preheat broiler. In a 10-in. ovenproof skillet, saute zucchini and shallots in oil and butter until tender.
2. In a small bowl, whisk eggs and water; stir in turkey and seasonings. Pour egg mixture into skillet; cover and cook over medium-low heat for 8-10 minutes or until eggs are nearly set.
3. Uncover skillet; sprinkle with cheese. Broil 6 in. from the heat for 2-3 minutes or until eggs are completely set. Cut into wedges.
1 PIECE: *171 cal., 11g fat (5g sat. fat), 175mg chol., 256mg sod., 3g carb. (1g sugars, 0 fiber), 14g pro.*

WINE PAIRINGS

With the varied and intense flavors in these Mediterranean-style bites, why not go with some surprising choices from the region? Spain, Italy and Greece have some amazing party-friendly options.

For a sparkling wine, try a Spanish **cava.** Made with red or white grapes, cava is a dry, light and minerally alternative to much more expensive champagnes.

A Greek **assyrtiko** is a natural match for shellfish, spinach and feta, but it's versatile enough to serve with other flavors as well. This dry white is fairly new to the import market and can be hard to find—but it's worth seeking out!

For a sweeter option, an Italian **moscato d'Asti** works well with the meat-based appetizers in this chapter. This is a semi sparkling wine, so you get a pleasant zing rather than full-on fizz. The Italians call this style of wine *frizzante.*

If you're looking beyond whites, a **lambrusco frizzante** is a good match for anything with balsamic vinegar or the classic tomato-herb-cheese trifecta. Lambruscos range from sweet to dry, so ask your wine seller for specific recommendations.

As an alternative to wine, a sparkling white grape juice would provide the same light, refreshing zing without the alcohol.

MOROCCAN EMPANADAS

My family goes for Moroccan flavors, so I make empanadas using apricot preserves and beef. A spicy dipping sauce adds to the appeal of these flaky hand pies.
—Arlene Erlbach, Morton Grove, IL

- -

PREP: 30 min. • **BAKE:** 15 min.
MAKES: 20 servings

- ¾ lb. ground beef
- 1 medium onion, chopped
- 3 oz. cream cheese, softened
- ⅓ cup apricot preserves
- ¼ cup finely chopped carrot
- ¾ tsp. Moroccan seasoning (ras el hanout) or ½ tsp. ground cumin plus ¼ tsp. ground coriander and dash cayenne pepper
- ¼ tsp. salt
- 3 sheets refrigerated pie crust
- 1 large egg yolk, beaten
- 1 Tbsp. sesame seeds

SAUCE
- ½ cup apricot preserves
- ½ cup chili sauce

1. Preheat oven to 425°. In a large skillet, cook beef and onion over medium heat until beef is no longer pink, breaking up beef into crumbles, 5-7 minutes; drain. Stir in cream cheese, preserves, carrot and seasonings. Cool slightly.

2. On a lightly floured work surface, unroll sheets of pie crust. Cut 40 circles with a floured 3-in. cookie cutter, rerolling crust as necessary. Place half of the circles 2 in. apart on parchment-lined baking sheets. Top each with 1 rounded Tbsp. beef mixture. Top with remaining crust circles; press edges with a fork to seal.

3. Brush tops with egg yolk; sprinkle with sesame seeds. Cut slits in tops. Bake until golden brown, 12-15 minutes. Remove from pan to a wire rack.

4. Meanwhile, in a microwave, warm sauce ingredients, stirring to combine. Serve with empanadas.

FREEZE OPTION: *Cover and freeze unbaked empanadas on waxed paper-lined baking sheets until firm. Transfer to a freezer container; freeze. To use, bake as directed, increasing time as necessary. Prepare sauce as directed.*

1 EMPANADA WITH ABOUT 2 TSP. SAUCE: *215 cal., 11g fat (5g sat. fat), 30mg chol., 256mg sod., 25g carb. (8g sugars, 0 fiber), 5g pro.*

SPICY BEEF SATAY

The fragrant spices and full flavors of North African cuisine make these appetizers a tasty party food.
—Roxanne Chan, Albany, CA

- -

PREP: 35 min. • **BROIL:** 5 min.
MAKES: 2 dozen (½ cup sauce)

- 1 cup white wine vinegar
- ¾ cup sugar
- ½ cup water
- 1 Tbsp. orange marmalade
- ¼ tsp. grated orange zest
- ¼ tsp. crushed red pepper flakes
- ½ cup finely chopped salted roasted almonds
- 2 Tbsp. minced fresh mint
- 1 green onion, finely chopped
- 1 Tbsp. lemon juice
- 1 garlic clove, minced
- ¼ tsp. each ground cinnamon, cumin and coriander
- 1 lb. lean ground beef (90% lean)
  Minced fresh parsley

1. Preheat broiler. In a small saucepan, combine the first 6 ingredients. Bring to a boil. Reduce heat; simmer, uncovered, about 25 minutes or until reduced to ½ cup.

2. Meanwhile, in a large bowl, combine almonds, mint, onion, lemon juice, garlic and spices. Crumble beef over the mixture and mix lightly but thoroughly.

3. Divide beef mixture into 24 pieces. Shape each piece into a 3x1-in. rectangle; insert a soaked wooden appetizer skewer into each.

4. Broil 6 in. from the heat 2-4 minutes on each side or until a thermometer reads 160°. Arrange on a serving platter. Drizzle with the sauce mixture and sprinkle with parsley.

1 APPETIZER WITH 1 TSP. SAUCE: *74 cal., 3g fat (1g sat. fat), 12mg chol., 25mg sod., 8g carb. (7g sugars, 0 fiber), 4g pro.*

HOLIDAY BASH ON A BUDGET

You can still throw a pull-out-the-stops holiday dinner party even if you're watching your dollars. These dishes make the most of budget-friendly ingredients to create a truly luxurious spread.

BLACKBERRY BEER COCKTAIL

This refreshing hard lemonade has a mild alcohol flavor. The beer adds just enough fizz to dance on your tongue as you sip. Sorry, adults only!
—Ginger Sullivan, Cutler Bay, FL

TAKES: 10 min. • **MAKES:** 10 servings

- 4 bottles (12 oz. each) beer, chilled
- 1 can (12 oz.) frozen raspberry lemonade concentrate, thawed
- ¾ cup fresh or frozen blackberries, thawed
- ½ cup vodka
  Ice cubes
  Lemon slices

In a large pitcher, combine the beer, lemonade concentrate, blackberries and vodka. Serve over ice and garnish with lemon slices.
¾ CUP: 151 cal., 0 fat (0 sat. fat), 0 chol., 6mg sod., 21g carb. (19g sugars, 1g fiber), 1g pro.

CORNMEAL ROLLS

Golden and buttery, these rolls have cornmeal flavor and a texture that goes perfectly with a hearty bowl of chili.
—Carol Forcum, Marion, IL

PREP: 30 min. + rising • **BAKE:** 20 min. • **MAKES:** 2 dozen

- 2¼ cups warm water (110° to 115°), divided
- ⅓ cup cornmeal
- ¼ cups sugar
- 3 Tbsp. canola oil
- 2 tsp. salt
- 2 pkg. (¼ oz. each) active dry yeast
- 2 large eggs, room temperature
- 5 to 5½ cups all-purpose flour
  Melted butter
  Additional cornmeal

1. In a large saucepan, combine 1¾ cups water, cornmeal, sugar, oil and salt. Cook and stir over medium heat until mixture comes to a boil, 9-11 minutes. Cool to 120°-130°. Place in a large bowl. Dissolve yeast in remaining ½ cup warm water; add to the cornmeal mixture. Add eggs; beat until smooth. Stir in enough flour to make a soft dough.
2. Turn dough onto a floured surface; knead until smooth and elastic, 6-8 minutes. Place in a greased bowl, turning once to grease top. Cover and let rise in a warm place until doubled, 45-60 minutes.
3. Punch dough down. Shape into 24 balls. Place on greased baking sheets; brush with butter and sprinkle with cornmeal. Let rise, uncovered, until doubled, about 30 minutes.
4. Bake at 375° until golden brown, 18-20 minutes. Immediately remove from pan; serve warm.
1 ROLL: 132 cal., 2g fat (0 sat. fat), 18mg chol., 203mg sod., 24g carb. (3g sugars, 1g fiber), 3g pro.

NEW ENGLAND BEAN & BOG CASSOULET

When I moved to New England, I embraced the local cuisine. My cassoulet with baked beans pays tribute to a French classic and to New England.
—Devon Delaney, Westport, CT

PREP: 20 min. • **BAKE:** 35 min.
MAKES: 8 servings (3½ qt.)

- 5 Tbsp. olive oil, divided
- 8 boneless skinless chicken thighs (about 2 lbs.)
- 1 pkg. (12 oz.) fully cooked Italian chicken sausage links, cut into ½-in. slices
- 4 shallots, finely chopped
- 2 tsp. minced fresh rosemary or ½ tsp. dried rosemary, crushed
- 2 tsp. minced fresh thyme or ½ tsp. dried thyme
- 1 can (28 oz.) fire-roasted diced tomatoes, undrained
- 1 can (16 oz.) baked beans
- 1 cup chicken broth
- ½ cup fresh or frozen cranberries
- 3 day-old croissants, cubed (about 6 cups)
- ½ tsp. lemon-pepper seasoning
- 2 Tbsp. minced fresh parsley

1. Preheat oven to 400°. In a Dutch oven, heat 2 Tbsp. oil over medium heat. In batches, brown chicken thighs on both sides; remove from pan, reserving the drippings. Add sausage; cook and stir until lightly browned. Remove from pan.
2. In same pan, heat 1 Tbsp. oil over medium heat. Add shallots, rosemary and thyme; cook and stir until shallots are tender, 1-2 minutes. Stir in tomatoes, beans, broth and cranberries. Return chicken and sausage to pan; bring to a boil. Bake, covered, until chicken is tender, 20-25 minutes.
3. Toss croissant pieces with the remaining 2 Tbsp. oil; sprinkle with lemon pepper. Arrange over the chicken mixture. Bake, uncovered, until croissants are golden brown, 12-15 minutes. Sprinkle with parsley.
1¾ CUPS: *500 cal., 26g fat (7g sat. fat), 127mg chol., 1050mg sod., 32g carb. (6g sugars, 5g fiber), 35g pro.*

ALL-DAY BRISKET WITH POTATOES

I think the slow cooker was invented with brisket in mind. This sweet and savory version is perfection itself. It's important to buy first-cut or flat-cut brisket, which has far less fat than other cuts.
—Lana Gryga, Glen Flora, WI

PREP: 30 min. • **COOK:** 8 hours
MAKES: 8 servings

- 2 medium potatoes, peeled and cut into ¼-in. slices
- 2 celery ribs, sliced
- 1 fresh beef brisket (3 lbs.)
- 1 Tbsp. canola oil
- 1 large onion, sliced
- 2 garlic cloves, minced
- 1 can (12 oz.) beer
- ½ tsp. beef bouillon granules
- ¾ cup stewed tomatoes
- ⅓ cup tomato paste
- ¼ cup red wine vinegar
- 3 Tbsp. brown sugar
- 3 Tbsp. Dijon mustard
- 3 Tbsp. soy sauce
- 2 Tbsp. molasses
- ½ tsp. paprika
- ¼ tsp. salt
- ⅛ tsp. pepper
- 1 bay leaf

1. Place potatoes and celery in a 5-qt. slow cooker. Cut brisket in half. In a large skillet, brown beef in oil on all sides; transfer to slow cooker. In the same pan, saute onion until tender. Add garlic; cook 1 minute longer. Add to slow cooker.
2. Add beer and bouillon to skillet, stirring to loosen browned bits from pan; pour over meat. In a large bowl, combine the remaining ingredients; add to slow cooker.
3. Cover and cook on low until the meat and vegetables are tender, 8-10 hours. Discard bay leaf. To serve, thinly slice across the grain.
NOTE: *This is a fresh beef brisket, not corned beef.*
1 SERVING: *352 cal., 9g fat (3g sat. fat), 72mg chol., 722mg sod., 25g carb. (13g sugars, 2g fiber), 38g pro.*
DIABETIC EXCHANGES: *5 lean meat, 1 starch, 1 vegetable, ½ fat.*

CLASSIC FRENCH ONION SOUP

Enjoy my signature soup the way my granddaughter Becky does. I make it for her in a French onion soup bowl complete with garlic croutons and gobs of melted Swiss cheese on top.
—Lou Sansevero, Ferron, UT

PREP: 20 min. • **COOK:** 2 hours
MAKES: 12 servings (2¼ qt.)

- 5 Tbsp. olive oil, divided
- 1 Tbsp. butter
- 8 cups thinly sliced onions (about 3 lbs.)
- 3 garlic cloves, minced
- ½ cup port wine
- 2 cartons (32 oz. each) beef broth
- ½ tsp. pepper
- ¼ tsp. salt
- 24 slices French bread baguette (½ in. thick)
- 2 large garlic cloves, peeled and halved
- ¾ cup shredded Gruyere or Swiss cheese

1. In a Dutch oven, heat 2 Tbsp. oil and butter over medium heat. Add the onions; cook and stir until softened, 10-13 minutes. Reduce heat to medium-low; cook, stirring occasionally, until deep golden brown, 30-40 minutes. Add minced garlic; cook 2 minutes longer.
2. Stir in wine. Bring to a boil; cook until liquid is reduced by half. Add the broth, pepper and salt; return to a boil. Reduce heat. Simmer, covered, stirring occasionally, for 1 hour.
3. Meanwhile, preheat oven to 400°. Place baguette slices on a baking sheet; brush both sides with remaining 3 Tbsp. oil. Bake until toasted, 3-5 minutes on each side. Rub toasts with halved garlic.
4. To serve, place twelve 8-oz. broiler-safe bowls or ramekins on baking sheets; place 2 toasts in each. Ladle with soup; top with cheese. Broil 4 in. from heat until cheese is melted.

¾ CUP SOUP WITH 1 SLICE BREAD AND 1 TBSP. CHEESE: 172 cal., 9g fat (3g sat. fat), 10mg chol., 773mg sod., 16g carb. (3g sugars, 1g fiber), 6g pro.

> ### Holiday Helper
> Common olive oil works better for cooking at high heat than virgin or extra virgin oil.

EASY TRUFFLES

These smooth, creamy chocolates are divine—and with just a few ingredients, they're easy to make anytime.
—Taste of Home *Test Kitchen*

PREP: 25 min. + chilling • **COOK:** 5 min.
MAKES: about 6 dozen

- 3 cups semisweet chocolate chips
- 1 can (14 oz.) sweetened condensed milk
- 1 Tbsp. vanilla extract
  Toasted finely chopped nuts or assorted jimmies

1. Place chocolate chips and milk in a microwave-safe bowl; microwave on high for 3 minutes, stirring halfway through. Stir in vanilla. Refrigerate, covered, until firm enough to shape, about 3 hours.
2. Shape into 1-in. balls; roll in nuts or jimmies. Place in a 15x10x1-in. pan; refrigerate until firm, about 1 hour.

1 TRUFFLE: 52 cal., 3g fat (2g sat. fat), 2mg chol., 8mg sod., 7g carb. (7g sugars, 0 fiber), 1g pro.

MASHED CAULIFLOWER AU GRATIN

Unless someone tells you, you might not know you're eating cauliflower. Even my grandchildren love this buttery, cheesy, creamy dish that tastes like mashed potatoes.
—Sandie Parker, Elk Rapids, MI

PREP: 40 min. • **COOK:** 40 min.
MAKES: 12 servings

- 2 **large heads cauliflower, broken into florets**
- 1½ **cups shredded Parmesan cheese**
- 1 **cup shredded Colby-Monterey Jack cheese**
- 6 **Tbsp. butter, cubed**
- ¾ **tsp. garlic salt**
- ½ **tsp. Montreal steak seasoning**

TOPPING
- 1 **cup Italian-style panko bread crumbs**
- ¼ **cup butter, melted**

1. Preheat oven to 350°. Place cauliflower in a stockpot; add water to cover. Bring to a boil. Reduce heat; simmer, uncovered, until very tender, 10-12 minutes. Drain; transfer to a large bowl. Mash cauliflower; stir in the cheeses, cubed butter and seasonings. Transfer to a greased 3-qt. or 13x9-in. baking dish.
2. In a small bowl, mix bread crumbs with melted butter until evenly coated; sprinkle over cauliflower mixture. Bake, uncovered, until heated through and topping is golden brown, 40-50 minutes.
FREEZE OPTION: *Cool unbaked casserole; cover and freeze. To use, partially thaw in refrigerator overnight. Remove from refrigerator 30 minutes before baking. Preheat oven to 350°. Bake casserole as directed, increasing time as necessary to heat through and for a thermometer inserted in center to read 165°.*
¾ CUP: *238 cal., 17g fat (10g sat. fat), 41mg chol., 612mg sod., 14g carb. (3g sugars, 4g fiber), 9g pro.*
Swiss Mashed Cauliflower: *Cook and mash cauliflower as directed. Add 1 cup shredded Swiss cheese, 2 Tbsp. butter, 1 tsp. salt, ½ tsp. pepper, ¼ tsp. garlic powder and ¼-⅓ cup 2% milk.*

ROAST SPICED CHICKEN

My mother's index card recipe is worn and food stains obscure the words—that's how much I've cooked this dish. Spiced chicken has been in our family more than 50 years.
—Cindy Kanwar, Blacklick, OH

PREP: 20 min. • **BAKE:** 1½ hours + standing
MAKES: 12 servings

- 3 **tsp. dried thyme**
- 2 **tsp. salt**
- 2 **tsp. seasoned salt**
- 2 **tsp. pepper**
- ½ **tsp. garlic powder**
- ⅔ **cup butter, cubed**
- ⅓ **cup lemon juice**
- 2 **Tbsp. Dijon mustard**
- 1½ **tsp. paprika**
- ½ **tsp. garlic salt**
- 1 **roasting chicken (6 to 7 lbs.)**
- 1 **lemon, quartered, optional**

1. Preheat oven to 425°. In a small bowl, mix the first 5 ingredients. In a small saucepan, melt butter; stir in lemon juice, mustard, paprika and garlic salt. Keep warm.
2. Sprinkle half the thyme mixture inside chicken; if desired, place a quartered lemon inside chicken. Place chicken on a rack in a shallow roasting pan, breast side up. Tuck wings under chicken; tie the drumsticks together.
3. Brush outside of chicken with ½ cup butter mixture; sprinkle with remaining thyme mixture. Roast 1 hour, basting every 15 minutes with the remaining butter mixture. (Cover loosely with foil if chicken browns too quickly.)
4. Roast until a thermometer inserted in thickest part of thigh reads 170°-175°, 30-60 minutes longer. Remove chicken from oven; tent with foil. Let stand for 15 minutes before carving.
1 SERVING: *390 cal., 27g fat (11g sat. fat), 132mg chol., 918mg sod., 2g carb. (0 sugars, 0 fiber), 33g pro.*

MULLED DR PEPPER

When neighbors or friends visit us on a chilly evening, I'll serve this warm beverage with ham sandwiches and deviled eggs.
—Bernice Morris, Marshfield, MO

PREP: 10 min. • **COOK:** 2 hours • **MAKES:** 10 servings

- 8 cups Dr Pepper
- ¼ cup packed brown sugar
- ¼ cup lemon juice
- ½ tsp. ground allspice
- ½ tsp. whole cloves
- ¼ tsp. salt
- ¼ tsp. ground nutmeg
- 3 cinnamon sticks (3 in.)

In a 3-qt. slow cooker, combine all ingredients. Cover and cook on low until heated through, about 2 hours. Discard the cloves and cinnamon sticks.

1 SERVING: *105 cal., 0 fat (0 sat. fat), 0 chol., 69mg sod., 27g carb. (26g sugars, 0 fiber), 0 pro.*

ONE BOUQUET, MANY CENTERPIECES

One of the best ways to decorate your house at the holidays is with flowers. But adorning your table, side tables, coffee tables and more can get expensive. Instead, to save money and still festoon your entertaining space with beautiful blooms, opt for one big bouquet and split it among small pots, vases and glasses. Since the flowers were chosen by the florist to go together, you'll be sure of a harmonious look, with everything coordinated and complementary. You can even pull your own houseplants into service as decoration, like the succulents pictured above.

BREAD PUDDING PIE

This unique dessert is a bread pudding-pie combo. It was created by my paternal grandmother's family. They had a farm and made their own bread, which made this a low-cost dessert.
—Kelly Barnes, Lexington, IN

- -

PREP: 15 min. • **BAKE:** 55 min. + chilling
MAKES: 8 servings

Pastry for single-crust pie
1 cup cubed bread
2 large eggs, room temperature
2 cups 2% milk
¾ cup sugar
½ tsp. vanilla extract
¼ tsp. ground nutmeg
2 tsp. butter

1. Preheat oven to 425°. On a lightly floured surface, roll the dough to a ⅛-in.-thick circle; transfer to a 9-in. pie plate. Trim crust to ½ in. beyond the rim of the plate; flute edge. Arrange bread in bottom of pie crust. In a large bowl, whisk eggs, milk, sugar and vanilla; pour over bread. Sprinkle with nutmeg and dot with butter. Bake 10 minutes. Reduce oven setting to 350°.
2. Bake until a knife inserted in the center comes out clean, 45-50 minutes longer. Cover edge loosely with foil during the last 15 minutes if needed to prevent overbrowning. Remove foil. Cool on a wire rack for 1 hour. Refrigerate for at least 3 hours before serving.
1 PIECE: *314 cal., 15g fat (9g sat. fat), 84mg chol., 230mg sod., 39g carb. (22g sugars, 1g fiber), 6g pro.*
PASTRY FOR SINGLE-CRUST PIE (9 IN.): *Combine 1¼ cups all-purpose flour and ¼ tsp. salt; cut in ½ cup cold butter until crumbly. Gradually add 3-5 Tbsp. ice water, tossing with a fork until dough holds together when pressed. Cover and refrigerate 1 hour.*

HERB & ROMANO CHEESE WREATH

After the wreath is baked and cooled, it can be wrapped in foil, placed in an airtight plastic bag and frozen until you are ready to serve it or give it away. Add some whipped butter on the side and it's the perfect gift.
—Linda Padia, Wauna, WA

- -

PREP: 30 min. + rising
BAKE: 30 min. + cooling
MAKES: 1 loaf (24 pieces)

1 pkg. (¼ oz.) active dry yeast
2 Tbsp. honey
1½ cups warm water (110° to 115°)
½ cup nonfat dry milk powder
2 large eggs, room temperature
½ cup butter, softened
4 Tbsp. grated Romano cheese, divided
2 tsp. minced fresh rosemary or ½ tsp. dried rosemary, crushed
2 tsp. minced fresh thyme or ½ tsp. dried thyme
1½ tsp. salt
5½ to 6 cups bread flour
1 Tbsp. butter, melted

1. In a small bowl, dissolve yeast and honey in warm water; stir in milk powder. In a large bowl, combine eggs, softened butter, 2 Tbsp. cheese, rosemary, thyme, salt, yeast mixture and 2 cups flour; beat on medium speed until smooth. Stir in enough remaining flour to form a soft dough (dough will be sticky).
2. Turn onto a floured surface; knead until dough is smooth and elastic, 6-8 minutes. Place in a greased bowl, turning once to grease the top. Cover and let rise in a warm place until doubled, about 1 hour.
3. Punch down dough. Turn onto a lightly floured surface; divide into thirds. Roll each into a 30-in. rope. Place ropes on a greased baking sheet and braid. Shape into a wreath and pinch ends to seal.
4. Cover with a kitchen towel; let rise in a warm place until almost doubled, about 45 minutes. Preheat oven to 375°.
5. Brush braid with melted butter; sprinkle with remaining 2 Tbsp. cheese. Bake until golden brown, 30-35 minutes. Remove from pan to a wire rack to cool.
1 PIECE: *174 cal., 6g fat (3g sat. fat), 27mg chol., 215mg sod., 25g carb. (2g sugars, 1g fiber), 5g pro.*

GINGERSNAP RUM APPLE CRISP

My mother makes incredible apple crisp, and I've added a few twists of my own. We think it's best warm, with ice cream on the side.
—Nancy Heishman, Las Vegas, NV

PREP: 25 min. • **BAKE:** 35 min. • **MAKES:** 8 servings

- ¾ cup packed brown sugar
- 3 Tbsp. all-purpose flour
- 2¼ tsp. ground cinnamon
- 1¼ tsp. ground allspice
- 1 tsp. salt
- ¼ tsp. ground ginger
- 6 cups thinly sliced peeled tart apples (about 6 medium)
- 6 caramels
- ⅓ cup rum or orange juice

TOPPING
- ¾ cup crushed gingersnap cookies (about 15 cookies)
- ¾ cup packed brown sugar
- ½ cup all-purpose flour
- ½ cup cold butter, cubed
    Vanilla ice cream

1. Preheat oven to 375°. In a large bowl, mix the first 6 ingredients. Add apples; toss to coat. In a small saucepan, combine caramels and rum. Cook and stir over medium-low heat until caramels are melted. Pour over apple mixture; toss to coat. Transfer to a greased 8-in. square baking dish.
2. For topping, in a small bowl, mix crushed cookies, brown sugar and flour; cut in butter until crumbly. Sprinkle over filling. Bake 35-40 minutes or until apples are tender. Cover loosely with foil if top browns too quickly. Serve warm with vanilla ice cream.
1 SERVING: *430 cal., 14g fat (8g sat. fat), 31mg chol., 483mg sod., 76g carb. (56g sugars, 2g fiber), 3g pro.*

PUMPKIN PECAN CUSTARD

My family loves pumpkin pie, but this is a delicious, creamy, healthier alternative, and we don't miss the crust at all.
—Abby Booth, Coweta, OK

PREP: 20 min. • **BAKE:** 35 min. + chilling • **MAKES:** 8 servings

- 1 can (15 oz.) pumpkin
- 1 can (12 oz.) reduced-fat evaporated milk
- ¾ cup egg substitute
- ⅓ cup packed brown sugar
- 1½ tsp. vanilla extract
- 1 tsp. ground cinnamon
- ½ tsp. ground ginger
- ¼ tsp. ground cloves
- ⅛ tsp. salt

TOPPING
- 3 Tbsp. all-purpose flour
- 3 Tbsp. brown sugar
- ½ tsp. ground cinnamon
- 2 Tbsp. cold butter
- ½ cup chopped pecans

1. Preheat oven to 325°. In a large bowl, combine the first 9 ingredients. Transfer to eight 6-oz. ramekins. Place in a baking pan; add 1 in. boiling water to pan. Bake, uncovered, 20 minutes.
2. Combine flour, brown sugar and cinnamon. Cut in butter until crumbly. Stir in pecans. Sprinkle over custards. Bake 15-20 minutes longer or until a knife inserted in center comes out clean.
3. Remove ramekins from water bath; cool for 10 minutes. Cover and refrigerate at least 4 hours.
½ CUP: *213 cal., 9g fat (3g sat. fat), 11mg chol., 160mg sod., 27g carb. (21g sugars, 3g fiber), 7g pro.*
DIABETIC EXCHANGES: *2 starch, 1½ fat.*

SPICY CHEESE CRACKERS

They're crisp and flaky with a touch of zip—so it's no wonder these crackers disappear in no time. They are a favorite at every gathering. We often make them en masse and freeze them for later.
—Donna Lindecamp, Morganton, NC

TAKES: 30 min. • MAKES: 32 crackers

- 1½ cups shredded extra-sharp cheddar cheese
- ¾ cup all-purpose flour
- ½ tsp. kosher salt
- ¼ tsp. crushed red pepper flakes
- ¼ cup cold butter, cubed
- 1 to 2 Tbsp. half-and-half cream

1. Preheat oven to 350°. Place cheese, flour, salt and pepper flakes in a food processor; process until blended. Add butter; pulse until butter is the size of peas. While pulsing, add just enough cream to form moist crumbs.
2. On a lightly floured surface, roll dough to ⅛-in. thickness. Cut with a floured 3-in. holiday-shaped cookie cutter. Place 2 in. apart on greased baking sheets. Reroll scraps and repeat.
3. Bake until crackers are golden brown, 13-17 minutes. Remove from pans to wire racks to cool completely. Store in an airtight container.

1 CRACKER: *45 cal., 3g fat (2g sat. fat), 9mg chol., 76mg sod., 2g carb. (0 sugars, 0 fiber), 2g pro.*

SALMON PARTY SPREAD

We're always proud to serve our delicious Alaskan salmon to guests. Set out some crackers, and this slightly smoky spread will be gone in no time!
—Kathy Crow, Cordova, AK

PREP: 10 min. + chilling • MAKES: 2 cups

- 1 pkg. (8 oz.) cream cheese, softened
- 1 can (7½ oz.) pink salmon, drained, flaked and cartilage removed
- 3 Tbsp. chopped fresh parsley
- 2 Tbsp. finely chopped green pepper
- 2 Tbsp. finely chopped sweet red pepper
- 2 tsp. lemon juice
- 1 tsp. prepared horseradish
- ½ tsp. liquid smoke, optional
  Finely chopped pecans or additional parsley
  Crackers

In a bowl, combine the first 8 ingredients; stir until well blended. Cover and chill for up to 24 hours. Transfer to a serving bowl; if desired, sprinkle with pecans or parsley. Serve with crackers.

2 TBSP.: *71 cal., 6g fat (3g sat. fat), 21mg chol., 115mg sod., 1g carb. (0 sugars, 0 fiber), 4g pro.*

TOMATO-BASIL PULL-APART ROLLS

My nephew helped me create these soft and colorful rolls. He named them "wheelies" because the spiral shapes reminded him of his toy trucks.
—Dianna Wara, Washington, IL

PREP: 30 min. + rising • **BAKE:** 20 min.
MAKES: 1 dozen

- 1 pkg. (¼ oz.) active dry yeast
- 2 Tbsp. sugar
- ¾ cup warm 2% milk (110° to 115°)
- 1 large egg, room temperature
- ¼ cup tomato paste
- 3 Tbsp. olive oil
- 1 tsp. salt
- 2¾ to 3¼ cups bread flour

FILLING
- 1 cup shredded Italian cheese blend
- 2 tsp. dried basil
- ½ tsp. garlic powder

1. Dissolve yeast and sugar in warm milk. In a large bowl, beat egg, tomato paste, oil, salt, yeast mixture and 1 cup flour on medium speed until smooth. Stir in enough remaining flour to form a soft dough (dough will be sticky).
2. Turn onto a floured surface; knead until smooth and elastic, 6-8 minutes. Place in a greased bowl, turning to grease the top. Cover; let rise in a warm place until doubled, about 45 minutes.
3. In a bowl, toss filling ingredients. Punch down dough; turn onto a lightly floured surface. Roll into a 16x12-in. rectangle. Sprinkle with filling to within ½ in. of edges. Roll up jelly-roll style, starting with a long side; pinch seam to seal. Cut into 12 slices.
4. Place, cut side down, in a parchment-lined 10-in. cast-iron skillet. Cover with a kitchen towel; let rise in a warm place until almost doubled, about 45 minutes. Preheat oven to 350°.
5. Bake until golden brown, 20-25 minutes. Remove rolls to a wire rack.
1 ROLL: *204 cal., 7g fat (2g sat. fat), 24mg chol., 284mg sod., 27g carb. (3g sugars, 1g fiber), 7g pro.*

MEATBALLS WITH CHIMICHURRI SAUCE

This South American condiment, featuring fresh cilantro and parsley, is more than just a sauce for tossing with meatballs. You'll want plenty for extra dipping.
—Amy Chase, Vanderhoof, BC

TAKES: 30 min.
MAKES: about 20 (⅔ cup sauce)

- 1 pkg. (22 oz.) frozen fully cooked Angus beef meatballs
- 3 garlic cloves, peeled
- 1 cup packed Italian flat leaf parsley
- ¼ cup packed fresh cilantro leaves
- 1 tsp. salt
- ¼ tsp. coarsely ground pepper
- 2 Tbsp. red wine vinegar
- ½ cup extra virgin olive oil

1. Prepare the meatballs according to package directions.
2. Meanwhile, place garlic in a small food processor; pulse until chopped. Add parsley, cilantro, salt and pepper; pulse until finely chopped. Add vinegar. While processing, gradually add oil in a steady stream.
3. In a large bowl, toss meatballs with a little more than half of the chimichurri sauce. Transfer to a platter. Serve with remaining sauce for dipping.
1 MEATBALL WITH ABOUT 2 TSP. SAUCE: *130 cal., 12g fat (4g sat. fat), 17mg chol., 318mg sod., 2g carb. (0 sugars, 0 fiber), 4g pro.*

ROASTED BALSAMIC SWEET POTATOES

The usual potato salad belongs to the summer months, while this warm, spicy side is perfect for cozy season!
—Karen Vande Slunt, Watertown, WI

PREP: 30 min. • **COOK:** 30 min.
MAKES: 12 servings

6	medium sweet potatoes, cubed
1	tsp. olive oil
½	tsp. salt
½	tsp. pepper
1	lb. bacon strips, chopped
4	celery ribs, chopped
1	medium onion, thinly sliced
3	garlic cloves, minced
1	cup beef stock
⅔	cup balsamic vinegar
4	tsp. paprika
¾	tsp. ground cumin, optional
6	green onions, chopped
	Minced fresh parsley, optional

1. Preheat oven to 375°. Place sweet potatoes in a 15x10x1-in. pan; drizzle with olive oil and sprinkle with salt and pepper. Turn to coat. Bake until tender, 30-35 minutes.
2. Meanwhile, in a large skillet, cook bacon over medium-low heat until crisp; drain. Discard all but 4 tsp. drippings.
3. Cook celery and onion in drippings over medium heat until tender, 6-8 minutes. Stir in garlic; cook 1 minute. Add beef stock and balsamic vinegar; simmer until liquid is reduced by half, 5-8 minutes. Add paprika and, if desired, cumin; cook 1 minute longer.
4. Pour the balsamic mixture over sweet potatoes; add bacon. Toss to coat. Top with green onions and, if desired, minced fresh parsley; serve immediately.

CRAN-ORANGE ICEBOX COOKIES

When we ranked our favorite Christmas treats, these cranberry, orange and pecan cookies were at the top of the list.
—Nancy Rollag, Kewaskum, WI

PREP: 30 min. + chilling
BAKE: 10 min./batch • **MAKES:** about 5 dozen

1	cup butter, softened
1	cup sugar
1	large egg, room temperature
2	Tbsp. 2% milk
1	tsp. vanilla extract
3	cups all-purpose flour
1½	tsp. baking powder
2	tsp. grated orange zest
⅔	cup chopped dried cranberries
¼	cup chopped pecans
8	to 10 drops red food coloring, optional

1. In a large bowl, cream butter and sugar until light and fluffy, 5-7 minutes. Beat in the egg, milk and vanilla. Combine flour and baking powder; gradually add to the creamed mixture and mix well.
2. Transfer 1 cup dough to a small bowl; stir in orange zest and set aside. To the remaining dough, add the cranberries, pecans and, if desired, food coloring; divide in half.
3. Line an 8x4-in. loaf pan with waxed paper. Press 1 portion of cranberry dough evenly into pan; top with orange dough, then remaining cranberry dough. Cover and refrigerate for 2 hours or until firm.
4. Preheat oven to 375°. Remove dough from pan; cut in half lengthwise. Cut each portion into ¼-in. slices. Place 1 in. apart on lightly greased baking sheets.
5. Bake until the edges begin to brown, 8-10 minutes. Remove to wire racks. Store in an airtight container.

STEAK CROSTINI WITH CARROT-HORSERADISH MARMALADE

I've been making little tweaks to this family favorite for years. Prep everything ahead, then layer up the crostini right before party time.
—Greg Fontenot, The Woodlands, TX

PREP: 1 hour • **COOK:** 30 min.
MAKES: 3½ dozen

- 1 French bread baguette (10½ oz.), cut into ¼-in. slices
- ¼ cup olive oil, divided
- 1 lb. medium carrots, grated
- 2 cups water
- 1½ cups sugar
- 1 to 2 Tbsp. prepared horseradish
- 1 Tbsp. butter
- 1 cup chopped onion
- 2 cups shredded Swiss cheese
- 1 carton (8 oz.) mascarpone cheese
- 2 Tbsp. mayonnaise
- 1 Tbsp. sour cream
- 1 boneless beef top loin steak (12 to 14 oz.)

1. Preheat oven to 350°. Place baguette slices on baking sheets; brush with 2 Tbsp. olive oil. Bake until toasted, about 10 minutes.

2. Place carrots and water in a large saucepan; bring to a boil over medium-high heat. Cook, uncovered, 10 minutes. Add sugar; cook on medium heat until thickened, about 15 minutes, stirring occasionally. Remove from heat; add desired amount of horseradish and mix well. Cool.

3. Meanwhile, in a small saucepan over medium-low heat, melt butter. Cook and stir onions until golden brown and tender, 10-12 minutes; cool. Stir in cheeses, mayonnaise and sour cream.

4. In a large cast-iron or other heavy skillet, heat the remaining 2 Tbsp. olive oil over medium-high heat. Add steak; cook until meat reaches desired doneness (for medium-rare, a thermometer should read 135°; medium, 140°; medium-well, 145°), 4-6 minutes on each side. Let stand for 5 minutes, then cut into thin slices.

5. To serve, spread cheese mixture on each baguette slice. Add a piece of steak; top with carrot mixture.

NOTE: *Top loin steak may be labeled as strip steak, Kansas City steak, New York strip steak, ambassador steak or boneless club steak in your region.*

1 APPETIZER: *125 cal., 7g fat (3g sat. fat), 16mg chol., 76mg sod., 13g carb. (8g sugars, 1g fiber), 4g pro.*

HOLIDAY FEASTS

*At the center of the holiday celebration is the feast—
a magnificent meal that will create wonderful memories.
Here are three full menus, plus some a la carte extras
to help you set your own unforgettable table.*

Turkey Feast

MAPLE-SAGE BRINED TURKEY

When the leaves start turning, it's turkey time at our house. We use a maple-sage brine to help brown the bird and make the meat incredibly juicy.
—Kimberly Forni, Laconia, NH

- -

PREP: 40 min. + brining
BAKE: 2½ hours + standing
MAKES: 20 servings

- 4 qt. water
- 1½ cups packed brown sugar
- 1 cup sea salt
- 1 cup maple syrup
- 1 cup cider vinegar
- 24 fresh sage leaves
- 6 bay leaves
- 2 Tbsp. yellow prepared mustard
- 2 Tbsp. coarsely ground pepper
- 1 tsp. ground cloves
- 4 qt. ice water
- 2 turkey-size oven roasting bags
- 1 turkey (14 to 16 lbs.)

TURKEY

- 2 Tbsp. olive oil
- ½ tsp. pepper
- ½ tsp. salt, optional

1. In a large stockpot, combine the first 10 ingredients; bring to a boil. Cook and stir until the sugar and salt are dissolved. Remove from heat. Add 4 qt. ice water to cool the brine to room temperature.
2. Put 1 turkey-size oven roasting bag inside the other; place in a large stockpot. Place turkey in inner bag; pour in cooled brine. Seal bags, pressing out as much air as possible. Refrigerate 18-24 hours.
3. Preheat oven to 350°. Remove turkey from brine; rinse and pat dry. Discard brine. Place turkey on a rack in a shallow roasting pan, breast side up. Tuck wings under turkey; tie drumsticks together. Rub oil over outside of turkey; sprinkle with pepper and, if desired, salt.
4. Roast, uncovered, until a thermometer inserted in thickest part of thigh reads 170°-175°, 2½-3 hours. (Cover loosely with foil if turkey browns too quickly.)
5. Remove turkey from oven; tent with foil. Let stand 20 minutes before carving.
7 OZ. COOKED TURKEY WITH SKIN: *384 cal., 18g fat (5g sat. fat), 172mg chol., 168mg sod., 0 carb. (0 sugars, 0 fiber), 51g pro.*

OYSTER SAUSAGE STUFFING

I've had this wonderful recipe for years and always use it during the holidays—it makes enough to stuff an 8- to 10-lb. turkey. But it's so rich and buttery that I often serve it with pork roast or stuffed pork chops during the year. It never fails to bring raves.
—Page Alexander, Baldwin City, KS

- -

PREP: 35 min. • **BAKE:** 40 min.
MAKES: 9 cups

- 1 envelope onion soup mix
- 2 cups boiling water
- ½ cup butter, cubed
- 10 cups cubed day-old bread, toasted
- 1 can (8 oz.) whole oysters, drained
- ½ lb. bulk pork sausage, cooked and drained
- ½ cup minced fresh parsley
- ¾ tsp. poultry seasoning

1. Preheat oven to 375°. Place soup mix in a bowl; add boiling water and let stand for 5 minutes. In Dutch oven, melt butter. Stir in the bread cubes and onion soup mixture. Cover and cook over low heat 5 minutes, stirring occasionally. Gently stir in the oysters, sausage, parsley and poultry seasoning.
2. Transfer to a large greased cast-iron skillet or 2½-qt. baking dish. Cover and bake until heated through, 40-50 minutes.
¾ CUP: *228 cal., 13g fat (6g sat. fat), 38mg chol., 590mg sod., 22g carb. (2g sugars, 1g fiber), 6g pro.*

GARLIC, BACON & STILTON MASHED POTATOES

Creamy and savory, these mashed potatoes are a perfect partner for nearly any entree. They're a snap to put together in advance.
—Jamie Brown-Miller, Napa, CA

PREP: 30 min. • **COOK:** 20 min.
MAKES: 8 servings

- 6 garlic cloves, peeled
- 1 tsp. olive oil
- 2½ lbs. small red potatoes, scrubbed
- 4 oz. cream cheese, softened
- ½ cup butter, cubed
- ½ cup 2% milk
- ½ tsp. salt
- ½ tsp. pepper
- ⅓ lb. Stilton cheese, crumbled
- 6 bacon strips, cooked and crumbled
- 3 Tbsp. minced fresh parsley, divided

1. Preheat the oven to 425°. Place garlic on a double thickness of heavy-duty foil. Drizzle with oil. Wrap foil around garlic. Bake for 15-20 minutes or until softened. Cool for 10-15 minutes.

2. Meanwhile, place potatoes in a large saucepan and cover with water. Bring to a boil. Reduce heat; cover and cook for 15-20 minutes or until tender. Drain; transfer to a large bowl.

3. Squeeze softened garlic into potatoes. Add the cream cheese, butter, milk, salt and pepper. Mash until the potatoes are desired consistency and ingredients are combined. Stir in Stilton cheese, bacon and 2 Tbsp. parsley. Just before serving, sprinkle with remaining 1 Tbsp. parsley and if desired, additional crumbled blue cheese and bacon.

¾ CUP: 364 cal., 25g fat (14g sat. fat), 71mg chol., 536mg sod., 25g carb. (2g sugars, 3g fiber), 11g pro.

FRESH HERBS AS DECOR

For a festive and aromatic touch, tuck fresh herbs through the napkin ring at each place setting. You can go with a single type of herb for the whole table, or give different herbs to the guests—may we recommend parsley, sage, rosemary and thyme? Don't overdo it, or your place setting will look as if it contains a bouquet garni, but a single sprig is a lovely touch.

MUSHROOM PASTRY PINWHEELS

Pinwheels make a pretty addition to any appetizer buffet, and when I serve them they disappear in a snap. These use purchased puff pastry, so they are easy to make.
—Mary Bettuchy, Saint Robert, MO

- -

PREP: 25 min. • **BAKE:** 20 min. • **MAKES:** 16 servings

- ½ lb. fresh mushrooms, finely chopped
- 2 Tbsp. butter
- 1 shallot, finely chopped
- 2 garlic cloves, minced
- 1 tsp. dried thyme
- ½ cup dry red wine or beef broth
- ⅛ tsp. salt
- ⅛ tsp. pepper
- 1 sheet frozen puff pastry, thawed
- 4 oz. spreadable garlic and herb cream cheese

1. Preheat oven to 400°. In a large skillet, saute mushrooms in butter until tender. Add shallot, garlic and thyme; saute 4-5 minutes longer.
2. Stir in the wine, salt and pepper; bring to a boil. Reduce heat; simmer, uncovered, for 8-10 minutes or until liquid is reduced by three-fourths. Remove from the heat; set aside.
3. On a lightly floured surface, unfold pastry. Roll into a 14x9-in. rectangle. Spread cheese over pastry; top with the mushroom mixture. Roll up jelly-roll style, starting from a short side; pinch seam to seal. Cut into ¾-in. pieces.
4. Place 2 in. apart on a parchment-lined baking sheet. Bake for 16-18 minutes or until golden brown. Serve warm.
1 APPETIZER: *119 cal., 8g fat (3g sat. fat), 13mg chol., 124mg sod., 10g carb. (1g sugars, 1g fiber), 2g pro.*

GREEN BEANS WITH CREAMY PISTACHIO SAUCE

I was asked to bring vegetables for a party and wasn't feeling inspired until I remembered how Mom served them with butter and evaporated milk. I love pistachios, so I added those. Everybody wanted the recipe, and I was really pleased—very little work and lots of happy family and friends!
—Loretta Ouellette, Pompano Beach, FL

- -

TAKES: 30 min. • **MAKES:** 10 servings

- 2 lbs. fresh green beans, trimmed
- 1 tsp. salt
- ½ cup butter, cubed
- ½ cup pistachios, coarsely chopped
- 1 cup evaporated milk
  Salt and pepper to taste

1. Place green beans and salt in a Dutch oven; add water to cover. Bring to a boil. Cook, uncovered, until tender, stirring occasionally, 5-8 minutes. Drain and remove from pan.
2. In the same pan, melt the butter over medium heat. Add pistachios; cook and stir until the pistachios begin to brown, 1-2 minutes. Stir in evaporated milk; bring to a boil. Cook until sauce is slightly thickened, 2-4 minutes. Add green beans; heat through, stirring to coat with sauce. Add salt and pepper to taste.
¾ CUP: *177 cal., 14g fat (7g sat. fat), 32mg chol., 365mg sod., 11g carb. (5g sugars, 4g fiber), 5g pro.*

1 PIECE: 430 cal., 23g fat (4g sat. fat), 109mg chol., 381mg sod., 53g carb. (30g sugars, 2g fiber), 7g pro.

PASTRY FOR SINGLE-CRUST PIE (9 IN.) Combine 1¼ cups all-purpose flour and ¼ tsp. salt; cut in ½ cup cold butter until crumbly. Gradually add 3-5 Tbsp. ice water, tossing with a fork until the dough holds together when pressed. Wrap dough and refrigerate 1 hour.

HOLIDAY RIBBON GELATIN

Layers of red and green make this festive salad a favorite during the Christmas season. Kids are sure to find it fun to eat, and adults will enjoy the combination of sweet-tart flavors.
—Jenny Hughson, Mitchell, NE

PREP: 40 min. + chilling • **MAKES:** 15 servings

- 2 pkg. (3 oz. each) lime gelatin
- 5 cups boiling water, divided
- 4 cups cold water, divided
- 1 pkg. (3 oz.) lemon gelatin
- ½ cup miniature marshmallows
- 1 pkg. (8 oz.) cream cheese, softened
- 1 cup mayonnaise
- 1 can (8 oz.) crushed pineapple, undrained
- 2 pkg. (3 oz. each) cherry gelatin

1. In a large bowl, dissolve lime gelatin in 2 cups boiling water. Add 2 cups of cold water; stir. Pour into a 13x9-in. dish; refrigerate until firm but not set, about 1 hour.

2. In a large bowl, dissolve the lemon gelatin in 1 cup boiling water. Stir in the marshmallows until melted. Cool for 20 minutes. In a small bowl, beat cream cheese and mayonnaise until smooth. Gradually beat in the lemon gelatin. Stir in the pineapple. Carefully spoon over lime layer. Chill until firm but not set.

3. Dissolve cherry gelatin in the remaining 2 cups boiling water. Add remaining 2 cups cold water; stir. Spoon over lemon layer. Refrigerate entire gelatin salad overnight. Cut into squares to serve.

1 SERVING: 236 cal., 17g fat (5g sat. fat), 22mg chol., 164mg sod., 19g carb. (18g sugars, 0 fiber), 3g pro.

PUMPKIN PECAN PIE

I've yet to meet a person who doesn't have room for a piece of this pie! It's a favorite at our little church (where I try out all my recipes on people who love to eat).
—Jean Lockwood, Bayfield, CO

PREP: 20 min. • **BAKE:** 55 min.
MAKES: 8 servings

- Pastry for single-crust pie (9 in.)
- 2 large eggs
- ¼ cup sugar
- ¼ cup packed brown sugar
- 1 tsp. all-purpose flour
- 1 tsp. pumpkin pie spice
- ¼ tsp. salt
- ⅔ cup canned pumpkin
- ⅔ cup 2% milk

PECAN TOPPING
- 2 large eggs
- ½ cup dark corn syrup
- 2 Tbsp. brown sugar
- 2 Tbsp. molasses
- 1 Tbsp. all-purpose flour
- 1 tsp. vanilla extract
- ½ tsp. salt
- ½ cup chopped pecans
- 1 cup pecan halves

1. Preheat oven to 425°. On a lightly floured surface, roll dough to a ⅛-in.-thick circle; transfer to a 9-in. deep-dish pie plate. Trim crust to ½ in. beyond rim of plate; flute edge. Chill crust while preparing filling.

2. Beat eggs, sugars, flour, pumpkin pie spice and salt until smooth. Mix in the pumpkin. Gradually beat in milk. Pour into the prepared pie crust.

3. Bake 10 minutes. Reduce temperature to 350° and bake 15 minutes longer.

4. For pecan topping, beat eggs in a bowl until foamy. Add corn syrup, brown sugar, molasses, flour, vanilla and salt. Pour over the filling. Sprinkle with chopped pecans; cover with pecan halves.

5. Bake at 350° for 30-35 minutes or until set. Cool completely. Store in the refrigerator.

Beef Wellington Feast

BEEF WELLINGTON WITH MADEIRA SAUCE

This impressive-looking yet easy-to-make dish can be made ahead. Just finish when your guests arrive.
—Janaan Cunningham, Greendale, WI

- -

PREP: 45 min. + chilling
BAKE: 40 min. + standing
MAKES: 16 servings

- 1 beef tenderloin roast (4 to 5 lbs.)
- 2 cans (10½ oz. each) condensed beef consomme, undiluted
- 2 Tbsp. tomato paste
- ½ tsp. beef bouillon granules
- 2 Tbsp. butter, softened
- 2 Tbsp. all-purpose flour
- ½ cup Madeira wine
- 2 cups chopped fresh mushrooms
- 4 shallots, chopped
- ¼ lb. sliced deli ham, chopped
- ¼ cup minced fresh parsley
- 1 pkg. (17.3 oz.) frozen puff pastry sheets, thawed
- 2 Tbsp. 2% milk
- 1 large egg, lightly beaten, optional

1. Preheat oven to 475°. Place tenderloin in a greased 15x10x1-in. baking pan; fold ends under tenderloin. Bake, uncovered, for 20-25 minutes or until browned. Cover and refrigerate until chilled for at least 2 hours.

2. For sauce, in a large saucepan, combine the consomme, tomato paste and bouillon granules. Bring to a boil. Reduce the heat; simmer, uncovered, for 20 minutes or until reduced to 2 cups.

3. Combine butter and flour until smooth. Stir into sauce, a teaspoon at a time. Bring to a boil; cook and stir for 2 minutes or until thickened. Remove from the heat; stir in Madeira and set aside.

4. For the filling, in a large skillet, combine mushrooms, shallots, ham and 2 Tbsp. Madeira sauce. Cook over low heat for 10 minutes, stirring occasionally. Stir in the parsley; cook 10 minutes longer or until liquid has evaporated, stirring occasionally. Set aside.

5. Preheat the oven to 425°. On a lightly floured surface, unfold both puff pastry sheets; moisten the short side of 1 sheet with water. Slightly overlap edge of the remaining sheet with the moistened edge; press edges together to seal. Transfer to an ungreased baking sheet.

6. Spread half the filling down the center of the pastry. Place the tenderloin on the filling. Spread the remaining filling over the top of meat. Bring the edges of the pastry over the filling and pinch together. Roll over to place seam side down. Brush pastry edges with milk; fold edges under meat. If desired, lightly score puff pastry with a sharp knife to form a diamond pattern and brush with beaten egg.

7. Bake, uncovered, until deep golden brown, 40 minutes. Cover lightly with foil if needed to prevent overbrowning (meat will be medium-rare). Transfer to a serving platter. Let stand for 15 minutes before slicing. Rewarm Madeira sauce if necessary. Serve with tenderloin.

1 PIECE: *363 cal., 17g fat (5g sat. fat), 56mg chol., 453mg sod., 21g carb. (2g sugars, 3g fiber), 30g pro.*

CREAMY CAULIFLOWER RICE

What began as a quick-fix dish has become a staple in our house. It's a wonderful way to add veggies to a meal, and it's a nice change from traditional cauliflower.
—Caresse Caton, Mobile, AL

- -

TAKES: 30 min. • **MAKES:** 10 servings

- 3 cups uncooked long grain rice
- 3 cups frozen cauliflower, thawed
- 6 cups reduced-sodium chicken broth
- 6 oz. cream cheese, cubed
- ¾ tsp. salt
- ¼ tsp. pepper

In a large saucepan, combine rice, cauliflower and broth; bring to a boil. Reduce heat; simmer, covered, for 15-20 minutes or until the liquid is absorbed and rice is tender. Remove from heat. Add cream cheese, salt and pepper; stir until melted.

¾ CUP: *301 cal., 6g fat (4g sat. fat), 17mg chol., 584mg sod., 52g carb. (2g sugars, 2g fiber), 8g pro.*

ROASTED BEETS WITH ORANGE GREMOLATA & GOAT CHEESE

My grandma pickled or canned her home-grown beets, but I prefer to prepare them differently. These roasted beets can be enjoyed all year—serve them warm or chilled.
—Courtney Archibeque, Greeley, CO

PREP: 25 min. • **BAKE:** 55 min. + cooling • **MAKES:** 12 servings

- 3 medium fresh golden beets (about 1 lb.)
- 3 medium fresh beets (about 1 lb.)
- 2 Tbsp. lime juice
- 2 Tbsp. orange juice
- ½ tsp. fine sea salt
- 1 Tbsp. minced fresh parsley
- 1 Tbsp. minced fresh sage
- 1 garlic clove, minced
- 1 tsp. grated orange zest
- 3 Tbsp. crumbled goat cheese
- 2 Tbsp. sunflower kernels

1. Preheat oven to 400°. Scrub beets and trim tops by 1 in. Place beets on a double thickness of heavy-duty foil (about 24x12 in.). Fold foil around beets, sealing tightly. Place on a baking sheet. Roast until tender, 55-65 minutes. Open foil carefully to allow steam to escape.
2. When cool enough to handle, peel, halve and slice beets; place in a serving bowl. Add the lime juice, orange juice and salt; toss to coat. Combine parsley, sage, garlic and orange zest; sprinkle over beets. Top with goat cheese and sunflower kernels.
¾ **CUP:** 49 cal., 1g fat (0 sat. fat), 2mg chol., 157mg sod., 9g carb. (6g sugars, 2g fiber), 2g pro.

KALE & BACON SALAD WITH HONEY-HORSERADISH VINAIGRETTE

Totally scrumptious and packed with nutrition, this salad was my response to friends who asked how they could incorporate kale into their diets without sacrificing taste. It is also wonderful made with collard or mustard greens prepared in the same fashion as the kale, or with a mix of spinach and arugula or watercress.
—Elizabeth Warren, Oklahoma City, OK

PREP: 35 min. • **MAKES:** 8 servings

- 10 kale leaves, stems removed, thinly sliced
- ¼ cup loosely packed basil leaves, thinly sliced
- ½ cup alfalfa sprouts
- 4 bacon strips, cooked and crumbled
- ½ cup crumbled feta cheese
- ½ medium ripe avocado, peeled and thinly sliced
- 1 hard-boiled large egg, chopped
- 1 cup grape tomatoes, chopped

VINAIGRETTE
- ⅓ cup olive oil
- 3 Tbsp. lemon juice
- 2 Tbsp. prepared horseradish
- 2 Tbsp. honey
- 1½ tsp. garlic powder
- 1½ tsp. spicy brown mustard
- ¼ tsp. crushed red pepper flakes
- ⅛ tsp. pepper
  Dash salt

1. On a serving platter or individual plates, arrange kale and basil. Top with sprouts, bacon, cheese, avocado, egg and tomatoes.
2. In a small bowl, whisk the vinaigrette ingredients. Drizzle over salad; serve immediately.
1 **SERVING:** 236 cal., 15g fat (3g sat. fat), 34mg chol., 248mg sod., 21g carb. (6g sugars, 4g fiber), 8g pro.

LOBSTER BISQUE

*My grandmother made lobster bisque all
the time, so I have always thought of it as
comfort food. If you don't care to cook live
lobsters, the store where you buy them can
usually cook them for you. Just be sure to
say you want to keep the shells; they are
key to the most delicious soup!*
—James Schend, Pleasant Prairie, WI

- -

PREP: 35 min. • **COOK:** 70 min.
MAKES: 2 qt.

- 2 live lobsters (about 1 lb. each)
- 2 medium carrots, peeled and
  chopped
- 1 medium onion, chopped
- 3 Tbsp. butter
- 2 Tbsp. tomato paste
- 2 garlic cloves, minced

- ¾ cup white wine or sherry
- 1 carton (32 oz.) seafood stock
- ⅔ cup uncooked long grain rice
- 2 cups heavy whipping cream
- 1 tsp. minced fresh thyme
- 1½ tsp. salt
- 1 tsp. coarsely ground pepper
  Minced fresh parsley, optional

1. In a Dutch oven, bring 2 in. of water
to a rolling boil. Add lobsters; cover and
steam for 8 minutes. Remove lobsters,
reserving liquid. When cool enough to
handle, remove meat from claws and
tail, reserving any juices; refrigerate
meat and juices.

2. In the same Dutch oven, cook carrots
and onion in butter over medium-high
heat until tender, 5-8 minutes. Stir in
tomato paste and cook until it starts to
caramelize, about 5 minutes. Add garlic;
cook 1 minute. Stir in wine and simmer
until reduced by half. Add lobster shells,
bodies, reserved cooking liquid, reserved
lobster juices and stock. Bring mixture to
a simmer; cook 1 hour.

3. Strain mixture, pressing to extract as
much liquid as possible; discard shells
and solids. Return liquid to Dutch oven.
Add rice and cook until extremely soft,
25-30 minutes.

4. Puree in a blender until smooth. Add
cream, thyme, salt and pepper. Bring
mixture to a very low simmer; add the
reserved lobster meat and cook until
heated through. If desired, sprinkle with
additional black pepper and parsley.

1 CUP: *373 cal., 26g fat (17g sat. fat), 127mg
chol., 942mg sod., 20g carb. (4g sugars,
1g fiber), 10g pro.*

COCONUT CRANBERRY ALASKA

This impressive treat is my favorite company dessert, and it's perfect for a holiday gathering! The recipe is easy to prepare in advance and makes such a beautiful presentation. I always receive raves when I serve it and predict that you will, too.
—Joan Hallford, North Richland Hills, TX

PREP: 30 min. + chilling
BAKE: 20 min. + cooling
MAKES: 16 servings

- 1 pkg. (9 oz.) white or yellow cake mix
- 2 envelopes unflavored gelatin
- ½ cup sugar, divided
- 1½ cups cranberry juice
- 1 can (14 oz.) whole-berry cranberry sauce
- 3 cups heavy whipping cream, divided
- ¼ cup chopped pecans
- 1½ cups sweetened shredded coconut, toasted

1. Prepare and bake cake according to package directions, using a greased 9-in. round baking pan. Cool on a wire rack.
2. In a large bowl, combine gelatin and ¼ cup sugar. Bring cranberry juice to a boil; stir into gelatin mixture until dissolved. Stir in cranberry sauce. Refrigerate until partially set.
3. In a small bowl, beat 1 cup cream until soft peaks form. Fold the whipped cream and pecans into gelatin mixture. Pour mixture into a 2-qt. bowl with a 9-in.-diameter rim coated with cooking spray. Refrigerate until set.
4. Place cake over gelatin mixture; trim if necessary. Invert dessert onto a serving plate. In a large bowl, beat the remaining 2 cups cream until it begins to thicken. Add remaining ¼ cup sugar; beat until stiff peaks form. Spread over the gelatin mixture and cake. Sprinkle with coconut.
1 PIECE: *396 cal., 27g fat (14g sat. fat), 86mg chol., 174mg sod., 37g carb. (27g sugars, 1g fiber), 4g pro.*

BRUSSELS SPROUTS SAUTE

Salty, savory and sprinkled with Parmesan, this dish appeals even to people who don't like Brussels sprouts. The onions and garlic add tremendous flavor.
—Deirdre Cox, Kansas City, MO

TAKES: 30 min. • **MAKES:** 8 servings

- 2 lbs. fresh Brussels sprouts, thinly sliced
- 3 Tbsp. canola oil
- 1 large onion, finely chopped
- 7 thin slices prosciutto or deli ham (about 5 oz.), cut into strips
- 4 garlic cloves, minced
- ½ tsp. pepper
- ¼ tsp. salt
- ⅔ cup plus 3 Tbsp. grated Parmesan cheese, divided

1. In a Dutch oven, bring 8 cups water to a boil. Add Brussels sprouts; cook, uncovered, 3-4 minutes or until tender. Drain sprouts.
2. In a large skillet, heat oil over medium-high heat. Add onion and prosciutto; cook and stir for 5-6 minutes or until onion is tender. Add garlic; cook 1 minute longer. Add Brussels sprouts, pepper and salt; heat through. Stir in ⅔ cup cheese. Sprinkle with remaining 3 Tbsp. cheese.
¾ CUP: *169 cal., 10g fat (2g sat. fat), 19mg chol., 474mg sod., 13g carb. (3g sugars, 5g fiber), 11g pro.*

Stuffed Pork Roast Feast

WILD RICE-STUFFED PORK LOIN

This recipe features wild rice and apricot stuffing tucked inside a tender pork roast.
—Kim Rubner, Worthington, IA

PREP: 20 min. • **BAKE:** 1½ hours + standing
MAKES: 10 servings

- 1 whole boneless pork loin roast (4 lbs.), trimmed
- 1 tsp. salt
- ½ tsp. garlic powder
- ¼ tsp. pepper
- 2 cups wild rice, cooked and drained
- 1½ cups coarsely chopped dried apricots
- 1 cup chopped onion
- ¾ cup finely chopped celery
- ¾ cup minced fresh parsley
- ½ tsp. rubbed sage
- ½ tsp. dried thyme
- ½ cup chicken broth
- 10 bacon strips
  Apricot preserves, optional

1. To butterfly the pork roast, cut a lengthwise slit down the center of the pork loin to within ½ in. of bottom. Open loin so it lies flat. On each half, make another lengthwise slit down the center to within ½ in. of bottom. Flatten to ¼-in. thickness. Sprinkle with salt, garlic powder and pepper.
2. Preheat oven to 350°. In a large bowl, combine the rice, apricots, onion, celery, parsley, sage, thyme and broth. Spread stuffing evenly over pork, ¼-½ in. thick. Roll up jelly-roll style, starting with a long side. Tie the roast at 1½-to-2-in. intervals with kitchen string. Place the remaining stuffing in a greased shallow 2-qt. baking dish; set aside.
3. Bake roast, uncovered, for 1 hour. Remove from oven; carefully remove string. Place bacon strips over top of roast, overlapping slightly. Bake until the bacon is browned and crisp and a thermometer reads 160°, 30-45 minutes longer. If needed, broil 4 in. from heat until bacon reaches desired crispness. Cover and bake remaining stuffing until heated through, about 30 minutes.
4. Let roast stand for 10 minutes before slicing. If desired, brush with apricot preserves before slicing.

1 SERVING: *436 cal., 20g fat (7g sat. fat), 109mg chol., 547mg sod., 23g carb. (10g sugars, 3g fiber), 41g pro.*

ELEGANT CRANBERRY PEAR SALAD

This salad recipe, with its combination of fresh ingredients and crunchy walnuts, is quick to make and yet looks very elegant—perfect for entertaining.
—Irene Fenlason, Helena, MT

TAKES: 15 min. • **MAKES:** 12 servings

- 9 cups torn red leaf lettuce
- 1 medium pear, chopped
- 1 small red onion, halved and sliced
- ½ cup crumbled blue cheese
- ⅓ cup dried cranberries
- ⅓ cup chopped walnuts, toasted

DRESSING
- ½ cup canola oil
- ¼ cup sugar
- ¼ cup red wine vinegar
- ½ tsp. poppy seeds
- ⅛ tsp. Worcestershire sauce

In a large serving bowl, combine the first 6 ingredients. In a jar with a tight-fitting lid, combine the dressing ingredients; shake well. Just before serving, shake the dressing again and pour over salad; toss to coat.
¾ CUP: *169 cal., 13g fat (2g sat. fat), 4mg chol., 73mg sod., 12g carb. (9g sugars, 1g fiber), 2g pro.*
DIABETIC EXCHANGES: *2½ fat, 1 vegetable, ½ starch.*

MAPLE-GINGERROOT VEGETABLES

My family loves the drizzling of golden maple syrup on these roasted vegetables. I prefer to use dark maple syrup. Either way, it's a great way to add a delectable sweetness to earthy root vegetables.
—Kelli Ritz, Innisfail, AB

PREP: 35 min. • **BAKE:** 45 min. • **MAKES:** 24 servings

- 5 medium parsnips, peeled and sliced
- 5 small carrots, sliced
- 3 medium turnips, peeled and cubed
- 1 large sweet potato, peeled and cubed
- 1 small rutabaga, peeled and cubed
- 1 large sweet onion, cut into wedges
- 1 small red onion, cut into wedges
- 2 Tbsp. olive oil
- 1 Tbsp. minced fresh gingerroot
- 1 tsp. salt
- ½ tsp. pepper
- 1 cup maple syrup

1. Place the first 7 ingredients in a large bowl; add the oil, ginger, salt and pepper. Toss to coat. Arrange vegetables in a single layer in two 15x10x1-in. baking pans coated with cooking spray. Bake, uncovered, at 425° for 25 minutes, stirring once.

2. Drizzle with syrup. Bake 20-25 minutes longer or until the vegetables are tender, stirring once more.

¾ **CUP:** *92 cal., 1g fat (0 sat. fat), 0 chol., 119mg sod., 20g carb. (13g sugars, 2g fiber), 1g pro.*
DIABETIC EXCHANGES: *1 starch.*

BAKED PARMESAN BROCCOLI

I began making this creamy side dish years ago as a way to get my kids to eat broccoli. They have since grown up but still request this satisfying casserole. It's truly a family favorite.
—Barbara Uhl, Wesley Chapel, FL

PREP: 30 min. • **BAKE:** 15 min. • **MAKES:** 12 servings

- 4 bunches broccoli, cut into florets
- 6 Tbsp. butter, divided
- 1 small onion, finely chopped
- 1 garlic clove, minced
- ¼ cup all-purpose flour
- 2 cups 2% milk
- 1 large egg yolk, beaten
- 1 cup grated Parmesan cheese
- ½ tsp. salt
- ⅛ tsp. pepper
- ½ cup seasoned bread crumbs

1. Preheat oven to 400°. Place half of the broccoli in a steamer basket; place in a large saucepan over 1 in. of water. Bring to a boil; cover and steam 3-4 minutes or until crisp-tender. Place in a greased 13x9-in. baking dish. Repeat with remaining broccoli.

2. Meanwhile, melt 4 Tbsp. butter in a small saucepan over medium heat. Add onion; cook and stir until tender. Add garlic; cook 1 minute longer.

3. Stir in flour until blended; gradually add milk. Bring to a boil; cook and stir 2 minutes or until thickened. Stir a small amount of hot mixture into the egg yolk; return all to the pan, stirring constantly. Cook and stir 1 minute longer. Remove from heat; stir in the cheese, salt and pepper. Pour over broccoli.

4. In a small skillet, cook bread crumbs in the remaining 2 Tbsp. butter until golden brown; sprinkle over the top.

5. Bake, uncovered, 15-18 minutes or until heated through.
¾ **CUP:** *191 cal., 10g fat (5g sat. fat), 41mg chol., 388mg sod., 19g carb. (7g sugars, 6g fiber), 11g pro.*

CHERRY & FONTINA STUFFED PORTOBELLOS

I developed this hearty appetizer for my mushroom-loving kids. They're grown now with families of their own, but they still lobby for these when they come home.
—Wendy Rusch, Cameron, WI

PREP: 30 min. • **BAKE:** 15 min.
MAKES: 12 servings

- 6 large portobello mushrooms
- ½ cup butter, cubed
- 1 medium onion, chopped
- 1 cup pecan halves, toasted
- 1 pkg. (5 oz.) dried tart cherries, coarsely chopped
- ½ tsp. poultry seasoning
- ½ tsp. dried thyme
- 7 oz. (about 4½ cups) seasoned stuffing cubes
- 1½ to 2 cups chicken broth
- 1½ cups shredded fontina cheese, divided

1. Preheat oven to 375°. Wipe mushroom caps clean with a damp paper towel; remove stems and gills and discard. Place caps on a foil-lined 15x10x1-in. baking pan.
2. In a large skillet, melt butter over medium heat until it begins to brown and smell nutty. Add onion; saute until translucent, stirring occasionally. Stir in pecans, cherries and seasonings; cook and stir 3 minutes. Remove from heat.
3. Combine onion mixture and stuffing cubes, tossing to coat evenly. Add 1½ cups broth to onion-stuffing mixture, stirring until well mixed. Add remaining broth as needed. Stir in 1 cup cheese.

4. Fill mushroom caps with stuffing until mounded, about 1 cup each. Sprinkle with the remaining ½ cup cheese. Bake until mushrooms are heated through and cheese is melted, 15-20 minutes. Cut in half; serve warm.
½ STUFFED PORTOBELLO: 301 cal., 19g fat (8g sat. fat), 37mg chol., 531mg sod., 27g carb. (8g sugars, 6g fiber), 8g pro.

¾ cup cake flour
Confectioners' sugar

FILLING

2⅓ cups fresh or frozen cranberries
1 cup sugar
6 Tbsp. water, divided
⅓ cup chopped candied orange peel, optional
1 Tbsp. orange liqueur, optional
1 tsp. grated orange zest, optional
2 Tbsp. cornstarch
Additional confectioners' sugar
Optional: Sugared cranberries and candied orange peel, for garnish

1. Place egg whites in a large bowl; let stand at room temperature for 30 minutes. Line a greased 15x10x1-in. baking pan with waxed paper; grease the paper and set aside.
2. Add vanilla, cream of tartar and salt to egg whites; beat on medium speed until soft peaks form. Gradually beat in sugar, 2 Tbsp. at a time, on high until stiff glossy peaks form and sugar is dissolved. Fold in flour, about ¼ cup at a time.
3. Carefully spread batter into prepared pan. Bake at 350° until cake springs back when lightly touched, 15-20 minutes. Cool for 5 minutes. Turn cake onto a kitchen towel dusted with confectioners' sugar. Gently peel off waxed paper. Roll up cake in the towel jelly-roll style, starting with a short side. Cool completely on a wire rack.
4. For filling, in a large saucepan, combine cranberries, sugar and ¼ cup water. Bring to a boil. Reduce heat; simmer, uncovered, for 5-6 minutes or until berries pop. Mash the berries; strain, reserving juice and discarding pulp.
5. Return juice to the pan. If desired, add chopped candied orange peel, orange liquor and orange zest. Combine the cornstarch and remaining 2 Tbsp. water until smooth; gradually add to cranberry juice mixture. Bring to a boil; cook and stir until thickened, about 2 minutes. Chill.
6. Unroll cake; spread the filling to within ½ in. of edges. Roll up again. Refrigerate for 1 hour. Dust with confectioners' sugar and, if desired, garnish with the candied orange peel and sugared cranberries. Refrigerate leftovers.
1 PIECE: *196 cal., 0 fat (0 sat. fat), 0 chol., 91mg sod., 46g carb. (36g sugars, 1g fiber), 3g pro.*

BUTTERNUT SQUASH CUSTARD

My husband first tried this comforting casserole more than 10 years ago when he was still my fiance. Having enjoyed it so much, he said I needed to offer it at every holiday dinner. I was happy to oblige!
—Maura Calusdian, Londonderry, NH

- -

PREP: 25 min. • **BAKE:** 55 min.
MAKES: 8 servings

1 medium butternut squash (2 to 3 lbs.), peeled, seeded and cubed
½ cup all-purpose flour
½ cup sugar
2 cups 2% milk
3 large eggs
2 Tbsp. butter, melted
⅛ tsp. salt
⅛ tsp. ground cinnamon
⅛ tsp. ground nutmeg

1. Place squash in a large saucepan and cover with water; bring to a boil. Reduce heat; cover and simmer until tender, 8-10 minutes. Drain.
2. In a large bowl, mash the squash with flour and sugar until blended; beat in the milk, eggs and butter. Pour into an ungreased 2½-qt. baking dish. Sprinkle with remaining ingredients.
3. Bake at 350° until center appears set, 55-65 minutes.
¾ CUP: *202 cal., 6g fat (3g sat. fat), 91mg chol., 118mg sod., 33g carb. (18g sugars, 3g fiber), 6g pro.*

CRANBERRY CAKE ROLL

This low-fat angel food cake roll makes a deliciously light finish to rich and filling meals—much appreciated during the holiday season!
—Paige Kowolewski, Topton, PA

- -

PREP: 45 min. + chilling
BAKE: 20 min. + cooling
MAKES: 12 servings

9 large egg whites
1½ tsp. vanilla extract
¾ tsp. cream of tartar
¼ tsp. salt
1 cup plus 2 Tbsp. sugar

More Choices for Christmas Menus

To make the feasts in this chapter just right for your family, swap any of the recipes for a course from this section. Or, if you like, create your own all-new personalized menu using these selections!

TOMATO-WALNUT PESTO SPREAD

Whenever I bring this popular spread to parties, I know I"ll need extra copies of the recipe. Once people taste the spread, they always ask how I make it. The red, green and white layers make it especially festive for Christmastime.

—Marsha Dawson, Appleton, WI

PREP: 15 min. + chilling • MAKES: 2⅓ cups

- 3 Tbsp. chopped oil-packed sun-dried tomatoes, patted dry
- 1 pkg. (8 oz.) cream cheese, softened
- ½ cup grated Parmesan cheese
- ¼ cup sour cream
- 2 Tbsp. butter, softened
- ½ cup finely chopped walnuts
- ½ cup prepared pesto
  Assorted crackers

1. Line a 4-cup mold with plastic wrap; coat with cooking spray. Place chopped tomatoes in bottom of mold; set aside.
2. In a large bowl, beat the cheeses, sour cream and butter until blended. In another bowl, combine walnuts and pesto. Spread cheese mixture over tomatoes in prepared mold; top with walnut mixture.
3. Bring edges of plastic wrap together over pesto; press down gently to seal. Refrigerate for at least 4 hours or until firm. Open plastic wrap; invert mold onto a serving plate. Serve with crackers.
2 TBSP.: *129 cal., 12g fat (5g sat. fat), 24mg chol., 137mg sod., 2g carb. (0 sugars, 0 fiber), 4g pro.*

SPECIAL SEAFOOD CASSEROLE

I first sampled this casserole at a baby shower and found myself going back for more. The trick is to add a bit of sherry or apple juice to the sauce.

—Angela Schwartz, Marietta, GA

PREP: 25 min. • BAKE: 25 min. + standing
MAKES: 6 servings

- ½ lb. sea scallops
- 1 small onion, finely chopped
- 1 celery rib, finely chopped
- 6 Tbsp. butter, cubed
- 7 Tbsp. all-purpose flour
- 1½ cups half-and-half cream

- 1 cup shredded sharp cheddar cheese
- 6 Tbsp. sherry or apple juice
- ¾ tsp. salt
- ¼ tsp. cayenne pepper
- 1 lb. cooked medium shrimp, peeled and deveined
- 1 can (6 oz.) crab
- 1 can (14 oz.) water-packed artichoke hearts, drained, rinsed, chopped and patted dry
- 1 can (8 oz.) sliced water chestnuts, drained
- ½ cup sliced almonds
- ¼ cup grated Parmesan cheese

1. Preheat oven to 350°. In a Dutch oven, saute scallops, onion and celery in butter until scallops are firm and opaque. Stir in flour until blended. Add cream. Bring to a boil; cook and stir 2 minutes or until thickened. Reduce heat; add cheddar cheese, sherry, salt and cayenne, stirring until the cheese is melted. Remove from heat; set aside.
2. In a greased 11x7-in. baking dish, layer the shrimp, crab, artichokes and water chestnuts. Top with sauce. Sprinkle with almonds and Parmesan cheese.
3. Bake, uncovered, for 25-30 minutes or until heated through. Let stand 10 minutes before serving.
1 SERVING: *518 cal., 30g fat (16g sat. fat), 236mg chol., 894mg sod., 19g carb. (5g sugars, 2g fiber), 38g pro.*

MUSHROOM & SWEET POTATO POTPIE

The last time I was in the U.S., I had an amazing mushroom and beer potpie at a small brew pub. It was so rich and comforting. I tried numerous versions when I got home and I think I've come pretty close!
—Iben Ravn, Copenhagen, Denmark

- -

PREP: 45 min. • **BAKE:** 30 min.
MAKES: 8 servings

⅓ cup olive oil, divided
1   lb. sliced fresh shiitake mushrooms
1   lb. sliced baby portobello mushrooms
2   large onions, chopped
2   garlic cloves, minced
1   tsp. minced fresh rosemary, plus more for topping
1   bottle (12 oz.) porter or stout beer
1½ cups mushroom broth or vegetable broth, divided
2   bay leaves

1   Tbsp. balsamic vinegar
2   Tbsp. reduced-sodium soy sauce
¼   cup cornstarch
3   to 4 small sweet potatoes, peeled and thinly sliced
¾   tsp. coarsely ground pepper
½   tsp. salt

1. Preheat oven to 400°. In a Dutch oven, heat 1 Tbsp. oil over medium heat. Add shiitake mushrooms and cook in batches until dark golden brown, 8-10 minutes; remove with a slotted spoon. Repeat with 1 Tbsp. oil and the portobello mushrooms.
2. In the same pan, heat 1 Tbsp. oil over medium heat. Add onions; cook and stir 8-10 minutes or until tender. Add garlic and 1 tsp. rosemary; cook for 30 seconds longer. Stir in the beer, 1 cup broth, bay leaves, vinegar, soy sauce and sauteed mushrooms.
3. Bring to a boil. Reduce heat; simmer, uncovered, 10 minutes. In a small bowl, mix cornstarch and remaining ½ cup broth until smooth; stir into mushroom

mixture. Return mixture to a boil, stirring constantly; cook and stir until thickened, 1-2 minutes. Remove and discard the bay leaves; transfer the mushroom mixture to 8 greased 8-oz. ramekins. Place on a rimmed baking sheet.
4. Layer sweet potatoes in a circular pattern on top of each ramekin; brush with remaining oil and sprinkle with pepper, salt and additional rosemary. Bake, covered, until potatoes are tender, 20-25 minutes. Remove cover and bake until lightly browned, 8-10 minutes. Let stand 5 minutes before serving.
1 SERVING: *211 cal., 10g fat (1g sat. fat), 0 chol., 407mg sod., 26g carb. (10g sugars, 4g fiber), 5g pro.*

Holiday Helper

Instead of beer, you could use dry red wine, Marsala or additional mushroom broth.

CURRIED PUMPKIN APPLE SOUP

Sweet apples and spicy curry make a tasty pair in this rich soup. It's everything you want on a chilly evening.
—*Jane Shapton, Irvine, CA*

PREP: 15 min. • **COOK:** 25 min. • **MAKES:** 8 servings (2 qt.)

- 2 medium Golden Delicious apples, peeled and coarsely chopped
- 1 medium onion, chopped
- 1 medium leek (white portion only), sliced
- 2 Tbsp. butter
- 3 garlic cloves, minced
- 2 to 3 tsp. curry powder
- 1 can (15 oz.) pumpkin
- 4 cups chicken broth
- 1 cup heavy whipping cream
  Salt to taste
  Fresh cilantro leaves, optional

1. In a large saucepan, saute the apples, onion and leek in butter until tender. Add the garlic and curry; cook 1 minute longer. Add pumpkin and broth; bring to a boil. Reduce the heat; cover and simmer for 20 minutes. Stir in cream; heat through (do not boil).
2. Remove from the heat; cool slightly. In a blender, process soup in batches until smooth. Season with salt. If desired, garnish with cilantro.
1 CUP: *187 cal., 15g fat (9g sat. fat), 48mg chol., 511mg sod., 13g carb. (8g sugars, 4g fiber), 3g pro.*

BUTTERNUT THYME TARTLETS

A teaser for what's to come, this light and crunchy appetizer is filled with my favorite late-fall flavors. Make the creamy filling a few days early, then fill the phyllo cups right before guests arrive.
—*Arlene Erlbach, Morton Grove, IL*

PREP: 25 min. • **BAKE:** 10 min. + cooling • **MAKES:** 2½ dozen

- 2 pkg. (1.9 oz. each) frozen miniature phyllo tart shells
- 1 pkg. (8 oz.) reduced-fat cream cheese
- 1½ cups frozen cubed butternut squash (about 8 oz.), thawed and patted dry
- ½ cup crumbled goat cheese
- 1 shallot, finely chopped
- 1 Tbsp. minced fresh thyme
- 1½ tsp. grated lemon zest
- ½ tsp. rubbed sage
- ⅛ tsp. salt
- ⅛ tsp. ground nutmeg
- ⅛ tsp. pepper
  Fresh thyme leaves

1. Preheat oven to 350°. Place shells in a 15x10x1-in. pan. Bake until golden brown, 8-10 minutes. Cool completely.
2. For filling, beat cream cheese on medium speed until fluffy, about 2 minutes. Coarsely chop squash; add to cream cheese. Add the goat cheese, shallot, minced thyme, lemon zest and seasonings; beat until blended.
3. To serve, spoon about 1 Tbsp. filling into each shell. Top with thyme. Refrigerate leftovers.
1 TARTLET: *49 cal., 3g fat (1g sat. fat), 8mg chol., 60mg sod., 4g carb. (1g sugars, 0 fiber), 2g pro.*

CRANBERRY RICOTTA GNOCCHI WITH BROWNED BUTTER SAUCE

To make light, airy gnocchi, work quickly and handle the dough as little as possible. You'll be pleased with the result!
—Sally Sibthorpe, Shelby Township, MI

- -

PREP: 30 min. + standing • **COOK:** 15 min.
MAKES: 8 servings

- ¾ cup dried cranberries, divided
- 2 cups ricotta cheese
- 1 cup all-purpose flour
- ½ cup grated Parmesan cheese
- 1 large egg, lightly beaten
- ¾ tsp. salt, divided
- 4 qt. water
- ¾ cup butter, cubed
- 2 Tbsp. minced fresh sage
- ½ cup chopped walnuts, toasted
- ⅛ tsp. white pepper

1. Finely chop ¼ cup cranberries. In a large bowl, combine ricotta cheese, flour, Parmesan cheese, egg, ½ tsp. salt and chopped cranberries; mix until blended. On a lightly floured surface, knead 10-12 times, forming a soft dough. Cover and let rest for 10 minutes.
2. Divide dough into 4 portions. On a floured surface, roll each portion into a ¾-in.-thick rope; cut into ¾-in. pieces. Press and roll each piece with a lightly floured fork.
3. In a Dutch oven, bring water to a boil. Cook gnocchi in batches 30-60 seconds or until they float. Remove with a slotted spoon; keep warm.
4. In a large heavy saucepan, cook butter over medium heat 5 minutes. Add sage; cook 3-5 minutes longer or until butter is golden brown, stirring occasionally. Stir in the walnuts, white pepper, remaining ½ cup cranberries and remaining ¼ tsp. salt. Add gnocchi; stir gently to coat.

¾ CUP: *411 cal., 30g fat (16g sat. fat), 101mg chol., 503mg sod., 26g carb. (11g sugars, 1g fiber), 13g pro.*

HERB BUTTERMILK DINNER ROLLS

When I couldn't find a recipe for dinner rolls, I created my own using a variety of herbs for extra flavor.
—Sue Friesen, Thorold, ON

- -

PREP: 20 min. + rising • **BAKE:** 25 min.
MAKES: 2 dozen

- 1 pkg. (¼ oz.) active dry yeast
- ¼ cup warm water (110° to 115°)
- ¾ cup warm buttermilk (110° to 115°)
- 4 Tbsp. butter, melted, divided
- 2 Tbsp. sugar
- 1½ tsp. salt
- ½ tsp. dried basil
- ½ tsp. dried marjoram
- ½ tsp. dried thyme
- ¼ tsp. baking soda
- 1 large egg, room temperature
- 2¾ to 3¼ cups all-purpose flour

1. Dissolve yeast in the warm water. Add buttermilk, 2 Tbsp. butter and the next 7 ingredients. Stir in 2 cups flour. Beat until smooth. Stir in enough remaining flour to form a soft dough, which will be sticky.
2. Turn dough onto a heavily floured surface; knead until smooth and elastic, 6-8 minutes. Place in a greased bowl, turning once to grease top. Cover and let rise in a warm place until doubled, about 75 minutes.
3. Punch dough down. Turn onto a lightly floured surface; divide into 4 portions. Divide each portion into 6 pieces; shape each piece into a ball. Place in a greased 13x9-in. baking pan. Cover and let rise until doubled, about 50 minutes.
4. Preheat oven to 375°. Bake rolls until golden brown, 25-30 minutes. Cool for 5 minutes before removing from pan to a wire rack. Brush with remaining 2 Tbsp. melted butter.

1 ROLL: *78 cal., 2g fat (1g sat. fat), 14mg chol., 186mg sod., 12g carb. (1g sugars, 0 fiber), 2g pro.*

HOLIDAY LETTUCE SALAD

My family always requests that I make this salad for get-togethers. It's light and very good; everyone goes back for seconds.
—Bryan Braack, Eldridge, IA

TAKES: 20 min. • **MAKES:** 14 servings

10	cups torn romaine
2	medium red apples, cubed
2	medium pears, cubed
1	cup shredded Swiss cheese
½	cup dried cranberries

DRESSING

6	Tbsp. lemon juice
3	Tbsp. canola oil
3	Tbsp. light corn syrup
1½	tsp. grated onion
1½	tsp. Dijon mustard
½	tsp. salt
½	cup chopped lightly salted cashews

1. In a large salad bowl, combine the first 5 ingredients.

2. For dressing, in a small bowl, whisk lemon juice, oil, corn syrup, onion, mustard and salt. Pour over romaine mixture; toss to coat. Sprinkle with chopped cashews.

1 CUP: *144 cal., 8g fat (2g sat. fat), 7mg chol., 134mg sod., 17g carb. (9g sugars, 3g fiber), 4g pro.*

DIABETIC EXCHANGES: *1½ fat, 1 starch, 1 vegetable.*

CARROT & KALE VEGETABLE SAUTE

Thanks to fresh veggie dishes like this one, I almost forget I'm wheat- and gluten-free. This gorgeous side dish is awesome topped with bacon.
—Darla Andrews, Boerne, TX

PREP: 15 min. • **COOK:** 20 min.
MAKES: 8 servings

8	bacon strips, coarsely chopped
4	large carrots, sliced
2	cups peeled cubed butternut squash (½-in. pieces)
1	poblano pepper, seeded and chopped
½	cup finely chopped red onion
1	tsp. smoked paprika
¼	tsp. salt
¼	tsp. pepper

2	plum tomatoes, chopped
2	cups chopped fresh kale

1. In a large skillet, cook bacon over medium heat until crisp, stirring occasionally. Using a slotted spoon, remove bacon to paper towels. Pour off all but 1 Tbsp. of the drippings.

2. Add carrots and squash to drippings; cook, covered, over medium heat for 5 minutes. Add poblano pepper and onion; cook until vegetables are tender, about 5 minutes, stirring occasionally. Stir in seasonings. Add tomatoes and kale; cook, covered, until kale is wilted, 2-3 minutes. Top with bacon.

¾ CUP: *101 cal., 5g fat (2g sat. fat), 10mg chol., 251mg sod., 11g carb. (4g sugars, 3g fiber), 4g pro.*

DIABETIC EXCHANGES: *1 vegetable, 1 fat, ½ starch.*

Holiday Helper

The sweet, rich flavor of smoked paprika is made by drying peppers over a fire for several weeks. If you can't find smoked paprika, chipotle powder makes a better substitute than regular paprika.

SPICED PUMPKIN TIRAMISU

I added pumpkin flavor and subtracted some of the coffee flavor in a tiramisu I developed for a special holiday dinner. A new Christmas tradition was born!
—Heather Clary, Downingtown, PA

PREP: 30 min. + chilling • **COOK:** 5 min.
MAKES: 12 servings

1 cup water
1 cup brewed coffee
⅔ cup sugar
⅔ cup hazelnut liqueur

PUMPKIN MIXTURE

2 cartons (8 oz. each) mascarpone cheese
¾ cup canned pumpkin
5 Tbsp. sugar, divided
1½ tsp. ground cinnamon
½ tsp. ground nutmeg
¼ tsp. ground ginger
¼ tsp. ground allspice
1¼ cups heavy whipping cream

ASSEMBLY

54 crisp ladyfinger cookies (about s16 oz.)
1 Tbsp. sugar
½ tsp. ground cinnamon

1. In a small saucepan, combine water, coffee, sugar and liqueur; cook and stir over medium-low heat until the sugar is dissolved, about 3 minutes. Transfer to a shallow bowl; cool completely.
2. In a large bowl, mix mascarpone cheese, pumpkin, 3 Tbsp. sugar and the spices just until blended. In a small bowl, beat cream until it begins to thicken. Add remaining 2 Tbsp. sugar; beat until soft peaks form. Fold into mascarpone mixture.
3. Quickly dip 18 ladyfingers into coffee mixture, allowing the excess to drip off. Arrange in a single layer in a 13x9-in. dish. Spread with 1⅔ cups cheese mixture. Repeat layers twice.
4. Mix sugar and cinnamon; sprinkle over top. Refrigerate, covered, at least 8 hours or overnight.
1 PIECE: *491 cal., 28g fat (15g sat. fat), 121mg chol., 88mg sod., 52g carb. (38g sugars, 1g fiber), 7g pro.*

SMOKED SALMON BITES WITH SHALLOT SAUCE

Dijon-mayo sauce adds zip to layers of crisp arugula, smoked salmon and shaved Asiago. I make these a couple of times a year.
—Jamie Brown-Miller, Napa, CA

TAKES: 30 min. • **MAKES:** 25 servings

1 sheet frozen puff pastry, thawed
2 shallots
2 Tbsp. Dijon mustard
1 Tbsp. mayonnaise
1 Tbsp. red wine vinegar
¼ cup olive oil
1 cup fresh arugula or baby spinach, coarsely chopped
4½ oz. smoked salmon or lox, thinly sliced
½ cup shaved Asiago cheese

1. Preheat oven to 400°. Unfold puff pastry; cut into 25 squares. Transfer to greased baking sheets. Bake until golden brown, 11-13 minutes.
2. Meanwhile, grate 1 shallot and finely chop the other. In a small bowl, combine the shallots, mustard, mayonnaise and vinegar. While whisking, gradually add oil in a steady stream.
3. Spoon a small amount of sauce onto each pastry; layer with arugula and salmon. Drizzle with remaining sauce and sprinkle with cheese.
1 APPETIZER: *41 cal., 3g fat (1g sat. fat), 3mg chol., 72mg sod., 1g carb. (0 sugars, 0 fiber), 2g pro.*

NEW SPINS ON HOLIDAY SIDES

*If the traditional sides that make their return
every year are becoming...expected, it's time to
bring new life to old favorites like green bean casserole,
cranberry sauce, mashed potatoes and more!*

MAPLE HORSERADISH BEETS

The bright crimson of beets makes them a natural choice for a Christmas table. An easy glaze adds a little zip and rich flavor to these sweet, earthy vegetables.
—Leslie Palmer, Swampscott, MA

PREP: 50 min. • **COOK:** 10 min. • **MAKES:** 6 servings

- 1¾ lbs. fresh beets
- 1 Tbsp. canola oil
- 2 Tbsp. butter
- ¼ cup maple syrup
- 3 Tbsp. prepared horseradish
- 2 Tbsp. cider vinegar
- ¼ tsp. salt
- ¼ tsp. pepper

1. Preheat oven to 400°. Peel beets and cut into wedges. Place in a 15x10x1-in. baking pan; drizzle with oil and toss to coat. Bake until beets are tender, 40-50 minutes.
2. In a small saucepan, melt butter. Stir in syrup, horseradish, vinegar, salt and pepper. Bring to a boil. Carefully stir in beets; cook until liquid is slightly thickened, 5-6 minutes, gently stirring occasionally.
¾ CUP: 152 cal., 6g fat (3g sat. fat), 10mg chol., 252mg sod., 23g carb. (19g sugars, 3g fiber), 2g pro.
DIABETIC EXCHANGES: 2 vegetable, 1 fat, ½ starch.

POMEGRANATE-HAZELNUT ROASTED BRUSSELS SPROUTS

I have converted many people to Brussels sprouts with this recipe, and it has become my most requested dish. The richness of the hazelnuts and the sweetness of pomegranate and orange elevate the sprouts to a new level.
—Melanie Stevenson, Reading, PA

TAKES: 25 min. • **MAKES:** 8 servings

- 2 lbs. fresh Brussels sprouts, trimmed and halved
- ¼ cup olive oil
- 1½ tsp. kosher salt
- 1 tsp. coarsely ground pepper
- 6 Tbsp. butter, cubed
- ⅔ cup chopped hazelnuts, toasted
- 1 Tbsp. grated orange zest
- ½ cup pomegranate seeds

1. Preheat oven to 400°. Place Brussels sprouts in a foil-lined 15x10x1-in. baking pan. Drizzle with oil; sprinkle with salt and pepper. Toss to coat. Roast for 15-20 minutes or until tender, stirring occasionally. Remove from oven.
2. Meanwhile, in a small heavy saucepan, melt butter over medium heat. Heat for 5-7 minutes or until golden brown, stirring constantly. Remove from heat; drizzle over Brussels sprouts. Add the hazelnuts and orange zest; gently toss to coat. Transfer to a serving bowl. Just before serving, sprinkle with pomegranate seeds.
¾ CUP: 248 cal., 22g fat (7g sat. fat), 23mg chol., 454mg sod., 13g carb. (4g sugars, 5g fiber), 5g pro.

FROZEN WALDORF SALAD

While I was growing up on a farm in western Kansas, we always had lots of hungry men around during the harvest. We served this salad often since it was easy to increase and we could prepare it ahead of time.
—Mildred Hall, Topeka, KS

PREP: 25 min. + freezing
MAKES: 12 servings

- 1 can (20 oz.) crushed pineapple
- 1 cup sugar
- 2 large eggs, beaten
  Dash salt
- 1 cup chopped celery
- 2 medium red apples, chopped
- 1 cup chopped pecans
- 1 cup heavy whipping cream, whipped
  Lettuce leaves, optional

1. Drain pineapple, reserving the juice. Set pineapple aside. In a saucepan, combine juice with sugar, eggs and salt. Cook, stirring constantly, over medium-low heat until slightly thickened. Remove from the heat; cool. Stir in pineapple, celery, apples and pecans. Fold in whipped cream.
2. Pour mixture into a 9-in. square pan. Cover and freeze until firm. Let stand at room temperature for about 15 minutes before cutting. Serve on lettuce-lined plates if desired.
1 PIECE: *257 cal., 15g fat (5g sat. fat), 63mg chol., 40mg sod., 30g carb. (26g sugars, 2g fiber), 3g pro.*

CREAMY PORTOBELLOS & CAULIFLOWER

When scalloped potatoes start to feel ho-hum, jazz things up with cauliflower and portobello mushrooms instead. We often serve this dish alongside rolls and a light salad.
—Donna Noel, Gray, ME

PREP: 35 min. • **BAKE:** 35 min.
MAKES: 8 servings

- 1 large head cauliflower, broken into florets (about 7 cups)
- 1 lb. sliced baby portobello mushrooms
- ¾ cup water
- 6 Tbsp. butter, divided
- 4 shallots, finely chopped
- ¼ cup all-purpose flour
- ½ tsp. salt
- ¼ tsp. paprika
- 1¼ cups half-and-half cream
- ¾ cup shredded white cheddar cheese
- ¼ cup panko bread crumbs

1. Preheat oven to 350°. Place 1 in. of water and the cauliflower in a 6-qt. stockpot; bring to a boil over high heat. Cook, covered, until florets are tender, 7-10 minutes. Drain.
2. In a large saucepan, combine sliced mushrooms and water; bring to a boil over medium-high heat. Reduce heat; simmer, covered, 10 minutes. Drain mushrooms, reserving ⅓ cup cooking liquid.

3. In the same saucepan, heat 3 Tbsp. butter over medium heat until hot. Add shallots and drained mushrooms; cook and stir until shallots are tender and lightly browned. Stir in flour, salt and paprika until blended; gradually stir in cream and reserved mushroom liquid. Bring to a boil, stirring constantly; cook and stir until thickened, 2-3 minutes.
4. Place cauliflower in a greased 1½-qt. or 11x7-in. baking dish; cover with the mushroom sauce. Sprinkle with cheese, then bread crumbs. Dot with remaining 3 Tbsp. butter. Bake, uncovered, until bubbly and golden brown, 35-40 minutes.
¾ CUP: *169 cal., 8g fat (5g sat. fat), 30mg chol., 275mg sod., 17g carb. (5g sugars, 3g fiber), 9g pro.*

NUTTY KALE PESTO PASTA WITH CARAMELIZED ONION

My bountiful garden and vegetarian daughter inspired me to create this nutritious, calcium-rich pasta sauce. No one would ever guess it can be prepared in about 30 minutes. For a gluten-free version, substitute quinoa pasta.
—Cindy Beberman, Orland Park, IL

PREP: 20 min. • **COOK:** 15 min.
MAKES: 8 servings

- ⅓ cup hazelnuts, toasted and skins removed
- 2 cups roughly chopped fresh kale, stems removed
- ¼ cup plus 2 Tbsp. grated Parmesan cheese, divided
- ¼ cup loosely packed basil leaves
- ¼ cup plus 2 Tbsp. extra virgin olive oil, divided
- ½ tsp. salt, divided
- 12 oz. uncooked whole wheat linguine
- 1 large sweet onion, thinly sliced
- 3 garlic cloves, minced
- 1 Tbsp. honey
- 3 large tomatoes, chopped

1. Pulse hazelnuts in food processor until finely ground. Add kale, ¼ cup Parmesan cheese, basil, ¼ cup olive oil and ¼ tsp. salt; pulse until smooth and creamy, adding oil if pesto seems dry.
2. In a large stockpot, cook the linguine according to the package directions. Meanwhile, in a large skillet, heat the remaining 2 Tbsp. olive oil over medium heat. Add onion; cook and stir until tender, about 5 minutes. Reduce heat to low; add minced garlic and honey. Cook, stirring occasionally, until onion caramelizes, about 5 minutes more.
3. Drain linguine, reserving ½ cup pasta water. In a large serving bowl, combine kale pesto, onion mixture, linguine, chopped tomato and remaining ¼ tsp. salt. Toss until well coated, adding reserved pasta water if needed to reach desired consistency. Top with the remaining 2 Tbsp. Parmesan cheese. Serve warm.
1 CUP: 314 cal., 15g fat (2g sat. fat), 3mg chol., 224mg sod., 42g carb. (7g sugars, 7g fiber), 8g pro.

SKILLET HASSELBACK SWEET POTATOES

Sweet potatoes dressed with buttery, herby, garlicky goodness make for a stunning, delicious side dish.
—Lauren McAnelly, Des Moines, IA

PREP: 25 min. • **BAKE:** 45 min.
MAKES: 8 servings

- 8 small sweet potatoes (about 7 oz. each)
- ½ cup butter, melted
- 3 Tbsp. finely chopped shallot
- 3 garlic cloves, minced
- 1½ tsp. salt
- ½ tsp. fresh ground pepper
- 2 tsp. minced fresh parsley
- 2 tsp. minced fresh thyme
- 2 tsp. minced fresh sage
- ½ cup soft whole wheat bread crumbs
- ¼ cup grated Parmesan cheese
- ½ cup chopped toasted nuts, optional

1. Preheat oven to 425°. Cut thin slices lengthwise from bottom of sweet potatoes to allow them to lie flat; discard slices. Place potatoes flat side down; cut crosswise into ⅛-in. slices, leaving them intact at the bottom. Arrange sweet potatoes in a 12-in. cast-iron or other ovenproof skillet.
2. Stir together the next 5 ingredients. Spoon half the butter mixture evenly over sweet potatoes. Bake 35 minutes.
3. Meanwhile, add herbs to the remaining butter mixture. Toss bread crumbs with Parmesan. Remove skillet from oven. Spoon remaining butter mixture over potatoes; top with bread crumb mixture.
4. Return to oven until potatoes are tender and topping is golden brown, 10-12 minutes. If desired, top potatoes with toasted nuts.
1 SWEET POTATO: 333 cal., 13g fat (8g sat. fat), 33mg chol., 620mg sod., 52g carb. (20g sugars, 6g fiber), 5g pro.

CITRUS WREATH

1. **TRIM AND SNIP** the greens into 8- to 12-in. lengths. Using covered binding wire, bind together 12-15 small bundles of assorted greenery at 3 points each, leaving wire tails long enough to secure each bundle to wire frame.

2. **POSITION EACH BUNDLE** of greens on front of wire frame, overlapping slightly; secure wires on back of frame as you go. Trim and tuck in ends.

3. **USING A TOOTHPICK,** poke a pattern of holes into 1 side of several pieces of fruit and insert whole cloves.

4. **ATTACH THE CITRUS** as desired using 20-gauge wire pieces. Thread a wire through each orange, lemon and clementine, bending wires gently down at a 90-degree angle on each side. Attach fruit to wire frame; secure wires on back. Trim and tuck in ends. (Avoid twisting wire too tightly or it will slice through the fruit.)

5. **MAKE KUMQUAT BUNDLES** by threading a 20-gauge wire through 2 kumquats. Gently bend wire ends down and twist together below kumquats. Repeat. Attach kumquat bundles to frame; secure wires. Trim and tuck in ends.

WHAT YOU NEED:
- 24-in. round wire wreath frame
- Covered binding wire
- 7 to 10 bunches of assorted greens (we used lemon leaf, bay leaf, rosemary, olive leaf and seeded eucalyptus)
- Toothpick
- 10 to 14 assorted citrus fruits: oranges, lemons, clementines and kumquats
- Whole cloves
- Eight to ten 18-in. pieces of 20-gauge wire
- Wire cutters

ORZO WITH CARAMELIZED BUTTERNUT SQUASH & BACON

The year my garden produced a bumper crop of butternut squash, I made so many new dishes trying to use up my bounty! This is a tasty, easy side with pretty colors, and it makes plenty to fill your hungry family. To make it into a main course, add shrimp or shredded chicken.
—Kallee Krong-McCreery, Escondido, CA

PREP: 20 min. • **COOK:** 20 min.
MAKES: 6 servings

- 1½ cups uncooked orzo pasta
- 4 bacon strips, chopped
- 2 cups cubed peeled butternut squash (½-in. cubes)
- ½ cup chopped onion
- 1 cup cut fresh or frozen cut green beans, thawed
- 1 garlic clove, minced
- 1 Tbsp. butter
- 1 tsp. garlic salt
- ¼ tsp. pepper
- ¼ cup grated Parmesan cheese
  Minced fresh parsley

1. In a large saucepan, cook the orzo according to package directions.
2. Meanwhile, in a large skillet, cook bacon over medium heat until crisp, stirring occasionally. Remove with a slotted spoon; drain on paper towels. Cook and stir squash and onion in the bacon drippings until tender, 8-10 minutes. Add beans and garlic; cook 1 minute longer.
3. Drain orzo; stir into the squash mixture. Add butter, garlic salt, pepper and reserved bacon; heat through. Sprinkle with Parmesan and parsley.
¾ CUP: 329 cal., 11g fat (4g sat. fat), 20mg chol., 533mg sod., 47g carb. (4g sugars, 3g fiber), 11g pro.

CHIPOTLE-ORANGE CRANBERRY SAUCE

My family prefers traditional dishes on Christmas, but I like to add in a few of my own unique creations. With brown sugar, cinnamon and chipotle powder for a little kick, this cranberry sauce will earn a permanent spot in your holiday lineup.
—Chris Michalowski, Dallas, TX

PREP: 15 min. + chilling • **MAKES:** 1¾ cups

- 1 medium orange
- 1 pkg. (12 oz.) fresh or frozen cranberries
- ½ cup packed brown sugar
- 1 cinnamon stick (3 in.)
- ¼ to ¾ tsp. ground chipotle pepper
- ¼ tsp. pepper

1. Finely grate zest from orange. Cut orange crosswise in half; squeeze juice from orange. Place zest and orange juice in a large saucepan. Add the remaining ingredients.
2. Bring to a boil, stirring to dissolve the sugar. Reduce heat to a simmer; cook, uncovered, until the cranberries pop, 5-7 minutes, stirring occasionally. Remove from heat.
3. Transfer to a small bowl; cool slightly. Refrigerate, covered, until cold.
¼ CUP: 103 cal., 0 fat (0 sat. fat), 0 chol., 10mg sod., 26g carb. (21g sugars, 2g fiber), 0 pro.

BBLT CHOPPED SALAD

My original recipe for this salad called for lettuce. One day I didn't have any, so I substituted spinach and made some healthier adjustments to the recipe. The rest is history!
—Cindy VanBeek, Randolph, WI

TAKES: 10 min. • **MAKES:** 4 servings

- 6 oz. (about 9 cups) fresh baby spinach, coarsely chopped
- 1 bunch broccoli, cut into small florets
- 2 cups grape tomatoes, halved
- 1 pkg. (2.52 oz.) ready-to-serve thick-cut fully cooked bacon, cut into 1-in. pieces
- 1 cup Miracle Whip
- 2 Tbsp. white vinegar
- 2 Tbsp. sugar

In a large bowl, combine the first 4 ingredients. In a small bowl, mix Miracle Whip, vinegar and sugar until blended. Just before serving, spoon dressing over salad; toss gently to coat.
2½ CUPS: *356 cal., 22g fat (4g sat. fat), 39mg chol., 906mg sod., 29g carb. (19g sugars, 6g fiber), 14g pro.*

AIR-FRYER CANDIED ACORN SQUASH SLICES

My grandma passed down her recipe for acorn squash, which she always served at the holidays. Now I make an air-fryer version of it whenever I'm feeling nostalgic.
—Rita Addicks, Weimar, TX

PREP: 15 min. • **COOK:** 15 min./batch • **MAKES:** 6 servings

- 2 medium acorn squash
- ⅔ cup packed brown sugar
- ½ cup butter, softened

1. Preheat air fryer to 350°. Cut squash in half lengthwise; remove and discard seeds. Cut each half crosswise into ½-in. slices; discard ends. In batches, arrange squash in a single layer on greased tray in air-fryer basket. Cook until just tender, 5 minutes per side.
2. Combine sugar and butter; spread over squash. Cook 3 minutes longer.
1 SERVING: *320 cal., 16g fat (10g sat. fat), 41mg chol., 135mg sod., 48g carb. (29g sugars, 3g fiber), 2g pro.*

SWEET ONION SPOON BREAD

This recipe has been a family-favorite secret for years. The layers of tangy cheese, sour cream and sweet onions in this moist cornbread taste so great together! Chopped green chiles could also add some fun zip.
—Heather Thomas, Fredericksburg, VA

PREP: 15 min. • **BAKE:** 25 min. • **MAKES:** 9 servings

1⅓ cups chopped sweet onions
1 Tbsp. butter
1 can (8¼ oz.) cream-style corn
1 pkg. (8½ oz.) cornbread/muffin mix
2 large egg whites, lightly beaten
2 Tbsp. fat-free milk
½ cup reduced-fat sour cream
⅓ cup shredded sharp cheddar cheese

1. Preheat oven to 350°. In a small nonstick skillet, saute onions in butter until tender; set aside.
2. In a large bowl, combine the corn, muffin mix, egg whites and milk. Pour into a 9-in. square baking dish coated with cooking spray. Combine sour cream and onions; spread over batter. Sprinkle with cheese.
3. Bake, uncovered, until a toothpick inserted in the center comes out clean, 25-30 minutes.
1 PIECE: *191 cal., 6g fat (3g sat. fat), 18mg chol., 361mg sod., 29g carb. (10g sugars, 1g fiber), 6g pro.*
DIABETIC EXCHANGES: *2 starch, ½ fat.*

SAUTEED TARRAGON RADISHES

Who says radishes only belong in salads? Sauteed in wine and tarragon, these may just change the way you look at radishes forever. They can be served on their own, or added to your favorite au gratin recipe.
—Taste of Home *Test Kitchen*

TAKES: 25 min. • **MAKES:** 12 servings

½ cup unsalted butter, cubed
6 lbs. radishes, quartered (about 9 cups)
¼ cup white wine or water
2 tsp. minced fresh tarragon or ½ tsp. dried tarragon
½ tsp. salt
¼ tsp. pepper

In a 6-qt. stockpot, heat butter over medium heat. Add radishes; cook and stir 2 minutes. Stir in wine; increase heat to medium-high. Cook, uncovered, until radishes are crisp-tender, 8-10 minutes. Stir in tarragon, salt and pepper.
¾ CUP: *108 cal., 8g fat (5g sat. fat), 20mg chol., 188mg sod., 8g carb. (4g sugars, 4g fiber), 2g pro.*

PORTOBELLO RISOTTO WITH MASCARPONE

Portobello mushrooms add a beefy flavor to this creamy classic. Each serving is topped with soft, buttery mascarpone cheese, which makes it extra special.
—Carmella Ryan, Rockville Centre, NY

- -

PREP: 20 min. • **COOK:** 25 min.
MAKES: 6 servings

1½ cups water
1 can (14 oz.) reduced-sodium beef broth
½ cup chopped shallots
2 garlic cloves, minced
1 Tbsp. canola oil
1 cup uncooked arborio rice
1 Tbsp. minced fresh thyme or 1 tsp. dried thyme
½ tsp. salt
½ tsp. pepper
½ cup white wine or additional reduced-sodium beef broth
1 cup sliced baby portobello mushrooms, chopped
¼ cup grated Parmesan cheese
½ cup mascarpone cheese

1. In a large saucepan, heat water and broth and keep warm. In a large saucepan, saute shallots and garlic in oil 2-3 minutes or until shallots are tender. Add the rice, thyme, salt and pepper; cook and stir for 2-3 minutes. Reduce heat; stir in white wine. Cook and stir until all the liquid is absorbed.

2. Add heated broth, ½ cup at a time, stirring constantly. Allow the liquid to absorb between additions. Cook just until risotto is creamy and rice is almost tender. (Cooking time is about 20 minutes.)

3. Add mushrooms and Parmesan cheese; stir gently until cheese is melted. Garnish each serving with a heaping tablespoon of mascarpone. Serve immediately.

FREEZE OPTION: *Before adding mascarpone cheese, freeze cooled risotto mixture in freezer containers. To use, partially thaw in refrigerator overnight. Heat through in a saucepan, stirring occasionally and adding a little broth or water if necessary. Garnish as directed.*

¾ CUP RISOTTO MIXTURE WITH 1 HEAPING TBSP. MARSCARPONE CHEESE: *350 cal., 21g fat (10g sat. fat), 51mg chol., 393mg sod., 31g carb. (1g sugars, 1g fiber), 7g pro.*

TWICE-BAKED RUTABAGAS

Mix it up by swapping your go-to spuds dish for these rutabagas with bacon, cheese and whipping cream. Even the skeptics won't be able to resist a bite!
—Lisa L. Bynum, Brandon, MS

PREP: 30 min. • BAKE: 20 min. • MAKES: 8 servings

- 4 small rutabagas, peeled and cut into 1-in. cubes
- 3 Tbsp. water
- 8 cooked bacon strips, chopped
- 1 cup heavy whipping cream
- ¼ cup butter, cubed
- 2 tsp. garlic powder
- ½ tsp. salt
- ¼ tsp. pepper
- 2 cups shredded cheddar cheese, divided
- 3 green onions, sliced, divided

1. Preheat oven to 350°. In a microwave-safe bowl, combine the rutabagas and water. Microwave, covered, on high for 16-20 minutes or until tender, stirring halfway. Mash rutabagas; add bacon, cream, butter, garlic powder, salt and pepper. Stir in 1 cup cheese and ¼ cup green onions.
2. Spoon mixture into 8 greased 6-oz. ramekins or custard cups. Sprinkle with remaining 1 cup cheese. Place ramekins on a baking sheet. Bake until rutabagas are bubbly and cheese is melted, 18-22 minutes. Sprinkle with the remaining green onions.
1 SERVING: *361 cal., 30g fat (17g sat. fat), 89mg chol., 592mg sod., 11g carb. (5g sugars, 2g fiber), 13g pro.*

SWEET POTATO MERINGUE BAKE

Here's a slightly sweet variation of a sweet potato casserole, minus the extra sugar. It's simple enough to throw together even after the holidays. For more sauce, you can add extra water, butter, brown sugar or maple syrup to the filling before baking. Rum, brandy or lemon zest can be added to change up the flavor.
—Kathy Kinomoto, Bothell, WA

PREP: 15 min. • BAKE: 40 min. • MAKES: 9 servings

- 5 medium sweet potatoes, peeled and cut into ¼-in. slices
- ½ cup packed brown sugar
- ½ cup chopped pecans
- ⅓ cup water
- 3 Tbsp. unsalted butter or ghee, melted
- 3 large egg whites, room temperature
- ½ tsp. vanilla extract
- ⅓ cup sugar

1. Preheat oven to 375°. Place sweet potatoes in a greased 8-in. square baking pan. Combine brown sugar, pecans, water and butter; pour over potatoes. Bake, uncovered, just until tender, 30-35 minutes.
2. Meanwhile, for meringue, in a small bowl, beat egg whites and vanilla on medium speed until foamy. Gradually add sugar, 1 Tbsp. at a time, beating on high after each addition, until sugar is dissolved. Continue beating until stiff glossy peaks form. Spread over hot potatoes. Bake 8-10 minutes longer or until meringue is golden brown.
1 SERVING: *265 cal., 8g fat (3g sat. fat), 10mg chol., 33mg sod., 46g carb. (30g sugars, 4g fiber), 4g pro.*

CELERIAC & GARLIC MASHED POTATOES

My family can't get enough of this comforting favorite, especially at the holidays. I love the addition of celeriac. Its mild celery flavor pairs well with the garlic and potato.
—Lynelle Martinson, Plover, WI

- -

PREP: 20 min. • **COOK:** 15 min.
MAKES: 6 servings

- 3 medium Yukon Gold potatoes, peeled and cubed
- 1 large celery root, peeled and chopped
- 3 garlic cloves, peeled
- 2 Tbsp. butter
- 2 Tbsp. 2% milk
- ½ tsp. salt
- ¼ tsp. pepper
- 1 Tbsp. minced chives

1. Place the potatoes, celery root and garlic in a Dutch oven; cover with water. Bring to a boil. Reduce heat; cover and cook just until tender, 15 minutes. Drain; cool slightly.
2. Mash vegetables with butter, milk, salt and pepper. Stir in chives.

¾ **CUP:** *135 cal., 4g fat (2g sat. fat), 10mg chol., 306mg sod., 23g carb. (3g sugars, 3g fiber), 3g pro.*
DIABETIC EXCHANGES: *1½ starch, ½ fat.*

RAISIN-STUDDED APPLE STUFFING

This is the only stuffing my family will permit on our holiday table. With Italian sausage and a blend of so many great flavors, it almost makes a meal in itself. No wonder it won first prize in a local recipe contest!
—Teri Lindquist, Gurnee, IL

- -

PREP: 30 min. • **BAKE:** 70 min.
MAKES: 18 cups

- 1 cup raisins
- 1½ cups orange juice, divided
- 2 cups chopped celery
- 1 large onion, chopped
- 1 cup butter, cubed, divided
- 1 lb. bulk Italian sausage
- 1 pkg. (14 oz.) crushed herb-seasoned stuffing

- 4 medium tart apples, peeled and chopped
- 1 cup chopped pecans
- 2 cups chicken broth
- 2 tsp. dried thyme
- ½ tsp. pepper

1. Preheat oven to 325°. In a saucepan, bring raisins and 1 cup orange juice to a boil. Remove from the heat; set aside (do not drain).
2. In a skillet, saute celery and onion in ½ cup butter until tender. Transfer to a large bowl. In the same skillet, cook sausage over medium heat until no longer pink; drain. Add the sausage, stuffing, apples, pecans, remaining orange juice and reserved raisins to the celery mixture.
3. In a saucepan, melt the remaining butter; add broth, thyme and pepper. Pour over the stuffing mixture; mix well.
4. Place in 2 greased 13x9-in. baking dishes. Cover and bake for 1 hour. Uncover; bake 10 minutes longer or until lightly browned. Refrigerate any leftovers.

1 **CUP:** *318 cal., 19g fat (8g sat. fat), 37mg chol., 645mg sod., 32g carb. (12g sugars, 3g fiber), 7g pro.*

GREEN BEAN MUSHROOM PIE

Fresh green bean flavor stands out in this pretty lattice-topped pie. A flaky golden crust holds the savory bean, mushroom and cream cheese filling. It tastes wonderfully different every time I make it, depending on the variety of mushrooms I use.
—Tara Walworth, Maple Park, IL

PREP: 45 min. • **BAKE:** 25 min.
MAKES: 10 servings

- 3 cups sliced fresh mushrooms
- 4 Tbsp. butter, divided
- 2½ cups chopped onions
- 6 cups cut fresh green beans (1-in. pieces)
- 2 tsp. minced fresh thyme or ¾ tsp. dried thyme
- ½ tsp. salt
- ¼ tsp. pepper
- 1 pkg. (8 oz.) cream cheese, cubed
- ½ cup 2% milk

CRUST
- 2½ cups all-purpose flour
- 2 tsp. baking powder
- 1 tsp. dill weed
- ¼ tsp. salt
- 1 cup cold butter, cubed
- 1 cup sour cream
- 1 large egg
- 1 Tbsp. heavy whipping cream

1. In a large skillet, saute mushrooms in 1 Tbsp. butter until tender; drain and set aside. In the same skillet, saute onions and beans in the remaining 3 Tbsp. butter until beans are crisp-tender, 18-20 minutes. Add the thyme, salt, pepper, cream cheese, milk and mushrooms. Cook and stir until the cheese is melted. Remove from the heat; set aside.

2. In a large bowl, combine flour, baking powder, dill and salt. Cut in butter until mixture resembles coarse crumbs. Stir in sour cream to form a soft dough.

3. Divide the dough in half. On a well-floured surface, roll out 1 portion to fit a deep-dish 9-in. pie plate; trim pastry even with edge.

4. Pour green bean mixture into crust. Roll out remaining pastry; make a lattice crust. Trim, seal and flute edge.

5. In a small bowl, beat the egg and cream; brush over lattice top. Bake at 400° until golden brown, 25-35 minutes.

1 SERVING: *503 cal., 37g fat (23g sat. fat), 127mg chol., 587mg sod., 35g carb. (7g sugars, 4g fiber), 9g pro.*

BUTTERNUT SQUASH & SAUSAGE SOUP

Soup comforts the soul and this creamy, healthy soup does just that. This makes a large pot and I love sharing it with others.
—Jerilyn Korver, Bellflower, CA

PREP: 50 min. • **COOK:** 45 min.
MAKES: 8 servings (3¼ qt.)

- 1 large butternut squash (4 to 4½ lbs.)
- 1 medium onion, chopped
- 1 medium tart apple, peeled and coarsely chopped
- 2 tsp. olive oil
- 6 garlic cloves, minced
- 2 tsp. dried thyme
- ½ tsp. pepper
- ½ tsp. dried marjoram
- ¼ tsp. salt
- ¼ tsp. ground cinnamon
- ⅛ tsp. ground nutmeg
- 6 cups reduced-sodium chicken broth
- 4 fully cooked Italian chicken sausage links, chopped
- 4 large carrots, chopped
- ⅔ cup reduced-fat plain Greek yogurt
- 4 tsp. minced fresh sage
- 1 tsp. cider vinegar
- Optional: Cornbread croutons and additional yogurt

1. Cut squash in half lengthwise; discard seeds. Place squash, cut side down, in a 15x10x1-in. baking pan coated with cooking spray. Bake, uncovered, at 400° until tender, 45-60 minutes. Cool slightly. Scoop out pulp; set aside.

2. In a Dutch oven, cook onion and apple in oil until tender. Add garlic; cook 1 minute longer. Stir in the seasonings; cook until fragrant, about 10 seconds. Add broth and squash; bring to a boil. Reduce heat; simmer, uncovered, 15-20 minutes. Cool slightly. In a blender, cover and process soup in batches until smooth. Return pureed mixture to pan; stir in sausage and carrots. Bring to a boil. Reduce heat; cover and simmer until carrots are tender, 15-20 minutes.

3. Just before serving, stir in ⅔ cup yogurt, sage and vinegar. Serve with croutons and additional yogurt if desired.
1½ CUPS: 222 cal., 5g fat (1g sat. fat), 34mg chol., 783mg sod., 33g carb. (11g sugars, 8g fiber), 14g pro.

LEEKS IN MUSTARD SAUCE

Leeks have a delicious onion flavor, and they are so wonderful in this side dish. The mustard sauce complements the leeks, and it goes well with many entrees.
—Taste of Home *Test Kitchen*

PREP: 15 min. • **COOK:** 20 min.
MAKES: 8 servings

- 10 medium leeks (white portion only)
- 2 green onions with tops, chopped
- 1 garlic clove, minced
- 1 Tbsp. olive oil

MUSTARD SAUCE
- 3 large egg yolks
- ¼ cup water
- 2 Tbsp. lemon juice
- 6 Tbsp. cold butter
- 1 Tbsp. Dijon mustard
- Dash white pepper

1. Cut leeks into 1½-in. slices, then julienne. In a large cast-iron or other heavy skillet, saute leeks, onions and garlic in oil until tender.

2. Meanwhile, in a small heavy saucepan, whisk the egg yolks, water and lemon juice. Cook and stir over low heat until mixture begins to thicken, bubbles around the edges and reaches 160°, about 20 minutes. Add butter, 1 Tbsp. at a time, whisking after each addition until melted. Remove from the heat; stir in mustard and pepper.

3. Transfer leek mixture to a serving bowl; top with mustard sauce.
½ CUP WITH ABOUT 4 TSP. SAUCE: 185 cal., 13g fat (6g sat. fat), 103mg chol., 160mg sod., 17g carb. (5g sugars, 2g fiber), 3g pro.

HOLIDAY DESSERT HACKS & HOW-TO'S

If holiday-worthy desserts seem difficult to pull off—don't worry! This collection of recipes comes with sweet bites of advice, clever kitchen tricks and how-to photos to lead you through the process of creating your masterpiece.

POMEGRANATE MAGIC BARS

Pomegranates make every dessert festive and bright with a burst of juicy sweetness.
—Lisa Keys, Kennett Square, PA

PREP: 45 min. • **BAKE:** 25 min. + cooling
MAKES: 3 dozen

- 1¼ cups all-purpose flour
- ¾ cup sugar
- ¼ cup baking cocoa
- ¾ cup cold butter, cubed
- 1 large egg, room temperature
- ½ tsp. vanilla extract
- 1 Tbsp. sesame seeds, toasted
- 1 cup sweetened shredded coconut, toasted
- ½ cup slivered almonds, toasted
- 2 cups (12 oz.) semisweet chocolate chips
- 1 can (14 oz.) sweetened condensed milk
- 1 cup pomegranate seeds

1. Preheat oven to 350°. Line a 13x9-in. pan with parchment, letting ends extend up sides. Lightly grease the parchment with cooking spray. In a food processor, combine flour, sugar and cocoa; pulse until combined. Add butter; pulse until mixture appears sandy. Add egg and vanilla; pulse just until combined. Press dough into the prepared pan.
2. Sprinkle dough with sesame seeds. Bake until top appears dry and toothpick comes out clean, 20-25 minutes. Remove from oven; sprinkle evenly with coconut, almonds and chocolate chips. Pour condensed milk evenly over top; return to oven. Bake until golden brown, 25-30 minutes. Cool on wire rack 10 minutes.
3. Sprinkle with pomegranate seeds; press seeds gently into warm topping with back of a spoon. Cool completely in pan on wire rack. Remove from pan and cut into bars.
1 BAR: *176 cal., 10g fat (6g sat. fat), 19mg chol., 55mg sod., 22g carb. (17g sugars, 1g fiber), 3g pro.*

> ## Holiday Helper
>
>
> For a quick how-to on removing pomegranate seeds, see p. 177.

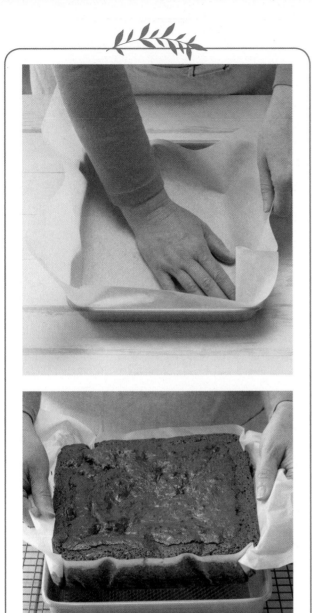

MAPLE BUTTERSCOTCH BROWNIES

I often make a double batch of these brownies—they go fast no matter where I take them! I've baked them for family-and-friend dinners and church suppers, and I always come back with an empty pan. They're easy to make and they freeze well.
—*Grace Vonhold, Rochester, NY*

PREP: 15 min. • **BAKE:** 30 min. + cooling • **MAKES:** 16 brownies

- 1½ cups all-purpose flour
- 1 tsp. baking powder
- 1¼ cups packed brown sugar
- ½ cup butter, melted
- 1½ tsp. maple flavoring
- 2 large eggs, room temperature
- 1 cup chopped walnuts
  Confectioners' sugar, optional

1. Preheat oven to 350°. Whisk together flour and baking powder.
2. In a large bowl, mix brown sugar, melted butter and maple flavoring. Beat in eggs, 1 at a time, mixing well after each addition. Stir in flour mixture and walnuts. Spread into a greased 9-in. square baking pan.
3. Bake until a toothpick inserted in center comes out clean, 27-32 minutes. Cool completely in pan on a wire rack. If desired, dust with confectioners' sugar. Cut into bars.
1 BROWNIE: *216 cal., 11g fat (4g sat. fat), 42mg chol., 98mg sod., 27g carb. (17g sugars, 1g fiber), 4g pro.*

LINE YOUR PAN WITH PARCHMENT

When making brownies or bars, line the baking pan with parchment paper so it extends up the sides. Since the high sugar content of these treats makes them more likely to stick, the parchment ensures that you can lift the entire panful of brownies out once they're cool. It also makes it easier to cut into even portions with clean cuts.

ARMAGNAC CHOCOLATE ALMOND TART

I am a pecan pie lover, and this is my twist on pecan pie. I use almonds instead of pecans and golden syrup instead of corn syrup. Both chocolate and Armagnac make this tart really special. Don't skip on toasting the almonds—it brings out the nuttiness of the pie.
—Phoebe Saad, Framingham, MA

PREP: 30 min. + chilling • **BAKE:** 35 min. + cooling • **MAKES:** 8 servings

- 1 cup all-purpose flour
- ¼ cup toasted ground almonds
- 1 Tbsp. sugar
- Dash salt
- ½ cup cold unsalted butter
- 2 to 4 Tbsp. ice water

FILLING

- 1½ cups slivered almonds, toasted
- 2 Tbsp. unsalted butter
- 1 oz. unsweetened chocolate, chopped
- 2 large eggs
- ½ cup sugar
- ⅓ cup golden syrup or light corn syrup
- 1½ Tbsp. Armagnac or Cognac
- ¼ tsp. vanilla extract
- ⅛ tsp. salt

1. In a large bowl, mix flour, ground almonds, sugar and salt; cut in butter until crumbly. Gradually add ice water, tossing with a fork until dough holds together when pressed. Shape into a disk; wrap and refrigerate 1 hour or overnight.

2. Preheat oven to 350°. On a lightly floured surface, roll dough to a ⅛-in.-thick circle; press onto bottom and up sides of an ungreased 9-in. tart pan with removable bottom. Place on a baking sheet.

3. For filling, sprinkle slivered almonds over crust. In top of a double boiler, melt the butter and chocolate; stir until smooth. Remove from heat. In a large bowl, beat eggs and sugar until thick and lemon-colored. Beat in golden syrup, Armagnac, vanilla and salt until well blended. Gradually beat in chocolate mixture. Slowly spoon filling over almonds.

4. Bake until set, 35-40 minutes. Cool completely on a wire rack.

1 SLICE: *462 cal., 29g fat (11g sat. fat), 85mg chol., 67mg sod., 44g carb. (27g sugars, 4g fiber), 9g pro.*

DOUBLES FOR A BOILER

If you don't have a double boiler, use a sturdy metal mixing bowl over a saucepan containing boiling water. Don't use too much water; the bottom of the bowl should not touch the surface of the water.

PALMIERS

It takes just two ingredients to make these impressive but easy-to-do French pastries, which are often called palm leaves.
—Taste of Home *Test Kitchen*

- -

PREP: 20 min. + freezing • **BAKE:** 10 min.
MAKES: 2 dozen

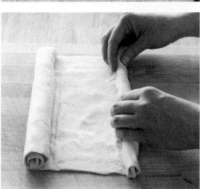

1 cup sugar, divided
1 sheet frozen puff pastry, thawed

1. Preheat oven to 425°. Sprinkle a work surface with ¼ cup sugar; unfold puff pastry sheet on surface. Sprinkle with 2 Tbsp. sugar. Roll into a 14x10-in. rectangle. Sprinkle with ½ cup sugar to within ½ in. of edges. Lightly press sugar into pastry.

2. With a knife, very lightly score a line crosswise across the middle of the pastry. Starting at a short side, roll up jelly-roll style, stopping at the score mark in the middle. Starting at the opposite side, roll up the pastry jelly-roll style to the score mark. Freeze until firm, 20-30 minutes. Cut into ⅜-in. slices.

3. Place slices 2 in. apart on parchment-lined baking sheets; sprinkle lightly with 1 Tbsp. sugar. Bake for 8 minutes. Turn pastries over and sprinkle with remaining 1 Tbsp. sugar. Bake until golden brown and glazed, about 3 minutes longer. Remove to wire racks to cool completely. Store in airtight containers.

1 PASTRY: *83 cal., 3g fat (1g sat. fat), 0 chol., 34mg sod., 14g carb. (8g sugars, 1g fiber), 1g pro.*

CITRUS CRANBERRY PIE

To showcase gorgeous bright red cranberries, we came up with this lattice-topped pie. A dollop of orange cream complements the slightly tart flavor.
—Taste of Home *Test Kitchen*

- -

PREP: 30 min. • **BAKE:** 50 min. + cooling
MAKES: 8 servings

3½ cups **fresh or frozen cranberries**
1 cup **sugar**
2 tsp. **grated lemon zest**
1 tsp. **grated orange zest**
1 **small navel orange, peeled, sectioned and chopped**
2 Tbsp. **butter, melted**
2 Tbsp. **all-purpose flour**
¼ tsp. **salt**
Pastry for double-crust pie
1 **large egg, lightly beaten**
Additional sugar

ORANGE CREAM
1 cup **heavy whipping cream**
1 Tbsp. **sugar**
2 tsp. **grated orange zest**
½ tsp. **orange extract, optional**

1. Preheat oven to 450°. Toss together first 8 ingredients. On a lightly floured surface, roll 1 half of dough to a ⅛-in.-thick circle; transfer to a 9-in. pie plate. Trim crust even with rim. Add filling.
2. Roll remaining dough to a ⅛-in.-thick circle; cut into strips. Arrange over filling in a lattice pattern. Trim and seal strips to edge of bottom crust; flute edge. Brush lattice with egg; sprinkle with sugar.
3. Bake 10 minutes. Reduce oven setting to 350°; bake until golden brown, 40-45 minutes, covering edge with foil if crust is getting too dark. Cool completely on a wire rack; refrigerate until serving.
4. Beat whipping cream until it begins to thicken. Add remaining ingredients; beat until soft peaks form. Refrigerate until serving. Serve with pie.

1 PIECE: *515 cal., 29g fat (15g sat. fat), 85mg chol., 323mg sod., 62g carb. (33g sugars, 2g fiber), 4g pro.*

PASTRY FOR DOUBLE-CRUST PIE (9 INCHES):
Combine 2½ cups all-purpose flour and ½ tsp. salt; cut in 1 cup cold butter until crumbly. Gradually add ⅓-⅔ cup ice water, tossing with a fork until dough holds together when pressed. Divide dough in half. Shape each into a disk; wrap and refrigerate 1 hour or overnight.

BERRIES WITH RICOTTA CREAM

Fresh, high-quality ingredients really make a difference in this dessert. If you don't have access to fresh-picked berries, use whatever fruit is in season near you.
—Thomas Faglon, Somerset, NJ

TAKES: 10 min. • **MAKES:** 6 servings

- 1   cup part-skim ricotta cheese
- ½   cup heavy whipping cream
- ¼   cup honey
- 2   cups fresh blueberries
- 2   cups fresh raspberries
- ½   cup chopped hazelnuts, toasted

In a large bowl, beat ricotta, cream and honey until combined. Divide berries among 6 dessert dishes. Top with cream and hazelnuts. Refrigerate until serving.

1 SERVING: *277 cal., 17g fat (7g sat. fat), 35mg chol., 48mg sod., 28g carb. (19g sugars, 5g fiber), 8g pro.*

MAKE YOUR OWN RICOTTA

Line a large strainer with 2 layers of dampened cheesecloth; place over a large bowl. In a Dutch oven, bring 2 qt. whole milk, 1 cup heavy whipping cream and ½ tsp. salt just to a boil over medium heat, stirring occasionally to prevent scorching. Remove from heat. Stir in 3 Tbsp. white vinegar; let stand until curds form, about 4 minutes. Pour into prepared strainer. Let stand until ricotta reaches desired consistency, 30-60 minutes. Discard liquid. Store ricotta in a covered container in the refrigerator for up to 5 days. Makes 2 cups.

CHOCOLATE CHIFFON CAKE

If you want to offer family and friends a dessert that really stands out from the rest, this is the cake to make. The beautiful high and airy sponge cake is drizzled with a succulent chocolate glaze.
—Erma Fox, Memphis, MO

PREP: 25 min. + cooling
BAKE: 1 hour + cooling • **MAKES:** 20 servings

- 7 large eggs, separated
- ½ cup baking cocoa
- ¾ cup boiling water
- 1¾ cups cake flour
- 1¾ cups sugar
- 1½ tsp. baking soda
- 1 tsp. salt
- ½ cup canola oil
- 2 tsp. vanilla extract
- ¼ tsp. cream of tartar

ICING
- ⅓ cup butter
- 2 cups confectioners' sugar
- 2 oz. unsweetened chocolate, melted and cooled
- 1½ tsp. vanilla extract
- 3 to 4 Tbsp. hot water
  Chopped nuts, optional

1. Let eggs stand at room temperature for 30 minutes. In a bowl, combine cocoa and water until smooth; cool for 20 minutes.
2. In a large bowl, combine flour, sugar, baking soda and salt. In a bowl, whisk the egg yolks, oil and vanilla; add to the flour mixture along with the cocoa mixture. Beat until well blended.
3. In another large bowl and with clean beaters, beat egg whites and cream of tartar on high speed until stiff peaks form. Gradually fold into egg yolk mixture.
4. Gently spoon batter into an ungreased 10-in. tube pan. Cut through the batter with a knife to remove air pockets. Bake on lowest rack at 325° for 60-65 minutes or until top springs back when lightly touched. Immediately invert pan; cool completely. Run a knife around sides and center tube of pan. Invert cake onto a serving plate.
5. For icing, melt butter in a saucepan. Remove from the heat; stir in the confectioners' sugar, chocolate, vanilla and water. Drizzle over cake. Sprinkle with nuts if desired.

1 PIECE: *268 cal., 11g fat (3g sat. fat), 73mg chol., 262mg sod., 40g carb. (30g sugars, 1g fiber), 4g pro.*

COOLING A CHIFFON CAKE

Chiffon cakes need to cool with the pan inverted so that gravity doesn't make the cake fall. Most foam cake pans have little feet to keep them elevated so air can circulate. If your pan doesn't have feet, make use of a wine bottle or other object that has a top diameter that will fit in the tube of the pan.

PUMPKIN CREME BRULEE

I've never met a creme brulee that I didn't love! I'm not usually a big pumpkin fan, but I think it's fantastic here.
—Tamara Leonard Merritt, Raleigh, NC

PREP: 20 min. • **BAKE:** 25 min. + chilling • **MAKES:** 8 servings

- 8 large egg yolks
- ⅓ cup plus ½ cup sugar, divided
- 3 cups heavy whipping cream
- ¾ cup canned pumpkin
- 1½ tsp. vanilla extract
- ½ tsp. ground cinnamon
- ¼ tsp. each ground ginger, nutmeg and cloves

1. In a small bowl, whisk egg yolks and ⅓ cup sugar. In a small saucepan, heat cream over medium heat until bubbles form around sides of pan. Remove from the heat; stir a small amount of hot cream into the egg yolk mixture. Return all to the pan, stirring constantly. Stir in the pumpkin, vanilla and spices.
2. Transfer to eight 6-oz. ramekins or custard cups. Place ramekins in a baking pan; add 1 in. boiling water to pan. Bake, uncovered, at 325° for 25-30 minutes or until centers are just set (mixture will jiggle). Remove ramekins from water bath; cool for 10 minutes. Cover and refrigerate for at least 4 hours.
3. If using a creme brulee torch, sprinkle with remaining sugar. Heat sugar with the torch until caramelized. Serve immediately.
4. If broiling the custards, place ramekins on a baking sheet; let stand at room temperature for 15 minutes. Sprinkle with remaining sugar. Broil 8 in. from the heat for 4-7 minutes or until sugar is caramelized. Refrigerate for 1-2 hours or until firm.
1 SERVING: *452 cal., 38g fat (22g sat. fat), 327mg chol., 43mg sod., 26g carb. (22g sugars, 1g fiber), 5g pro.*

USE TONGS TO LIFT RAMEKINS

It can be tricky to remove ramekins from a hot water bath to cool. The solution: Use canning tongs. Because the edges are rounded and nonslip, they make it easy to lift the ramekins out of the hot water without the risk of burning yourself or splashing water into the custard.

HONEYED PEARS IN PUFF PASTRY

This cozy dessert has plenty of the wow factor, and is an alluring variation on poached pears as a light and lovely ending to a filling holiday feast. Wrapped in puff pastry, it resembles a beehive.
—Heather Baird, Knoxville, TN

PREP: 25 min. • **BAKE:** 25 min. • **MAKES:** 4 servings

- 4 small pears
- 4 cups water
- 2 cups sugar
- 1 cup honey
- 1 small lemon, halved
- 3 cinnamon sticks (3 in.)
- 6 to 8 whole cloves
- 1 vanilla bean
- 1 sheet frozen puff pastry, thawed
- 1 large egg, lightly beaten

1. Core pears from bottom, leaving the stems intact. Peel pears; cut ¼ in. from the bottom of each to level if necessary.
2. In a large saucepan, combine the water, sugar, honey, lemon halves, cinnamon and cloves. Split vanilla bean and scrape seeds; add bean and seeds to the sugar mixture. Bring to a boil. Reduce heat; place pears on their sides in the saucepan and poach, uncovered, until almost tender, basting occasionally with poaching liquid, 16-20 minutes.
3. Remove pears with a slotted spoon; cool slightly. Strain and reserve 1½ cups of the poaching liquid; set aside.
4. Unfold puff pastry on a lightly floured surface. Cut into ½-in.-wide strips. Brush lightly with beaten egg. Starting at the bottom of a pear, wrap a pastry strip around pear, adding additional strips until the pear is completely wrapped in pastry. Repeat with the remaining pears and puff pastry.
5. Transfer to a parchment-lined 15x10x1-in. baking pan. Bake on a lower oven rack at 400° until golden brown, 25-30 minutes.
6. Meanwhile, bring reserved poaching liquid to a boil; cook until liquid is thick and syrupy, about 10 minutes. Place pears on dessert plates and drizzle with syrup. Serve warm.
1 PEAR WITH 3 TBSP. SYRUP: 518 cal., 17g fat (4g sat. fat), 0 chol., 205mg sod., 92g carb. (49g sugars, 9g fiber), 5g pro.

BLOOD ORANGE CARAMEL TARTE TATIN

Blood orange season is pretty short, so when I can get them, I use them in everything I possibly can. I had never had blood oranges until moving to California and I've found that the perfect combination is that sweet orange flavor combined with brown sugar. Whenever I have something to go to, my friends demand I bring this dessert.
—Pamela Butkowski, Hermosa Beach, CA

PREP: 20 min. • **BAKE:** 20 min. + cooling • **MAKES:** 6 servings

- ½ cup butter, cubed
- ½ cup packed brown sugar
- 1 tsp. vanilla extract
- 1 medium blood orange, thinly sliced
- 1 sheet frozen puff pastry, thawed
  Vanilla ice cream, optional

1. Preheat oven to 400°. In an 8-in. cast-iron or other ovenproof skillet, melt butter over medium heat; stir in brown sugar and vanilla until dissolved. Arrange orange slices in a single layer over brown sugar.
2. On a lightly floured surface, unfold the puff pastry. Roll to a 9-in. square; place over oranges, tucking in corners.
3. Bake until tart is golden brown and filling is heated through, 20-25 minutes. Cool 10 minutes before inverting onto a serving plate. Serve warm, with ice cream if desired.
1 SLICE: 416 cal., 26g fat (12g sat. fat), 41mg chol., 262mg sod., 43g carb. (19g sugars, 3g fiber), 3g pro.

PUFF PASTRY SHORTCUT

Frozen puff pastry makes a marvelous shortcut to magnificent desserts. When cutting puff pastry, use a very sharp knife for the cleanest edge possible; compressing the layers of dough will prevent it from rising properly.

CANDY CANE SOUFFLE

I came up with this recipe by modifying one of my mom's gelatin-based desserts. The pretty pink sweet is a welcome sight on the table.
—Joni Hilton, Rocklin, CA

PREP: 15 min. • **COOK:** 15 min. + chilling
MAKES: 10 servings

- 2 envelopes unflavored gelatin
- 1 cup cold water
- 12 candy canes, crushed (about 1 cup)
- 2 tsp. peppermint extract
- 6 large egg whites
- ½ cup sugar
  Dash salt
- 3 cups heavy whipping cream
  Optional: Whipped cream and additional crushed candy canes

1. In a small saucepan, sprinkle gelatin over cold water; let stand for 1 minute. Add crushed candy canes. Heat over low heat, stirring until gelatin is completely dissolved. Stir in extract; set aside.

2. In a large heavy saucepan, combine the egg whites and sugar. With a hand mixer, beat on low speed for 1 minute. Place over low heat and continue beating until the egg mixture reaches 160°, about 15 minutes. Transfer to a bowl. Add salt; beat until stiff glossy peaks form and the sugar is dissolved.

3. In a large bowl, beat cream until it begins to thicken. Add reserved candy cane mixture; beat until slightly thickened. Fold in egg white mixture.

4. Pour into a large glass dessert bowl or ten 6-oz. dessert dishes. Refrigerate for 6 hours or overnight. Garnish with whipped cream and additional crushed candy if desired.

¾ CUP (CALCULATED WITHOUT GARNISHES): 394 cal., 26g fat (16g sat. fat), 98mg chol., 86mg sod., 35g carb. (25g sugars, 0 fiber), 5g pro.

CRUSHING CANDY CANES

To quickly (and neatly!) crush candy canes, place the candies in a heavy-duty resealable bag and crush them with a rolling pin.

GINGERSNAP SWEET POTATO PRALINE PIE

This luscious mix of sweet potatoes, spices and nuts is like serving pecan pie and sweet potato pie together. Bake it and watch everyone devour it.
—Emily Hobbs, Ozark, MO

PREP: 35 min. • BAKE: 30 min. + chilling
MAKES: 8 servings

- 1½ cups crushed gingersnap cookies (about 30 cookies)
- ¼ cup butter, melted
- ¼ cup butter, softened
- 1 cup plus 3 Tbsp. packed brown sugar, divided
- 1½ cups mashed sweet potatoes
- 1 tsp. ground cinnamon
- ½ tsp. ground ginger
- ¼ tsp. ground nutmeg
- ¼ tsp. salt
- 3 large egg yolks
- 1 can (5 oz.) evaporated milk
- 1 tsp. vanilla extract
- 1¼ cups pecan halves

TOPPING
- 1 cup heavy whipping cream
- 3 Tbsp. maple syrup

1. Preheat oven to 325°. In a small bowl, mix crushed cookies and melted butter. Press onto bottom and up sides of an ungreased 9-in. pie plate. Bake until set, 8-10 minutes. Cool on a wire rack.

2. Increase oven setting to 375°. Cream softened butter and 1 cup brown sugar until light and fluffy, 5-7 minutes. Beat in mashed sweet potatoes, spices and salt until blended. Beat in egg yolks, milk and vanilla. Pour into crust.

3. Arrange pecans over filling; sprinkle with the remaining 3 Tbsp. brown sugar. Bake for 30-35 minutes or until a knife inserted in the center comes out clean. Cover edge loosely with foil during the last 20 minutes if needed to prevent overbrowning. Cool completely on a wire rack. Refrigerate at least 2 hours before serving.

4. In a small bowl, beat cream until it begins to thicken. Add maple syrup; beat until stiff peaks form. Serve with pie.

1 PIECE WITH ¼ CUP WHIPPED CREAM: 659 cal., 39g fat (17g sat. fat), 140mg chol., 353mg sod., 74g carb. (49g sugars, 4g fiber), 7g pro.

PRESSING CRUMBS INTO A PIE PLATE

When making a crumb crust, use the bottom of a measuring cup or glass with a rounded edge to press the crumbs into the pan. It'll give you a nice firm and level crust with no finger dents.

CRAN-APPLE PECAN CRISP

Even folks who claim not to like cranberries rave about this dish. I cherish the recipe from my mother, who inspired my love of cooking.
—Debbie Daly, Florence, KY

PREP: 20 min. • BAKE: 40 min. • MAKES: 12 servings

- 1 cup sugar
- 1 Tbsp. cornstarch
- 3 cups chopped tart apples
- 2 cups fresh or frozen cranberries
- 1 cup old-fashioned oats
- ½ cup packed brown sugar
- ½ cup chopped pecans
- ⅓ cup all-purpose flour
- ⅓ cup cold butter

Preheat oven to 375°. In a large bowl, combine sugar and cornstarch; stir in the apples and cranberries. Transfer to a greased 2-qt. baking dish. In another bowl, combine the oats, brown sugar, pecans and flour; cut in butter until mixture is crumbly. Sprinkle over apple mixture. Bake, uncovered, for 40-45 minutes or until golden brown. Serve warm.
½ CUP: 244 cal., 9g fat (4g sat. fat), 14mg chol., 56mg sod., 41g carb. (30g sugars, 3g fiber), 2g pro.

CRANBERRY CAKE WITH TANGERINE FROSTING

Sugary cranberries and candied citrus dress up this smartly elegant cake. It's my favorite Christmas dessert for its sheer impressiveness.
—*Sandy Gaulitz, Spring, TX*

PREP: 30 min. • **BAKE:** 35 min. + cooling • **MAKES:** 16 servings

- ¼ cup butter, softened
- 2 cups sugar
- 2 tsp. vanilla extract
- 4 cups plus 2 Tbsp. cake flour, divided
- 2 Tbsp. baking powder
- 1 tsp. salt
- 2 cups 2% milk
- 4 cups fresh or frozen cranberries

FROSTING

- 2 pkg. (8 oz. each) cream cheese, softened
- ¾ cup butter, softened
- 4 cups confectioners' sugar
- 2 Tbsp. tangerine or orange juice
- ½ tsp. grated tangerine or orange zest
  Optional toppings: Sugared cranberries, candied tangerine or orange slices, and red sprinkles

1. Preheat oven to 400°. Line the bottoms of 2 greased 8-in. square or 9-in. round baking pans with parchment; grease paper. In a large bowl, beat butter and sugar until crumbly, about 2 minutes. Beat in vanilla.

2. In another bowl, mix 4 cups flour, baking powder and the salt; add to the butter mixture alternately with milk, beating well after each addition. In a large bowl, toss cranberries with remaining 2 Tbsp. flour; fold into batter.

3. Transfer batter to prepared pans. Bake for 35-40 minutes or until a toothpick inserted in center comes out clean. Cool for 10 minutes before removing from pans to wire racks; remove parchment. Cool completely.

4. For frosting, in a large bowl, beat cream cheese and butter until smooth. Gradually beat in the confectioners' sugar, tangerine juice and zest. Spread between cake layers and over top and sides of cake. Refrigerate, covered, until serving. If desired, garnish with sugared cranberries, candied citrus and sprinkles.

1 PIECE: *572 cal., 22g fat (13g sat. fat), 62mg chol., 524mg sod., 89g carb. (58g sugars, 2g fiber), 6g pro.*

MAKING CANDIED CITRUS

For candied citrus, bring 2½ cups sugar and 2 cups of water to a boil. Add thin tangerine or orange slices and reduce heat to medium. Cook until slices are translucent, about 20 minutes, turning occasionally. Reduce heat; simmer until tender, about 10 minutes, turning occasionally. With a slotted spoon or tongs, remove slices to a parchment-lined baking sheet or wire rack. Let stand at room temperature or overnight to dry.

MAKING SUGARED CRANBERRIES

Stir together 2 Tbsp. water and 2 Tbsp. pasteurized liquid egg whites. Lightly coat 12 oz. fresh or frozen cranberries in mixture. Place the cranberries on a baking pan and sprinkle with ½ cup coarse sugar and ½ cup superfine sugar until coated. Dry at room temperature for 2 hours.

CHOCOLATE GINGERBREAD YULE LOG

If you've tasted a yule log sponge cake, you'll love this version with fresh ginger and spices. This stunner can be made ahead.
—Lauren McAnelly, Des Moines, IA

PREP: 1¼ hours • **BAKE:** 10 min. + cooling
MAKES: 16 servings

- 5 large eggs, separated
- ¾ cup cake flour
- 1 to 1½ tsp. each ground ginger and cinnamon
- ¼ tsp. each ground nutmeg and pepper
- ¼ tsp. salt
- ⅓ cup packed dark brown sugar
- ¼ cup molasses
- 2 Tbsp. canola oil
- 1 Tbsp. grated fresh gingerroot
- ⅛ tsp. cream of tartar
- ¼ cup sugar
  Baking cocoa

FILLING
- 1 carton (8 oz.) mascarpone cheese
- ⅓ cup confectioners' sugar
- 2 Tbsp. heavy whipping cream
- ⅛ tsp. salt
- ⅓ cup crystallized ginger, dried cranberries or miniature semisweet chocolate chips

CHOCOLATE BARK
- 4 to 6 oz. high-quality bittersweet chocolate, melted

BUTTERCREAM
- 2 large egg whites
- ½ cup sugar
- ⅛ tsp. salt
- ¾ cup unsalted butter, softened
- 4 oz. high-quality milk chocolate, melted and cooled

1. Place egg whites in a large bowl; let stand at room temperature 30 minutes. Preheat oven to 350°. Line bottom of a greased 15x10x1-in. baking pan with parchment; grease paper. Sift flour, spices and salt together twice.

2. In a large bowl, beat egg yolks until slightly thickened. Gradually add brown sugar, beating on high speed until thick. Beat in molasses, oil and fresh ginger. Fold in flour mixture (batter will be thick).

3. Add cream of tartar to egg whites; with clean beaters, beat on medium until soft peaks form. Gradually add sugar, 1 Tbsp. at a time, beating after each addition until sugar is dissolved. Beat on high until stiff, glossy peaks form. Using a large spatula, fold a fourth of the whites into batter, then fold in remaining whites. Transfer to prepared pan, spreading evenly.

4. Bake 10-12 minutes or until top springs back when lightly touched. Cool 5 minutes. Invert onto a tea towel dusted with cocoa. Gently peel off paper. Roll up cake in towel jelly-roll style. Cool completely on a wire rack.

5. For filling, in a small bowl, mix mascarpone cheese, confectioners' sugar, cream and salt just until blended; stir in ginger. Refrigerate, covered.

6. For bark, line the underside of a 15x10x1-in. baking pan with parchment. Using an offset spatula, spread melted chocolate in a thin, even layer on parchment. Refrigerate until set, about 30 minutes.

7. For buttercream, place egg whites, sugar and salt in a heatproof bowl; whisk until blended. Place bowl over simmering water in a large saucepan over medium heat. Whisking constantly, heat mixture until a thermometer reads 160°, 1-2 minutes.

8. Remove from heat. With the whisk attachment of a mixer, beat on high speed until stiff glossy peaks form and mixture has cooled, about 5 minutes. Gradually beat in butter, a few tablespoons at a time, on medium speed until smooth. Beat in cooled chocolate.

9. To assemble, unroll cake; spread filling over cake to within ¼ in. of edges. Roll up again, without towel; trim ends. Transfer to a platter. Spread buttercream over the cake.

10. To decorate cake, lift chilled chocolate with fingers and break carefully into shards; arrange over buttercream, overlapping slightly. If chocolate becomes too soft, return to refrigerator as necessary.

11. Refrigerate cake, loosely covered, until serving. Using a serrated knife, cut cake into slices.

1 SLICE: *373 cal., 24g fat (13g sat. fat), 103mg chol., 121mg sod., 38g carb. (29g sugars, 1g fiber), 5g pro.*

CRUMB-TOPPED APPLE & PUMPKIN PIE

This special recipe combines all the warm, delicious flavors of the season and makes a truly unique presentation. It gets rave reviews each year and has become a holiday tradition at our house.
—Trisha Fox, Plainfield, IL

PREP: 35 min. • **BAKE:** 50 min. + cooling
MAKES: 10 servings

- 1 sheet refrigerated pie crust
- 2 cups thinly sliced peeled tart apples
- ¼ cup sugar
- 2 tsp. all-purpose flour
- 1 tsp. lemon juice
- ¼ tsp. ground cinnamon

PUMPKIN FILLING

- 1½ cups canned pumpkin
- 1 cup fat-free evaporated milk
- 2 large eggs
- ½ cup sugar
- ¾ tsp. ground cinnamon
- ¼ tsp. salt
- ⅛ tsp. ground nutmeg

TOPPING

- ½ cup all-purpose flour
- 3 Tbsp. sugar
- 4½ tsp. cold butter
- 3 Tbsp. chopped walnuts

1. Preheat oven to 375°. On a lightly floured surface, unroll crust. Transfer crust to a 9-in. deep-dish pie plate. Trim crust to ½ in. beyond edge of plate; flute edge. In a large bowl, combine the apples, sugar, flour, lemon juice and cinnamon. Spoon into crust.

2. Whisk together the pumpkin filling ingredients. Pour over apple mixture. Bake for 30 minutes.

3. For topping, combine flour and sugar. Cut in butter until crumbly; stir in walnuts. Sprinkle over pie.

4. Bake 20-25 minutes longer or until a knife inserted into pumpkin layer comes out clean (cover edge with foil during the last 15 minutes to prevent overbrowning if necessary). Cool on a wire rack. Refrigerate leftovers.

1 PIECE: *282 cal., 10g fat (4g sat. fat), 47mg chol., 198mg sod., 44g carb. (26g sugars, 2g fiber), 6g pro.*

GETTING EGGS TO ROOM TEMP

If your recipe calls for room temperature eggs, and you forgot to take them out of the refrigerator, you can bring them up to temperature quickly by placing them in hot water while you prepare your recipe. They'll be ready by the time you need them.

MUDSLIDE CHEESECAKE

*Change up cheesecakes with different liqueur flavorings.
This mudslide version with coffee and Irish cream is my
husband's favorite.*
—Sue Gronholz, Beaver Dam, WI

PREP: 30 min. • **BAKE:** 1 hour + cooling • **MAKES:** 16 servings

  1 cup chocolate wafer crumbs
  3 Tbsp. sugar
  2 Tbsp. butter, melted

FILLING
  1 cup semisweet chocolate chips
  4 pkg. (8 oz. each) cream cheese, softened
1½ cups sugar
  4 Tbsp. all-purpose flour
  4 large eggs, room temperature
  2 tsp. vanilla extract
  2 Tbsp. coffee liqueur
  ¾ cup Irish cream liqueur

GANACHE
  ½ cup semisweet chocolate chips
  ¼ cup heavy whipping cream

1. Preheat oven to 325°. Wrap a double thickness of heavy-duty
foil (about 18 in. square) around a greased 9-in. springform
pan. Mix cookie crumbs and sugar; stir in butter. Press onto the
bottom of the prepared pan.

2. To prepare filling, microwave chocolate chips on high until
melted, about 1 minute. Beat cream cheese and sugar until
smooth. Add flour; mix well. Add eggs and vanilla; beat on low
just until blended. Measure out 2 cups batter, and stir in coffee
liqueur; add melted chocolate chips and stir until blended. Pour
over crust. Add Irish cream liqueur to remaining batter; spoon
over chocolate layer. Place springform pan in a larger baking
pan; add 1 in. hot water to the larger pan.

3. Bake until the center is just set and the top appears dull,
60-75 minutes. Remove springform pan from water bath. Cool
cheesecake on a wire rack 10 minutes. Loosen sides from
pan with a knife; remove foil. Cool 1 hour longer. Refrigerate
overnight, covering when completely cooled.

4. For ganache, microwave chocolate chips and whipping cream
on high until the chips melt; cool slightly. Remove rim from pan;
spread ganache over top of chilled cheesecake.

1 PIECE: *485 cal., 31g fat (16g sat. fat), 118mg chol., 280mg sod.,
44g carb. (37g sugars, 1g fiber), 6g pro.*

WATER BATH FOR CHEESECAKES

Even if your recipe doesn't call for it, a water
bath is a good idea when baking cheesecakes—
keeping the air in the oven humid helps prevents
cracking. Wrap the springform pan in foil,
set it in a larger roasting pan, and add about
an inch of hot water to the larger pan.
It's safest to add the water after you've
filled the springform pan with batter.

GREAT GANACHE

When making ganache, don't overheat the cream—remove it from the heat just when it reaches boiling temperature. Too hot, and it can overheat the fat in the chocolate and cause it to separate. Cover the bowl and let it sit for up to 10 minutes before whisking. Whisk too soon and you'll cool the cream too quickly; the ganache could become grainy. If it does get grainy, put it on the stove on the lowest setting—just enough to remelt the chocolate—whisking constantly.

SPECIAL-OCCASION CHOCOLATE CAKE

This recipe won Grand Champion at the Alaska State Fair, and with one bite, you'll see why! The decadent chocolate cake boasts a luscious ganache filling and fudge buttercream frosting.
—*Cindi DeClue, Anchorage, AK*

- -

PREP: 40 min. + chilling • **BAKE:** 25 min. + cooling
MAKES: 16 servings

- 1 cup baking cocoa
- 2 cups boiling water
- 1 cup butter, softened
- 2¼ cups sugar
- 4 large eggs, room temperature
- 1½ tsp. vanilla extract
- 2¾ cups all-purpose flour
- 2 tsp. baking soda
- ½ tsp. baking powder
- ½ tsp. salt

GANACHE
- 10 oz. semisweet chocolate, chopped
- 1 cup heavy whipping cream
- 2 Tbsp. sugar

FROSTING
- 1 cup butter, softened
- 4 cups confectioners' sugar
- ½ cup baking cocoa
- ¼ cup 2% milk
- 2 tsp. vanilla extract

GARNISH
- ¾ cup sliced almonds, toasted

1. Preheat oven to 350°. Combine cocoa and water; set aside to cool completely. In a large bowl, cream butter and sugar until light and fluffy, 5-7 minutes. Add eggs, 1 at a time, beating well after each addition. Beat in vanilla. Whisk together the flour, baking soda, baking powder and salt; add to creamed mixture alternately with cocoa mixture, beating well after each addition.
2. Pour into 3 greased and floured 9-in. round baking pans. Bake until a toothpick inserted in the center comes out clean, 25-30 minutes. Cool for 10 minutes before removing from pans to wire racks to cool completely.
3. For ganache, place chocolate in a bowl. In a small heavy saucepan over low heat, bring cream and sugar to a boil. Pour over chocolate; whisk gently until smooth. Allow to cool until it reaches a spreadable consistency, stirring occasionally.
4. For frosting, in a large bowl, beat butter until fluffy. Add the confectioners' sugar, cocoa, milk and vanilla; beat until smooth.
5. Place 1 cake layer on a serving plate; spread with 1 cup frosting. Top with second layer and 1 cup ganache; sprinkle with ½ cup almonds. Top with third layer; frost top and sides of cake. Warm ganache until pourable; pour over cake, allowing some to drape down the sides. Sprinkle with remaining ¼ cup almonds. Refrigerate until serving.
1 PIECE: *736 cal., 39g fat (22g sat. fat), 125mg chol., 454mg sod., 86g carb. (63g sugars, 3g fiber), 8g pro.*

PUMPKIN CREAM TIRAMISU

Pumpkin isn't only for pies. Now you can take the classic vegetable and enjoy it in a tiramisu-style dessert. After one bite, you'll add this recipe to your keeper files.
—Pam Peters, Fernie, BC

- -

PREP: 1 hour + chilling
BAKE: 10 min./batch + cooling
MAKES: 12 servings

½ cup butter, softened
1 cup sugar
1 large egg, room temperature
¼ cup honey
½ cup solid-pack pumpkin
1 tsp. dark rum
2⅓ cups all-purpose flour
2 tsp. ground cinnamon
1½ tsp. baking soda
1½ tsp. ground ginger
1 tsp. ground cloves
½ tsp. salt

TIRAMISU

2¼ cups solid-pack pumpkin
1½ tsp. ground cinnamon
¾ tsp. ground ginger
¼ tsp. ground cloves
3 cups heavy whipping cream
¾ cup sugar
12 oz. cream cheese, softened
¼ cup dark rum
½ tsp. ground cinnamon or nutmeg

1. Preheat oven to 350°. In a large bowl, cream the butter and sugar until light and fluffy, 5-7 minutes. Gradually beat in egg and honey. Add pumpkin and rum; mix well. In another bowl, whisk the flour, cinnamon, baking soda, ginger, cloves and salt; gradually beat into creamed mixture.
2. Cut a ¾-in. hole in the tip of a pastry bag or in a corner of a food-safe plastic bag. Working in batches, pipe dough to form 2½-in. logs, 2 in. apart, onto parchment-lined baking sheets. Bake for 12-14 minutes or until cookies are golden and set. Cool on a wire rack.
3. In a large bowl, mix pumpkin and spices. In a small bowl, beat cream until it begins to thicken. Add sugar; beat until soft peaks form.
4. Fold a third of the whipped cream mixture into the pumpkin mixture. In a small bowl, beat cream cheese until smooth. Beat in remaining whipped cream until combined.
5. Arrange a third of the cookies in a single layer in a 13x9-in. baking dish; brush with rum. Top with a third of the pumpkin filling. Spread with a third of the cream cheese mixture. Repeat layers twice. Refrigerate, covered, 8 hours or overnight. Sprinkle with cinnamon.
1 PIECE: *635 cal., 40g fat (25g sat. fat), 132mg chol., 432mg sod., 63g carb. (40g sugars, 3g fiber), 7g pro.*

SNOWED IN:
ROMANTIC CHRISTMAS FOR TWO

The wind is howling and the snow is flying, but all is well when you and your sweetheart are cozied up by a crackling fire while Bing Crosby croons in the background. This year, enjoy a delicious small-scale meal perfect for two.

IRISH COFFEE

Creme de menthe adds a festive and colorful touch to the cream floating atop these yummy drinks. The drink would also be delicious with a little Irish cream liqueur stirred in.
—Taste of Home *Test Kitchen*

TAKES: 10 min. • **MAKES:** 2 servings

- 2 tsp. sugar
- 2 oz. Irish whiskey
- 2 cups hot strong brewed coffee (French or other dark roast)
- ¼ cup heavy whipping cream
- 1 tsp. green creme de menthe

Divide the sugar and whiskey between 2 mugs; stir in coffee. In a small bowl, beat the cream and creme de menthe until thickened. Gently spoon onto tops of drinks, allowing cream to float. Serve immediately.

1 CUP: *203 cal., 11g fat (7g sat. fat), 41mg chol., 21mg sod., 8g carb. (6g sugars, 0 fiber), 1g pro.*

> ### *Holiday Helper*
> If you're short on time or simply prefer plain whipped cream, simply top the coffee with a dollop of canned whipped cream.

SPICE-RUBBED LAMB CHOPS

Lamb chops are one of my favorite dinner entrees. My girls, Hanna and Amani, love watching me make my delicious chops, but they love eating them even more.
—Nareman Dietz, Beverly Hills, MI

PREP: 15 min. + chilling • **BAKE:** 5 min. • **MAKES:** 2 servings

- 2 tsp. lemon juice
- 2 tsp. Worcestershire sauce
- 1½ tsp. pepper
- 1¼ tsp. ground cumin
- 1¼ tsp. curry powder
- 1 garlic clove, minced
- ½ tsp. sea salt
- ½ tsp. onion powder
- ½ tsp. crushed red pepper flakes
- 4 lamb rib chops
- 1 Tbsp. olive oil

1. Mix first 9 ingredients; spread over chops. Refrigerate, covered, overnight.

2. Preheat oven to 450°. In an ovenproof skillet, heat oil over medium-high heat; brown chops, about 2 minutes per side. Transfer to oven; roast until desired doneness (for medium-rare, a thermometer should read 135°; medium, 140°), 3-4 minutes.

2 LAMB CHOPS: *290 cal., 17g fat (4g sat. fat), 90mg chol., 620mg sod., 5g carb. (1g sugars, 2g fiber), 29g pro.*
DIABETIC EXCHANGES: *4 lean meat, 1½ fat.*

LI'L PECAN PIES

I love having all the rich, traditional flavors of a full-size pecan pie in an adorable size. These mini baked treats are perfect for my husband and me.
—Christine Boitos, Livonia, MI

PREP: 15 min. + chilling
BAKE: 35 min. + cooling • **MAKES:** 2 servings

- ½ cup all-purpose flour
- ⅛ tsp. salt
- 3 Tbsp. shortening
- 4 tsp. cold water

FILLING
- ⅓ cup pecan halves
- 1 large egg
- ⅓ cup packed brown sugar
- ⅓ cup corn syrup
- ½ tsp. vanilla extract
   Whipped cream, optional

1. In a small bowl, combine flour and salt; cut in shortening until crumbly. Gradually add water, tossing with a fork until dough forms a ball. Cover and refrigerate for at least 30 minutes.

2. Divide dough in half. Roll each half into a 6-in. circle. Transfer to two 4½-in. tart pans; fit pastry into pans, trimming if necessary. Arrange pecans in shells.

3. In another small bowl, whisk egg, brown sugar, corn syrup and vanilla. Pour over pecans. Place shells on a baking sheet. Bake at 375° for 35-40 minutes or until a knife inserted in the center comes out clean. Cool on a wire rack. Top with whipped cream if desired.

1 PIE: *734 cal., 34g fat (6g sat. fat), 106mg chol., 260mg sod., 104g carb. (65g sugars, 3g fiber), 8g pro.*

ORANGE ROSEMARY CARROTS

My family loves rosemary, and I grow it along with carrots in my garden every year. Both ingredients shine in this delicious dish.
—Arlene Butler, Ogden, UT

TAKES: 30 min. • **MAKES:** 2 servings

- 1 Tbsp. butter
- 1 Tbsp. finely chopped shallot or red onion
- 1 garlic clove, minced
- 3 medium carrots, cut into ½-in. slices
- 1 Tbsp. brown sugar
- 1 Tbsp. water
- 1 Tbsp. thawed frozen orange juice concentrate
- ½ tsp. minced fresh rosemary
- ⅛ tsp. salt
- ⅛ tsp. pepper
   Minced fresh parsley, optional

1. In a small saucepan, melt butter over medium-high heat. Add shallot; cook and stir until tender, 2-3 minutes. Add garlic; cook 1 minute longer.

2. Stir in carrots. Add the brown sugar, water, orange juice concentrate, fresh rosemary, salt and pepper. Reduce the heat to medium-low. Cook, covered, until carrots are crisp-tender, 15-20 minutes. Uncover and cook until liquid is reduced by half, 1-2 minutes. If desired, sprinkle with fresh parsley.

¾ CUP: *133 cal., 6g fat (4g sat. fat), 15mg chol., 260mg sod., 20g carb. (14g sugars, 3g fiber), 1g pro.*

HERB-STUFFED ROASTED CORNISH HENS

If you're looking for an elegant dinner for two, try these delightful Cornish game hens. As a bonus, crisp, tasty potatoes cook right alongside.
—Taste of Home *Test Kitchen*

PREP: 20 min. • **BAKE:** 70 min.
MAKES: 2 servings

- 2 Cornish game hens (20 to 24 oz. each)
- 12 fresh sage leaves
- 4 lemon wedges
- 6 green onions, cut into 2-in. lengths, divided
- 2 Tbsp. butter, melted
- 1 Tbsp. olive oil
- 1 Tbsp. lemon juice
- 2 garlic cloves, minced
- 1 tsp. kosher salt or sea salt
- ¼ tsp. coarsely ground pepper
- 6 small red potatoes, halved

1. Preheat oven to 375°. Gently lift skin from hen breasts and place sage leaves under skin. Place lemon wedges and a third of the onions in the cavities. Tuck wings under hens; tie legs together. Place in a small greased roasting pan.
2. Combine butter, oil, lemon juice and garlic; spoon half of mixture over hens. Sprinkle with salt and pepper.
3. Bake 30 minutes. Add potatoes and remaining onions to pan. Brush hens with remaining butter mixture. Bake until a thermometer inserted in thickest part of thigh reads 170°-175° and potatoes are tender, 40-45 minutes longer.
4. Remove hens to a serving platter. Stir potatoes and onions to coat with pan drippings. Serve with hens.
1 SERVING: *980 cal., 67g fat (22g sat. fat), 379mg chol., 1,398mg sod., 29g carb., 4g fiber, 63g pro.*

CRAB-STUFFED MANICOTTI

I love pasta, and my husband loves seafood. I combined them to create this special dish. He raved that it's the best meal ever.
—Sonya Polfliet, Anza, CA

PREP: 25 min. • **BAKE:** 25 min.
MAKES: 2 servings

- 4 uncooked manicotti shells
- 1 Tbsp. butter
- 4 tsp. all-purpose flour
- 1 cup fat-free milk
- 1 Tbsp. grated Parmesan cheese
- 1 cup lump crabmeat, drained
- ⅓ cup reduced-fat ricotta cheese
- ¼ cup shredded part-skim mozzarella cheese
- ¼ tsp. lemon-pepper seasoning
- ¼ tsp. pepper
- ⅛ tsp. garlic powder
- Minced fresh parsley

1. Preheat oven to 350°. Cook manicotti shells according to package directions; drain. Meanwhile, in a small saucepan, melt butter. Stir in flour until smooth; gradually add milk. Bring to a boil; cook and stir until thickened, about 2 minutes. Remove from heat; stir in Parmesan.
2. In a small bowl, combine the crab, ricotta cheese, mozzarella cheese, lemon-pepper seasoning, pepper and garlic powder. Stuff shells with crab mixture. Spread ¼ cup sauce in an 8-in. square baking dish coated with cooking spray. Top with stuffed manicotti. Pour remaining sauce over top.
3. Bake, covered, until heated through, 25-30 minutes. Just before serving, sprinkle with parsley and, if desired, additional grated Parmesan cheese.
2 STUFFED SHELLS: *359 cal., 12g fat (7g sat. fat), 98mg chol., 793mg sod., 38g carb. (11g sugars, 1g fiber), 26g pro.*
DIABETIC EXCHANGES: *2 starch, 2 lean meat, 1 fat, ½ fat-free milk.*

MUSHROOM PORK RAGOUT

My savory slow-cooked pork is served in a delightful tomato gravy over noodles. It's a nice change from regular pork roast. I serve it with broccoli or green beans on the side.
—Connie McDowell, Greenwood, DE

- -

PREP: 20 min. • **COOK:** 3 hours
MAKES: 2 servings

1	pork tenderloin (¾ lb.)
⅛	tsp. salt
⅛	tsp. pepper
1	Tbsp. cornstarch
¾	cup canned crushed tomatoes, divided
1	Tbsp. chopped sun-dried tomatoes (not packed in oil)
1¼	tsp. dried savory
1½	cups sliced fresh mushrooms
⅓	cup sliced onion
1½	cups hot cooked egg noodles

1. Rub pork with salt and pepper; cut in half. In a 1½-qt. slow cooker, combine the cornstarch, ½ cup crushed tomatoes, sun-dried tomatoes and savory. Top with the mushrooms, onion and pork. Pour the remaining tomatoes over pork. Cover and cook on low for 3-4 hours, until the meat is tender.

2. Remove meat and cut into slices. Stir cooking juices until smooth; serve with pork and noodles.

1 SERVING: *360 cal., 7g fat (2g sat. fat), 122mg chol., 309mg sod., 32g carb. (3g sugars, 3g fiber), 40g pro.*
DIABETIC EXCHANGES: *5 lean meat, 2 vegetable, 1 starch.*

Baked Mushroom Pork Ragout:
Assemble as directed, using a greased 1½-qt. baking dish. Cover and bake at 425° for 30-35 minutes or until a thermometer reads 160°. Serve as directed.

MINTY BAKED ALASKA

I've made this dessert on a few special occasions for my husband and me. He loves it. It's so simple, but looks and tastes like you spent all day in the kitchen. Crushed peppermint candy adds a special taste and decorative touch. It never fails to impress.
—Brenda Mast, Clearwater, FL

- -

TAKES: 30 min. • **MAKES:** 2 servings

2	large egg whites
¼	cup sugar
¼	tsp. cream of tartar
¼	tsp. vanilla extract
	Dash salt
1	Tbsp. crushed peppermint candy
⅔	cup mint chocolate chip ice cream
2	individual round sponge cakes

1. In a heatproof bowl of a stand mixer, whisk the egg whites, sugar and cream of tartar until blended. Place over simmering water in a large saucepan over medium heat. Whisking constantly, heat mixture until a thermometer reads 160°, 4-5 minutes. Remove from heat; add vanilla and salt. With the whisk attachment of a stand mixer, beat on high speed until stiff glossy peaks form and meringue has slightly cooled, 7-9 minutes. Fold in peppermint candy.

2. Preheat broiler. Place the sponge cakes on an ungreased foil-lined baking sheet and top each cake with ⅓ cup ice cream. Immediately spread meringue over ice cream and cake, sealing it to foil on sheet. Broil 8 in. from heat until lightly browned, 3-5 minutes. Serve immediately.

1 BAKED ALASKA: *326 cal., 9g fat (5g sat. fat), 44mg chol., 333mg sod., 54g carb. (46g sugars, 0 fiber), 6g pro.*

CHANCE OF SNOW

Arrange swirls of paper to make a pretty winter ornament. Quilling, a craft technique for rolling paper strips into pretty designs, produces this charming snowflake.

1. Using a quilling needle tool, wrap 16-in.-long paper strips to make six 1½-in. circles. Glue ends in place.
2. Pinch 1 side of the circles to make a teardrop. Use needle tool and wrap another strip into a 1-in. circle. Glue the teardops around the circle, pointed sides out.
3. Using a quilling looper tool (it looks a bit like a comb), wrap a strip around top prong and glue down. Wrap around next prong and up and over top prong. Wrap around third prong and up and over top prong. Repeat to end of strip and glue end.
4. Slide off tool and pinch 1 end. Repeat to make 6 small, tight teardrops. Glue these into place between the larger teardrops, pointed side in.
5. Fold a paper strip in half and roll each end outward into a circle to form a Y-shape scroll. Repeat for 6 total Y's. Cut at folds and glue to outer sides of larger teardrops.
6. Create 6 marquise shapes by rolling 6 scrolls and pinching the outer edges on 2 opposite sides. Glue between the Y scroll loops. Spray entire piece with adhesive.
7. Sprinkle glitter all over. Repeat on other side. Dry completely. Tie ribbon in a loop to hang.

BUTTERSCOTCH MARTINIS

The rich flavors of butterscotch and chocolate pair up for a nightcap that will satisfy any sweet tooth.
—*Clara Coulson Minney, Washington Court House, OH*

TAKES: 10 min. • **MAKES:** 2 servings

      Ice cubes
2   oz. clear creme de cacao
2   oz. creme de cacao
1½ oz. vodka
1½ oz. butterscotch schnapps liqueur
6   semisweet chocolate chips
    Soft butterscotch candies, optional

1. Fill a shaker three-fourths full with ice. Add the creme de cacao, vodka and schnapps.
2. Cover and shake until condensation forms on outside of shaker, 10-15 seconds. Divide the chocolate chips between 2 chilled cocktail glasses; strain butterscotch mixture over chips. If desired, garnish with butterscotch candies.
1 SERVING: *322 cal., 1g fat (0 sat. fat), 0 chol., 4mg sod., 29g carb. (29g sugars, 0 fiber), 0 pro.*

SIMPLE SWISS CHEESE FONDUE

When I was growing up, my friend's mother would make this fondue whenever I spent the night. It brings back fond memories every time I make it. I love the rich flavor. Happy dipping!
—Tracy Lawson, Plain City, UT

TAKES: 20 min. • **MAKES:** ⅔ cup

- 1 cup shredded Swiss cheese
- 1 Tbsp. all-purpose flour
- ⅛ tsp. ground mustard
  Dash ground nutmeg
- ¼ cup half-and-half cream
- ¼ cup beer or nonalcoholic beer
  French bread cubes

1. In a small bowl, combine the cheese, flour, ground mustard and nutmeg. In a small saucepan, heat cream and beer over medium heat until bubbles form around sides of pan. Stir in the cheese mixture. Bring just to a gentle boil; cook and stir until combined and smooth, 1-2 minutes.
2. Transfer to a small fondue pot and keep warm. Serve with bread cubes.
⅓ **CUP:** 280 cal., 20g fat (12g sat. fat), 65mg chol., 117mg sod., 6g carb. (2g sugars, 0 fiber), 16g pro.

CHOCOLATE BREAD PUDDING

Try my yummy chocolate twist on traditional bread pudding. It's a rich, comforting dessert.
—Mildred Sherrer, Fort Worth, TX

PREP: 15 min. + standing • **BAKE:** 30 min. • **MAKES:** 2 servings

- 2 oz. semisweet chocolate
- ½ cup half-and-half cream
- ⅔ cup sugar
- ½ cup 2% milk
- 1 large egg, room temperature
- 1 tsp. vanilla extract
- ¼ tsp. salt
- 4 slices day-old bread, crusts removed, cut into cubes (about 3 cups)
  Optional: Confectioners' sugar and whipped cream

1. In a small microwave-safe bowl, melt chocolate; stir until smooth. Stir in cream; set aside.
2. In a large bowl, whisk the sugar, milk, egg, vanilla and salt. Stir in chocolate mixture. Add bread cubes and toss to coat. Let stand for 15 minutes.
3. Spoon into 2 greased 2-cup souffle dishes. Bake at 350° until a knife inserted in the center comes out clean, 30-35 minutes.
4. If desired, sprinkle with confectioners' sugar and top with a dollop of whipped cream.
1 SERVING: 622 cal., 17g fat (9g sat. fat), 145mg chol., 656mg sod., 105g carb. (79g sugars, 2g fiber), 12g pro.

SCENTED RICE IN BAKED PUMPKIN

This easy, delicious and healthy side is a showpiece that always delights. You can use grain, squash, fruits and nuts to suit your taste. It's impossible to go wrong!
—Lynn Heisel, Jackson, MO

PREP: 30 min. • **BAKE:** 35 min.
MAKES: 2 servings

- 1 small pie pumpkin (about 2 lbs.)
- 1 Tbsp. olive oil
- ½ cup uncooked brown rice
- 1 cup water
- ¼ cup coarsely chopped pecans, toasted
- 3 dried apricots, chopped
- 2 Tbsp. raisins
- ¼ tsp. salt
- ¼ tsp. curry powder
- ⅛ tsp. ground cinnamon
- ⅛ tsp. ground cardamom, optional
- ⅛ tsp. ground cumin

1. Wash pumpkin; cut into 6 wedges. Remove loose fibers and seeds from the inside, and discard seeds or save them for toasting. Brush wedges with oil. Place on an ungreased 15x10x1-in. baking sheet. Bake at 400° until tender, 35-40 minutes.
2. Meanwhile, in a small saucepan, bring rice and water to a boil. Reduce heat; cover and simmer until liquid is absorbed and rice is tender, 20-25 minutes. Stir in pecans, dried apricots, raisins, salt, curry, cinnamon and, if desired, cardamom.
3. Set 4 pumpkin wedges aside for another use. Sprinkle cumin onto the remaining wedges; top with rice mixture.
1 SERVING: *389 cal., 15g fat (2g sat. fat), 0 chol., 309mg sod., 62g carb. (13g sugars, 5g fiber), 7g pro.*

Holiday Helper
Use the leftover roasted pie pumpkin any way you would use cooked winter squash puree: add to soup, mash for a side dish, or cube and stir into stuffing or pilaf.

MINESTRONE-STYLE SHRIMP SALAD

My shrimp salad is the perfect dish to serve as a small dinner for two. It's refreshing, light and loaded with healthy ingredients.
—Roxanne Chan, Albany, CA

PREP: 20 min. • COOK: 10 min.
MAKES: 2 servings

- 1 cup uncooked tricolor spiral pasta
- 2 Tbsp. lemon juice
- 2 Tbsp. olive oil
- 2 Tbsp. prepared pesto
- 1 garlic clove, minced
- ¼ tsp. salt
- ¼ tsp. pepper

SALAD

- 1 cup canned white kidney or cannellini beans, rinsed and drained
- 1 medium tomato, chopped
- ¼ cup fresh corn
- 2 Tbsp. sliced celery
- 2 Tbsp. diced red onion
- 2 Tbsp. diced carrot
- 2 Tbsp. roasted sweet red peppers, diced
- 2 Tbsp. minced fresh parsley
- 2 cups Italian-blend salad greens
- 8 peeled and deveined cooked large shrimp
  Grated Parmesan cheese, optional

1. Cook pasta according to package directions. Meanwhile, in a small bowl, whisk together the lemon juice, oil, pesto, garlic, salt and pepper. Rinse pasta with cold water; drain.
2. In a large bowl, combine the pasta, beans, tomato, corn, celery, onion, carrot, red peppers, parsley and dressing. Divide salad greens between 2 plates; top with pasta mixture and shrimp. If desired, sprinkle with Parmesan cheese.
1 SERVING: *535 cal., 23g fat (4g sat. fat), 48mg chol., 719mg sod., 63g carb. (6g sugars, 10g fiber), 21g pro.*

ROASTED GARLIC TWICE-BAKED POTATO

The creamy texture and roasted garlic flavor make this side dish a winner. It's easy to prepare and a perfect choice to pair with a hearty meat entree.
—Nancy Mueller, Menomonee Falls, WI

PREP: 1 hour • BAKE: 25 min.
MAKES: 2 servings

- 1 large baking potato
- 1 tsp. canola oil, divided
- 6 garlic cloves, unpeeled
- 2 Tbsp. butter, softened
- 2 Tbsp. 2% milk
- 2 Tbsp. sour cream
- ¼ tsp. minced fresh rosemary or dash dried rosemary, crushed
- ⅛ tsp. salt
- ⅛ tsp. pepper

1. Scrub and pierce potato; rub with ½ tsp. oil. Place garlic cloves on a double thickness of heavy-duty foil. Drizzle with remaining oil. Wrap foil around garlic. Place potato and garlic on a baking sheet. Bake at 400° for 15 minutes. Remove the garlic; bake potato until tender, about 45 minutes longer.
2. When cool enough to handle, cut potato in half lengthwise. Scoop out the pulp, leaving thin shells.
3. Squeeze softened garlic into a small bowl; add potato pulp and mash. Stir in remaining ingredients. Spoon into potato shells. Place on an ungreased baking sheet. Bake, uncovered, at 350° until heated through, 25-30 minutes.
1 SERVING: *318 cal., 17g fat (9g sat. fat), 41mg chol., 253mg sod., 38g carb. (4g sugars, 3g fiber), 6g pro.*

BACON-WRAPPED FILETS WITH SCOTCHED MUSHROOMS

I got the idea for this recipe when I came across bacon-wrapped filets on sale in the grocery store. The rest was inspired my husband, because he once made a Scotch and ginger ale sauce. This recipe is for two, but it can easily be doubled.
—Mary Kay LaBrie, Clermont, FL

TAKES: 30 min. • **MAKES:** 2 servings

- 2 bacon strips
- 2 beef tenderloin steaks (5 oz. each)
- ¼ tsp. salt
- ¼ tsp. coarsely ground pepper
- 3 tsp. olive oil, divided
- 2 cups sliced baby portobello mushrooms
- ¼ tsp. dried thyme
- 2 Tbsp. butter, divided
- ¼ cup Scotch whiskey
- ½ cup diet ginger ale
- 1 Tbsp. brown sugar
- 1½ tsp. reduced-sodium soy sauce
- ¼ tsp. rubbed sage

1. In a small skillet, cook bacon over medium heat until partially cooked but not crisp. Remove to paper towels to drain.
2. Preheat oven to 375°. Sprinkle steaks with salt and pepper; wrap a strip of bacon around the sides of each steak and secure with toothpicks.
3. In a small ovenproof skillet coated with cooking spray, cook steaks in 1½ tsp. oil over medium-high heat, 2 minutes on each side.
4. Bake, uncovered, until meat reaches desired doneness (for medium-rare, a thermometer should read 135°; medium, 140°; medium-well, 145°), 8-12 minutes.
5. Meanwhile, in a large skillet, saute mushrooms and thyme in 1 Tbsp. butter and remaining oil until tender; remove from heat. Add whiskey, stirring to loosen browned bits from pan. Stir in ginger ale, brown sugar, soy sauce and sage.
6. Bring to a boil. Reduce heat; simmer, uncovered, until reduced by half, 3-5 minutes. Stir in remaining butter. Serve with steaks.

1 FILET WITH ⅓ CUP MUSHROOM MIXTURE: *581 cal., 37g fat (15g sat. fat), 108mg chol., 729mg sod., 10g carb. (8g sugars, 1g fiber), 35g pro.*

CRANBERRY-SESAME SPINACH SALAD

We love this snappy salad that balances sweet and sour with good crunch from almonds and sesame seeds. It makes a great small-scale starter for any occasion.
—Stephanie Smoley, Rochester, MN

TAKES: 25 min. • **MAKES:** 2 servings

- 1 tsp. butter
- 2 Tbsp. slivered almonds
- 2½ cups fresh baby spinach
- 2 Tbsp. dried cranberries

DRESSING
- 2 Tbsp. canola oil
- 1 Tbsp. sugar
- 1 Tbsp. cider vinegar
- 2 tsp. toasted sesame seeds
- ½ tsp. dried minced onion
- ½ tsp. poppy seeds
- ⅛ tsp. salt
    Dash paprika

1. In a small skillet, heat the butter over medium heat. Add almonds; cook and stir until lightly browned. Remove from heat.
2. Place spinach and cranberries in a bowl. In a small bowl, whisk dressing ingredients until blended. Add to the salad and toss to coat. Sprinkle with the toasted almonds. Serve immediately.

1¼ CUPS: *257 cal., 21g fat (3g sat. fat), 5mg chol., 207mg sod., 16g carb. (12g sugars, 3g fiber), 3g pro.*

SPICY HONEY MUSTARD GREEN BEANS

I love fresh beans, but was getting tired of my usual method of steaming and eating them plain. I whipped up this honey-mustard combination to amp up the flavor of this simple side dish.
—*Carol Traupman-Carr, Breinigsville, PA*

TAKES: 20 min. • **MAKES:** 2 servings

- ½ lb. fresh green beans, trimmed
- ¼ cup thinly sliced red onion
- 2 Tbsp. spicy brown mustard
- 2 Tbsp. honey
- 1 Tbsp. snipped fresh dill or 1 tsp. dill weed

1. In a large saucepan, bring 6 cups water to a boil. Add beans; cook, uncovered, just until crisp-tender, 3-4 minutes. Drain beans and immediately drop into ice water. Drain and pat dry; transfer to a small bowl.
2. In another bowl, combine onion, mustard, honey and dill. Pour over beans; toss to coat.
1 SERVING: *122 cal., 0 fat (0 sat. fat), 0 chol., 159mg sod., 27g carb. (21g sugars, 4g fiber), 2g pro.*

POMEGRANATE COSMO

Every soiree needs a signature drink, even if it's a party for two. Sugar dresses up this simple cosmo that lets you enjoy a cozy evening with your sweetheart and still shake things up.
—*Taste of Home Test Kitchen*

TAKES: 10 min. • **MAKES:** 1 serving

- 1 Tbsp. coarse red sugar
- ¾ to 1 cup ice cubes
- 1½ oz. lemon-lime soda
- 1½ oz. pomegranate liqueur or cranberry-pomegranate juice
- 1 oz. X-Rated Fusion liqueur
- ½ oz. Triple Sec
- 1 oz. cranberry-pomegranate juice
  Lemon zest strip, optional

1. Sprinkle red sugar on a plate. Moisten rim of a cocktail glass with water; dip rim in sugar to coat.
2. Fill a shaker three-fourths full with ice. Add soda, liqueurs and juice; cover and shake until condensation forms on outside of shaker, 10-15 seconds. Strain into prepared glass. If desired, garnish with lemon zest.
1 SERVING: *209 cal., 0 fat (0 sat. fat), 0 chol., 6mg sod., 29g carb. (28g sugars, 0 fiber), 0 pro.*

SALMON PUFFS

Convenient puff pastry shells turn these salmon bites into an elegant appetizer. You can bake the unfilled shells ahead and freeze for future use.
—Carolyn Moseley, Mount Pleasant, SC

TAKES: 30 min. • **MAKES:** 2 servings

- 2 frozen puff pastry shells or 2 slices toast
- ½ cup apricot preserves
- 1 Tbsp. prepared horseradish
- 2 tsp. cider vinegar
- 1 cup fully cooked salmon chunks or 1 can (7½ oz.) salmon, drained, bones and skin removed
  Minced chives, optional

Bake the pastry shells according to the package directions. Meanwhile, combine preserves, horseradish and vinegar in a saucepan. Cook over medium heat until heated through, about 5 minutes. Stir in salmon and heat through. Spoon into pastry shells or over toast. If desired, top with minced chives. Serve immediately.

1 SERVING: *566 cal., 21g fat (5g sat. fat), 84mg chol., 728mg sod., 68g carb. (37g sugars, 1g fiber), 30g pro.*

Holiday Helper
Thaw puff pastry shells at room temperature for about 20 minutes before handling. Handle as little as possible to avoid stretching and tearing. Baked filled pastries are best enjoyed the day they are made. Baked unfilled pastry may be frozen in airtight containers for up to 6 weeks.

SPEEDY CREAM OF WILD RICE SOUP

Add simple homemade touches to a can of potato soup to get comfort food on the table quickly. The result is a thick and creamy dish textured with wild rice and flavored with smoky bacon.
—Joanne Eickhoff, Pequot Lakes, MN

TAKES: 20 min. • **MAKES:** 2 servings

- ½ cup water
- 4½ tsp. dried minced onion
- ⅔ cup condensed cream of potato soup, undiluted
- ½ cup shredded Swiss cheese
- ½ cup cooked wild rice
- ½ cup half-and-half cream
- 2 bacon strips, cooked and crumbled

In a small saucepan, bring water and onion to a boil. Reduce heat. Stir in the potato soup, Swiss cheese, rice and cream; heat through (do not boil). Garnish with bacon.

1 CUP: *333 cal., 18g fat (11g sat. fat), 68mg chol., 835mg sod., 24g carb. (5g sugars, 2g fiber), 15g pro.*

SEASONAL GET-TOGETHERS

*The holidays are the time for festive gatherings—
whether it's a kid-friendly bash, an adults-only brunch,
or a musical singalong for the whole family. Here are
the perfect menus to go with each party!*

Brunch &
Bloody Marys

The traditional cocktail for a morning
gathering of grown-ups, a great
Bloody Mary can be a feast in and
of itself! Here are some amazing
dishes to add for a complete
holiday brunch spread.

UNCLE MERLE'S BLOODY MARY

I had a very good friend who was not related to me, but everyone called him Uncle Merle. He gave me this recipe and made me promise not to give it to anyone until he passed away. Uncle Merle is gone now, but his recipe lives on.
—Ronald Roth, Three Rivers, MI

TAKES: 10 min. • **MAKES:** 5 servings

- 4 cups tomato juice
- 1 Tbsp. white vinegar
- 1½ tsp. sugar
- 1½ tsp. Worcestershire sauce
- 1 tsp. beef bouillon granules
- ½ tsp. salt
- ¼ tsp. onion powder
- ¼ tsp. celery salt
- ¼ tsp. pepper
- ⅛ tsp. garlic powder
- 1 drop hot pepper sauce
  Dash ground cinnamon, optional
  Ice cubes
- 7½ oz. vodka
  Optional garnishes: Celery ribs, cooked shrimp, cherry tomatoes, jalapeno peppers, string cheese, lemon wedges, cooked bacon, beef snack sticks, olives, cucumber spears, cubed cheese, Old Bay seasoning and celery salt

In a pitcher, mix the first 11 ingredients until blended. If desired, stir in cinnamon. For each serving, pour ¾ cup mixture over ice; stir in 1½ Tbsp. of vodka. Garnish as desired.

1 CUP: *119 cal., 1g fat (0 sat. fat), 0 chol., 961mg sod., 9g carb. (7g sugars, 1g fiber), 2g pro.*

CRANBERRY-WALNUT BELGIAN WAFFLES

Belgian waffles have larger squares and deeper pockets than American waffles do. I make mine with nutrition boosters— whole wheat, flaxseed, cranberries and toasted walnuts.
—Laura McDowell, Portland, ME

PREP: 20 min. • **COOK:** 5 min./batch
MAKES: 6 servings

- 1¼ cups whole wheat flour
- ¾ cup old-fashioned oats
- ¼ cup packed brown sugar
- 2 Tbsp. ground flaxseed
- 4 tsp. baking powder
- 2 tsp. ground cinnamon
- ¼ tsp. salt, divided
- 2 large eggs, room temperature
- 1½ cups 2% milk
- ⅓ cup butter, melted
- 1 tsp. vanilla extract
- 1¾ cups fresh or frozen thawed cranberries, divided
- ⅓ cup chopped walnuts, toasted
- ½ cup maple syrup
- ¼ cup granulated sugar
- ¼ cup water
- 1 Tbsp. lemon juice

1. Grease a Belgian waffle iron with cooking spray; preheat to medium-high. Whisk together first 6 ingredients and ⅛ tsp. salt. In a separate bowl, whisk together eggs, milk, butter and vanilla. Add to flour mixture; stir until just combined. Fold in ¾ cup cranberries and walnuts.

2. Pour ⅓ cup batter into each quarter of the waffle iron, spreading batter to the edges. Close; cook until the waffle iron stops steaming and the waffle is golden brown, about 4 minutes. Repeat with remaining batter.

3. Meanwhile, in a small saucepan, combine maple syrup, granulated sugar, water, remaining 1 cup cranberries and remaining ⅛ tsp. salt. Bring to a boil; reduce heat, and simmer, 6-8 minutes. Remove from heat; stir in lemon juice. Serve with waffles.

2 WAFFLES WITH ABOUT 2 TBSP. SAUCE: *477 cal., 20g fat (9g sat. fat), 94mg chol., 506mg sod., 69g carb. (38g sugars, 7g fiber), 10g pro.*

PECAN COFFEE CAKE MUFFINS

With heaps of crumb topping and a moist, cakelike texture, these muffins are simply the perfect way to greet company for brunch. Give the muffins a pretty dusting of powdered sugar for a true coffee shop feel.

—Shannon Saltsman, Olmsted Falls, OH

PREP: 25 min. • **BAKE:** 20 min.
MAKES: 15 muffins

½ cup butter, softened
1 cup packed brown sugar
1 cup all-purpose flour
1 tsp. ground cinnamon
½ cup chopped pecans

BATTER
1 cup butter, softened
¾ cup packed brown sugar
½ cup sugar
2 eggs, room temperature
⅓ cup half-and-half cream
1½ tsp. vanilla extract
2 cups all-purpose flour
2 tsp. baking powder
½ tsp. salt
Confectioners' sugar, optional

1. Preheat oven to 350°. For streusel, in a small bowl, combine butter, brown sugar, flour and cinnamon until crumbly. Stir in pecans; set aside.

2. In a large bowl, cream butter and sugars until light and fluffy, 5-7 minutes. Add eggs, 1 at a time, beating well after each addition. Beat in cream and vanilla. Combine the flour, baking powder and salt; add to the creamed mixture just until moistened.

3. Fill greased or paper-lined muffin cups one-quarter full. Drop 1 Tbsp. streusel into the center of each muffin cup; cover with batter. Sprinkle tops with the remaining streusel.

4. Bake until a toothpick inserted in muffin comes out clean, 20-22 minutes. Cool in pan 5 minutes. Remove from pans to wire rack to cool completely. Dust with confectioners' sugar if desired. Serve muffins warm.

1 MUFFIN: *420 cal., 22g fat (12g sat. fat), 79mg chol., 284mg sod., 52g carb. (32g sugars, 1g fiber), 4g pro.*

BACON SWISS QUICHE

With a quiche like this, you don't need a lot of heavy side dishes. It's got everything—eggs, bacon, cheese and a touch of apple juice. I serve it with grapes or other fresh fruit, or a simple green salad.
—Colleen Belbey, Warwick, RI

PREP: 15 min. • BAKE: 40 min. + standing
MAKES: 6 servings

- 1   sheet refrigerated pie crust
- ¼   cup sliced green onions
- 1   Tbsp. butter
- 6   large eggs
- 1½ cups heavy whipping cream
- ¼   cup unsweetened apple juice
- 1   lb. sliced bacon, cooked and crumbled
- ⅛   tsp. salt
- ⅛   tsp. pepper
- 2   cups shredded Swiss cheese

1. Preheat oven to 350°. Line a 9-in. pie plate with crust; trim and flute edges. Set aside. In a small skillet, saute green onions in butter until tender.
2. In a large bowl, whisk the eggs, cream and juice. Stir in bacon, salt, pepper and green onions. Pour into crust; sprinkle with cheese.
3. Bake until a knife inserted in the center comes out clean, 40-45 minutes. Let stand 10 minutes before cutting.

FREEZE OPTION: *Securely wrap individual portions of cooled quiche in parchment and foil; freeze. To use, partially thaw in refrigerator overnight. Remove from refrigerator 30 minutes before baking. Unwrap quiche; reheat in a 350° oven until heated through and a thermometer inserted in center reads 165°.*
1 PIECE: *739 cal., 60g fat (31g sat. fat), 359mg chol., 781mg sod., 22g carb. (4g sugars, 0 fiber), 27g pro.*

HAM QUICHE: Omit apple juice. Increase heavy whipping cream to 1¾ cup. Substitute 3 cups diced cooked ham for the bacon and cheddar cheese for the Swiss cheese. Proceed as directed.

HAM BROCCOLI QUICHE: Follow directions for Ham Quiche. Add 1 cup chopped broccoli florets to the egg mixture.

CHEESY BACON & GRITS CASSEROLE

I was craving grits for breakfast and had fresh corn from the farmers market, and leftover bacon. I put everything together and came up with this masterpiece! Serve with avocado and hot sauce.
—Rebecca Yankovich, Springfield, VA

PREP: 30 min. • BAKE: 35 min. + standing
MAKES: 8 servings

- 6   bacon strips, chopped
- 3   cups water
- 1   cup whole milk
- ¾   tsp. salt
- 1   cup uncooked old-fashioned grits
- 2   cups shredded Colby-Monterey Jack cheese, divided
- 2   large eggs, room temperature, lightly beaten
- 1   cup fresh or frozen corn, thawed
- ¼   tsp. pepper
     Sliced avocado, optional

1. Preheat oven to 350°. In a large skillet, cook bacon over medium heat until crisp, stirring occasionally. Remove with a slotted spoon; drain on paper towels.

2. Meanwhile, in a Dutch oven, bring water, milk and salt to a boil. Slowly stir in grits. Reduce heat to low; cook, covered, until thickened, 15-20 minutes, stirring occasionally. Remove from heat. Stir in 1½ cups cheese until melted. Slowly stir in eggs until blended. Stir in bacon, corn and pepper. Transfer to a greased 2-qt. baking dish. Sprinkle with remaining ½ cup cheese.
3. Bake, uncovered, until the edges are golden brown and cheese is melted, 35-40 minutes. Let stand 10 minutes before serving. If desired, serve with avocado.

FREEZE OPTION: *Cool unbaked casserole; cover and freeze. To use, partially thaw in refrigerator overnight. Remove casserole from the refrigerator 30 minutes before baking. Bake grits as directed until heated through and a thermometer inserted in center reads 165°, increasing time to 45-55 minutes.*
¾ CUP: *261 cal., 13g fat (8g sat. fat), 81mg chol., 534mg sod., 23g carb. (3g sugars, 1g fiber), 13g pro.*

WHAT'S THE BEST BACON?

As a garnish to a perfect Bloody Mary or an ingredient in many of these great brunch recipes, there's nothing like perfectly cooked bacon. Our Test Kitchen experts experimented to find the way to get the bacon you like best.

◄ **CAST-IRON SKILLET:** Arrange bacon in a single layer in a cold cast-iron skillet. Cook on medium-low. Turn occasionally with tongs. Drain on paper towels.
1. Chewy: 12 min.
2. Crisp-chewy: 14:30 min.
3. Crisp: 16 min.

► **NONSTICK SKILLET:** Arrange bacon in a single layer in a cold nonstick skillet. Cook on medium-low. Turn occasionally with tongs. Drain on paper towels.
4. Chewy: 14:45 min.
5. Crisp-chewy: 16:20 min.
6. Crisp: 19:30 min.

▲ **MICROWAVE:** Place 2-3 paper towels in a microwave-safe dish. Arrange bacon in a single layer on paper towels. Place 1-2 paper towels over bacon. Microwave on high for about 1 minute per piece of bacon. Remove bacon to a serving platter and let stand for 1 minute. Bacon should look undercooked as it comes out of the microwave—there will be carry-over cooking.
7. Chewy: 40 seconds/strip
8. Crisp-chewy: 50 seconds/strip
9. Crisp: 60 seconds/strip

▼ **ON BAKING RACK OVER SHEET PAN:** Place a wire rack in a 15x10x1-in. baking pan. Lightly spritz rack with cooking spray. Arrange bacon in a single layer on prepared rack. Bake at 400°; remove to paper towels.
13. Chewy: 17 min.
14. Crisp-chewy: 23 min.
15. Crisp: 26:30 min.

▲ **DIRECTLY ON SHEET PAN:** Arrange bacon in a single layer in a 15x10x1-in. baking pan. Bake at 400°; remove bacon to paper towels.
10. Chewy: 16:40 min.
11. Crisp-chewy: 17:30 min.
12. Crisp: 25 min.

MAPLE & BACON BARS

This bacon maple bar recipe is the perfect treat when you're craving both sweet and salty. Its aroma will taunt and tempt you while it's baking in the oven!
—Taste of Home *Test Kitchen*

PREP: 15 min. • **BAKE:** 20 min. + cooling
MAKES: 9 servings

- ½ cup butter, softened
- ¾ cup packed brown sugar
- 2 large eggs, room temperature
- 1 Tbsp. 2% milk
- 1 tsp. vanilla extract
- ¾ cup all-purpose flour
- ¾ cup quick-cooking oats
- ½ tsp. baking powder
- ¼ tsp. salt
- 4 bacon strips, cooked and crumbled
- ⅓ cup chopped pecans, toasted

MAPLE GLAZE
- 1 cup confectioners' sugar
- 2 Tbsp. maple syrup
- ½ to 1 tsp. maple flavoring, optional

1. Preheat oven to 350°. In a large bowl, cream butter and brown sugar until light and fluffy, 5-7 minutes. Beat in eggs, milk and vanilla. Combine flour, oats, baking powder and salt; gradually add to creamed mixture. Fold in bacon and pecans.
2. Spread into a greased 9-in. square baking pan. Bake until a toothpick inserted in center comes out clean, 20-25 minutes. Cool on a wire rack.
3. For the glaze, mix confectioners' sugar, syrup and if desired, maple flavoring. Drizzle over bars; let stand until set.
1 BAR: *351 cal., 16g fat (8g sat. fat), 72mg chol., 261mg sod., 48g carb. (34g sugars, 1g fiber), 5g pro.*

CIOPPINO-MIXED GREEN SALAD

Living in California, the salad bowl of the United States, I'm inspired to cook nutritious meals. Whenever my friends and I get together, this salad—a spin on the classic seafood stew—is the top request.
—Cleo Gonske, Redding, CA

PREP: 20 min. + marinating
MAKES: 10 servings

- 1 cup Italian salad dressing
- 1 Tbsp. minced fresh basil
- ¼ cup dry white wine, optional
- ¾ lb. peeled and deveined cooked shrimp (31-40 per lb.)
- 2 cups lump crabmeat (about 10 oz.), drained
- 16 cups torn mixed salad greens
- 2 large tomatoes, seeded and coarsely chopped
- 2 jars (7½ oz. each) marinated quartered artichoke hearts, drained
- 1 large red onion, thinly sliced and separated into rings
- 1 can (6 oz.) pitted ripe olives, drained and quartered
- 6 hard-boiled large eggs, quartered lengthwise
  Optional: Minced fresh parsley and lemon wedges

1. Mix dressing, basil and, if desired, wine. Add shrimp and crab; toss gently to combine. Refrigerate, covered, 2 hours.
2. Add the greens, tomatoes, artichoke hearts, onion, olives and eggs; toss gently to combine. If desired, sprinkle with parsley and serve with lemon wedges.
2 CUPS: *285 cal., 17g fat (3g sat. fat), 190mg chol., 888mg sod., 13g carb. (6g sugars, 3g fiber), 18g pro.*

Christmas Pickle Party

Each year, children have fun finding an ornament hidden somewhere on the Christmas tree. While they search the boughs for the elusive shiny green pickle, these kid-friendly dishes will keep everyone fed and happy.

AIR-FRYER PICKLES

Like deep-fried pickles? You'll love this version even more. Dill pickle slices are coated with panko bread crumbs and spices, then air-fried until crispy. Dip them in ranch dressing for an appetizer you won't soon forget.
—Nick Iverson, Denver, CO

- -

PREP: 20 min. + standing
COOK: 15 min./batch • **MAKES:** 32 slices

- 32 dill pickle slices
- ½ cup all-purpose flour
- ½ tsp. salt
- 3 large eggs, lightly beaten
- 2 Tbsp. dill pickle juice
- ½ tsp. cayenne pepper
- ½ tsp. garlic powder
- 2 cups panko bread crumbs
- 2 Tbsp. snipped fresh dill
  Cooking spray
  Ranch salad dressing, optional

1. Preheat air fryer to 400°. Let pickles stand on a paper towel until liquid is almost absorbed, about 15 minutes.
2. Meanwhile, in a shallow bowl, combine flour and salt. In another shallow bowl, whisk eggs, pickle juice, cayenne and garlic powder. Combine panko and dill in a third shallow bowl.
3. Dip pickles in flour mixture to coat both sides; shake off excess. Dip in egg mixture, then in crumb mixture, patting to help coating adhere. In batches, place pickles in a single layer on greased tray in air-fryer basket. Cook until golden brown and crispy, 7-10 minutes. Turn pickles; spritz with cooking spray. Cook until golden brown and crispy, 7-10 minutes longer. Serve immediately. If desired, serve with ranch dressing.
1 PICKLE SLICE: *26 cal., 1g fat (0 sat. fat), 13mg chol., 115mg sod., 4g carb. (0 sugars, 0 fiber), 1g pro.*

> ### Holiday Helper
> If you don't have an air fryer, make these pickles in the oven instead! Use 2 eggs instead of 3, reduce the bread crumbs to ½ cup and the fresh dill to 1 Tbsp. Bake at 500° on a greased rack on a rimmed baking sheet for 20-25 minutes.

SPICED SWEET POTATO FRIES

A spicy homemade seasoning blend shakes up everyone's favorite finger food in this rendition of sweet potato fries.
—Taste of Home *Test Kitchen*

- -

TAKES: 25 min. • **MAKES:** 6 servings

- 1 pkg. (19 oz.) frozen french-fried sweet potatoes
- ½ tsp. garlic powder
- ½ tsp. curry powder
- ½ tsp. pepper
- ¼ tsp. chili powder
- ⅛ tsp. ground cinnamon
- ⅛ tsp. salt

Bake the fries according to package directions. Meanwhile, in a small bowl, combine the remaining ingredients. Sprinkle over fries; toss to coat.
1 SERVING: *129 cal., 3g fat (1g sat. fat), 0 chol., 241mg sod., 24g carb. (10g sugars, 2g fiber), 0 pro.*

A CHRISTMAS... PICKLE?

A common—in some parts—tradition challenges guests and family members to find a pickle ornament hidden somewhere on the Christmas tree. Asked by befuddled outsiders to explain, the story goes like this: Hiding a pickle ornament (*die Weihnachtsgurke*) in the tree is an old German tradition. The first child to find it on Christmas morning receives a special gift and is blessed with good luck.

However, according to a 2016 *New York Times* article, a poll of more than 2,000 native Germans revealed that the vast majority of them (91%!) had never heard of such a thing.

Two different legends are linked to the tradition, but neither really seems likely as a foundation myth. In the first, two children are kidnapped by an evil innkeeper and stuffed in a pickle barrel, only to be rescued by St. Nicholas. The suffering individual in the second story is a captured Civil War soldier who, as his dying wish, asked for a pickle, which—amazingly enough—revived him so that he eventually made his way home safely.

Both these amazing stories started to gain traction in the 1880s...right around the time the F.W. Woolworth Co. started selling imported German glass ornaments, many of which were in the shapes of various fruits and vegetables. Perhaps, just perhaps, the stories were the invention of savvy sales reps who saw no earthly reason why people might otherwise buy a pickle ornament to hang on their Christmas tree.

Whatever the tradition's origin, many families love it, and kids get a kick out of the whole race to find the pickle. So if you have a pickle ornament, hide it in your tree. And if die Weihnachtsgurke is new to you, hang one up and feel free to spin your own yarn. Fun family traditions, no matter what the source, create treasured memories to last a lifetime.

PUMPKIN MILK SHAKES

My son loved this festive milk shake growing up—it's nicely spiced and tastes like pumpkin pie. I like cutting off both ends of a licorice twist and serving it as a straw.
—Joan Hallford, North Richland Hills, TX

- -

TAKES: 10 min. • **MAKES:** 6 servings

- 1   cup orange juice
- 4   cups vanilla ice cream
- 1   cup canned pumpkin
- ½   cup packed brown sugar
- 1   tsp. ground cinnamon
- ½   tsp. ground ginger
- ½   tsp. ground nutmeg
    Black licorice twists, optional

In batches, place the first 7 ingredients in a blender. Cover and process until smooth, 20-30 seconds. Serve immediately, with licorice stirrers if desired.

1 CUP: *287 cal., 10g fat (6g sat. fat), 39mg chol., 78mg sod., 47g carb. (42g sugars, 2g fiber), 4g pro.*

BEST EVER MAC & CHEESE

To make this amazing mac, I make a sauce loaded with three different cheeses to toss with the noodles. When baked, it's ooey-gooey and cheesy good. And don't get me started on the crunchy topping!
—Beth Jacobson, Milwaukee, WI

PREP: 40 min. • **BAKE:** 10 min.
MAKES: 12 servings

- 1 pkg. (16 oz.) uncooked elbow macaroni
- 4 slices hearty white bread (4 oz.), torn into large pieces
- 6 Tbsp. butter, cubed and divided
- ½ cup grated Parmesan cheese
- 1 tsp. salt, divided
- 1 tsp. pepper, divided
- ¼ cup finely chopped onion
- 1 tsp. ground mustard
- ¼ tsp. cayenne pepper
- ¼ cup all-purpose flour
- 3 cups whole milk
- 2 cups half-and-half cream
- 1 cup (4 oz.) cubed process cheese (Velveeta)
- 1 block (8 oz.) sharp cheddar cheese, shredded
- 1 block (8 oz.) Monterey Jack cheese, shredded
- 1 tsp. Worcestershire sauce

1. Preheat oven to 400°. In a stockpot or Dutch oven, cook pasta according to package directions for al dente; drain and return to pan.
2. Pulse bread, 2 Tbsp. butter, Parmesan, ½ tsp. salt and ½ tsp. pepper in a food processor until coarsely ground; set aside.
3. In a large skillet over medium heat, melt remaining 4 Tbsp. butter. Add onions and cook until tender, about 3 minutes. Add ground mustard and cayenne; stir until blended. Stir in flour until smooth, about 3 minutes. Slowly whisk in milk and cream; bring to a boil. Reduce heat to medium-low; simmer, stirring constantly, until thickened, about 5 minutes.
4. Remove from heat; stir in Velveeta. Slowly add remaining cheeses a handful at a time, stirring until cheese is melted. Add Worcestershire and remaining salt and pepper. Pour over pasta; toss to coat.
5. Transfer to a greased 13x9-in baking dish. Sprinkle bread crumbs over top of casserole. Bake until topping is golden brown and sauce is bubbly, 10-12 minutes.
1 CUP: *762 cal., 43g fat (25g sat. fat), 134mg chol., 1138mg sod., 61g carb. (10g sugars, 3g fiber), 32g pro.*

BACON CHEESEBURGER SLOPPY JOES

My family doesn't even like sloppy joes— but we are all big fans of this recipe!
—Janine Smith, Columbia, SC

TAKES: 25 min. • **MAKES:** 8 servings

- 1½ lbs. ground turkey
- 1 large red onion, finely chopped
- 12 bacon strips, cooked and crumbled
- 2 medium tomatoes, chopped
- ¾ cup ketchup
- ½ cup chopped dill pickle
- 2 Tbsp. yellow mustard
- 1½ cups shredded cheddar cheese
- 8 hamburger buns, split

1. In a large skillet, cook and crumble the turkey with onion over medium heat until turkey is no longer pink, 6-8 minutes. Stir in bacon, tomatoes, ketchup, pickle and mustard; heat through.
2. Stir in cheese until melted. Spoon meat mixture onto bun bottoms. Replace tops.
1 SANDWICH: *431 cal., 20g fat (8g sat. fat), 90mg chol., 1022mg sod., 32g carb. (11g sugars, 2g fiber), 31g pro.*

MINI PB&J CHEESECAKES

I got hooked on these mini cheesecakes when a friend made them. She let me steal her recipe, and now I'm sharing this tasty treat with you!
—Elizabeth King, Duluth, MN

- -

PREP: 35 min. • **BAKE:** 15 min. + cooling
MAKES: about 2½ dozen

- 1 cup creamy peanut butter
- ½ cup sugar
- 1 large egg, room temperature

CHEESECAKE LAYER

- 1 pkg. (8 oz.) cream cheese, softened
- ½ cup sugar
- 1 large egg, room temperature, lightly beaten
- 1 tsp. vanilla extract
- ¼ cup strawberry jelly, warmed

OPTIONAL DRIZZLE

- ½ cup confectioners' sugar
- 2 to 3 Tbsp. heavy whipping cream

1. Preheat oven to 350°. In a small bowl, beat the peanut butter and sugar until blended. Beat in egg. Press 2 tsp. of the mixture into each of 32 paper-lined mini-muffin cups.
2. For the cheesecake layer, beat cream cheese and sugar until smooth. Beat in egg and vanilla. Spoon a scant 2 tsp. cream cheese mixture into each cup. Drop jelly by ¼ teaspoonfuls over tops. Cut through the batter with a toothpick to swirl.
3. Bake 12-14 minutes or until centers are set. Cool completely on a wire rack.
4. If desired, mix confectioners' sugar and enough cream to reach desired consistency; drizzle over cheesecakes. Refrigerate until serving.
1 MINI CHEESECAKE: *119 cal., 7g fat (3g sat. fat), 20mg chol., 61mg sod., 12g carb. (11g sugars, 0 fiber), 3g pro.*

> ### Holiday Helper
>
> This recipe is flexible, so try it with different jellies and jams that you have on hand. Orange juice and marmalade would also work deliciously here! Apple jelly is also a great stand-in.

FLAKY CHICKEN WELLINGTON

This cozy chicken Wellington takes a classic recipe and makes it super easy! I like to cook the chicken a day or so ahead of time to make it even simpler to put together on busy nights or for parties.
—Kerry Dingwall, Wilmington, NC

- -

PREP: 30 min. • **BAKE:** 15 min.
MAKES: 6 servings

- 2 cups cubed cooked chicken
- 1 pkg. (10 oz.) frozen chopped spinach, thawed and squeezed dry
- 3 hard-boiled large eggs, chopped
- ½ cup finely chopped dill pickles
- ⅓ cup finely chopped celery
- 2 tubes (8 oz. each) refrigerated crescent rolls
- 2 tsp. prepared mustard, divided
- 1 cup sour cream
- 2 Tbsp. dill pickle juice

1. Preheat oven to 350°. In a large bowl, combine the first 5 ingredients. Unroll 1 tube of crescent dough into 1 long rectangle; press perforations to seal.
2. Spread half the mustard over dough; top with half the chicken mixture to within ¼ in. of edges. Roll up jelly-roll style, starting with a long side; pinch seam to seal. Place cut side down on a parchment-lined baking sheet. Cut slits in top. Repeat with remaining tube of crescent dough, 1 tsp. mustard and chicken mixture.
3. Bake until golden brown, 15-20 minutes. Meanwhile, combine the sour cream and pickle juice; serve with pastries.
FREEZE OPTION: *Cover and freeze unbaked pastries on a parchment-lined baking sheet until firm. Transfer to a freezer container; return to freezer. To use, bake the pastries on a parchment-lined baking sheet in a preheated 350° oven until golden brown, 30-35 minutes. Prepare sauce as directed.*
⅓ PASTRY WITH ABOUT 3 TBSP. SAUCE: *495 cal., 28g fat (6g sat. fat), 144mg chol., 830mg sod., 37g carb. (10g sugars, 2g fiber), 25g pro.*

Carol-oke Party

Gather your loved ones to sing along with your favorite holiday music for a karaoke party with a festive spin. In between performances, they can enjoy this casual collection of pure comfort foods, just right for singers of all ages.

CHICKEN MARSALA BOWTIES

I won first place at a state fair cooking contest with this recipe. I absolutely love mushrooms and this dish is full of them! You can substitute Italian dressing mix for the ranch with equally delicious results.
—Regina Farris, Mesquite, TX

- -

PREP: 20 min. • **COOK:** 25 min.
MAKES: 8 servings

- 2 cups uncooked bow tie pasta
- ⅓ cup all-purpose flour
- ½ tsp. salt
- ½ tsp. garlic powder
- ½ tsp. dried thyme
- 1¾ lbs. boneless skinless chicken breasts, cut into ½-in. cubes
- 3 Tbsp. olive oil
- 6 Tbsp. butter, cubed
- ½ lb. sliced baby portobello mushrooms
- 3 shallots, finely chopped
- ½ cup Marsala wine or chicken broth
- 1 can (10¾ oz.) condensed golden mushroom soup, undiluted
- 1 pkg. (3 oz.) cream cheese, cubed
- ½ cup heavy whipping cream
- 1 envelope ranch salad dressing mix
- ⅓ cup grated Parmesan cheese
  Minced fresh parsley, optional

1. Cook the pasta according to package directions. Meanwhile, combine flour, salt, garlic powder and thyme. Add chicken, a few pieces at a time, tossing to coat.
2. In a Dutch oven, heat oil over medium heat. Add chicken in batches; cook and stir until no longer pink, 5-7 minutes. Remove from pan; set aside.
3. In the same pan, heat butter over medium-high heat. Add mushrooms and shallots; cook and stir until tender, 2-3 minutes. Stir in wine; bring to a boil. Cook until liquid is reduced by half. Stir in soup, cream cheese, cream and dressing mix; stir until cream cheese is melted.
4. Drain pasta. Add pasta and chicken to the mushroom mixture; heat through, tossing to coat. Sprinkle with Parmesan cheese and parsley.
1 CUP: 468 cal., 28g fat (13g sat. fat), 108mg chol., 870mg sod., 28g carb. (3g sugars, 2g fiber), 27g pro.

PERFECT WINTER SALAD

This is my most-requested salad recipe. It is delicious as a main dish with grilled chicken breast or as a side salad. It's so good, I sometimes eat it at the end of the meal, instead of dessert!
—DeNae Shewmake, Burnsville, MN

- -

TAKES: 20 min. • **MAKES:** 12 servings

- ¼ cup reduced-fat mayonnaise
- ¼ cup maple syrup
- 3 Tbsp. white wine vinegar
- 2 Tbsp. minced shallot
- 2 tsp. sugar
- ½ cup canola oil
- 2 pkg. (5 oz. each) spring mix salad greens
- 2 medium tart apples, thinly sliced
- 1 cup dried cherries
- 1 cup pecan halves
- ¼ cup thinly sliced red onion

1. In a small bowl, mix first 5 ingredients; gradually whisk in canola oil until blended. Refrigerate, covered, until serving.
2. To serve, place remaining ingredients in a large bowl; toss with dressing.
1 CUP: 235 cal., 18g fat (1g sat. fat), 2mg chol., 47mg sod., 20g carb. (15g sugars, 2g fiber), 2g pro.

VINTAGE DECOR

If you're looking for a new way to decorate your home for your holiday party, why not make use of the antique red wagon in your basement? Loaded up with birch logs and holiday branches, berries and pine cones, it makes a lovely piece of decor, laden with memories of Christmas past. And if the wheels make it easy to move out of the way when more floor space is needed for the carol-oke singers, that bit of practicality is an added bonus!

COCONUT NUTELLA BROWNIES

My parents were coming over for dinner at the holidays and I wanted a fast go-to brownie. My mom loves coconut, chocolate and brownies, so this was the perfect treat.
—Danielle Lee, West Palm Beach, FL

PREP: 15 min. • **BAKE:** 25 min. + cooling • **MAKES:** 2 dozen

- ½   cup butter, softened
- 1⅓ cups sugar
- ½   cup Nutella
- 4   large eggs, room temperature
- 1   tsp. vanilla extract
- 1   cup all-purpose flour
- ½   cup whole wheat flour
- ⅔   cup Dutch-processed cocoa
- ½   cup flaked coconut
- ½   cup old-fashioned oats

1. Preheat oven to 350°. In a large bowl, beat butter, sugar and Nutella until blended. Add eggs, 1 at a time, beating well after each addition. Beat in vanilla. In another bowl, whisk flours and cocoa; gradually beat into butter mixture, mixing well. Fold in coconut and oats.

2. Spread into a greased 13x9-in. baking pan. Bake until a toothpick comes out with moist crumbs (do not overbake), 22-25 minutes. Cool completely in pan on a wire rack. Cut into bars.

1 BROWNIE: *186 cal., 9g fat (5g sat. fat), 41mg chol., 50mg sod., 26g carb. (16g sugars, 4g fiber), 4g pro.*

SPICY PUMPKIN GINGERBREAD

I have been making this gingerbread for years and it's won several blue ribbons. Serve it with whipped cream and caramel sauce or dust with confectioners' sugar after it cools. It's delicious!
—Marina Castle Kelley, Canyon Country, CA

PREP: 25 min. • **BAKE:** 30 min. + cooling
MAKES: 16 servings

- ½ cup butter, softened
- ½ cup packed dark brown sugar
- 2 large eggs, room temperature
- ½ cup canned pumpkin
- ½ cup molasses
- 2 Tbsp. grated orange zest
- 2½ cups all-purpose flour
- 1 tsp. baking soda
- 1 tsp. ground ginger
- 1 tsp. ground cinnamon
- ½ tsp. salt
- ½ tsp. ground ancho chili pepper
- ¾ cup buttermilk
- ⅓ cup shelled pumpkin seeds, chopped and toasted
- Optional: Whipped cream, caramel sundae syrup or confectioners' sugar

1. Preheat oven to 325°. In a large bowl, cream butter and brown sugar until light and fluffy, 5-7 minutes. Add eggs, 1 at a time, beating well after each addition. Beat in pumpkin, molasses and orange zest (mixture will appear curdled).
2. In a small bowl, combine flour, baking soda, ginger, cinnamon, salt and chili pepper. Add to the creamed mixture alternately with buttermilk, beating well after each addition. Stir in pumpkin seeds.
3. Pour batter into a greased 9-in. square baking pan. Bake until a toothpick inserted in center comes out clean, 28-32 minutes. Cool completely on a wire rack. Serve with toppings as desired.
1 PIECE: *209 cal., 8g fat (4g sat. fat), 39mg chol., 242mg sod., 31g carb. (15g sugars, 1g fiber), 4g pro.*

CHERRY-LIME SHRUB

This festive beverage is perfect for the holidays. The vinegar portion can be made up to a week ahead to save time.
—Gina Nistico, Denver, CO

PREP: 20 min. • **COOK:** 10 min. + chilling
MAKES: 2 cups

- 1 medium lime
- 1½ cups fresh or frozen dark sweet cherries, pitted and crushed
- 1 cup cider vinegar
- 1½ cups sugar
- ½ cup water
- Optional: Ice cubes, sparkling water, fresh cherries, mint and lime slices

1. Finely grate zest from lime. Place zest and cherries in a sterilized pint jar. Bring vinegar just to a boil; pour over fruit, leaving ¼-in. headspace. Center lid on jar; screw on band until fingertip tight. Refrigerate for 1 week.
2. Strain the vinegar mixture through a fine-mesh strainer into another sterilized pint jar. Press the solids to extract juice; discard remaining fruit.
3. Bring sugar and water to a boil. Reduce heat; simmer until sugar is dissolved. Cool slightly. Stir into vinegar mixture; shake well. Store in the refrigerator for up to 2 weeks.
4. Serve in 1-2 Tbsp. portions or add to a glass of ice, top with sparkling water and garnish with fresh cherries and lime.
2 TBSP. SYRUP: *86 cal., 0 fat (0 sat. fat), 0 chol., 1mg sod., 21g carb. (20g sugars, 0 fiber), 0 pro.*

SAVORY STUFFED PEPPERS

Our family's holiday dinners always include a giant antipasto, and the showpiece when we were growing up was Mom's stuffed hot peppers on top of the display. Regardless of how spicy the peppers were, every year we kids would sneak into the refrigerator and steal one of those thrilling little flavor bombs! There isn't a holiday that we don't make them in my mother's honor. These stuffed peppers are remarkable hot or cold. Serve with a nice loaf of Italian bread and a glass of wine.
—Donna Scarano, East Hanover, NJ

PREP: 20 min. • **BAKE:** 40 min.
MAKES: about 3 dozen

- 3 jars (16 oz. each) pickled hot cherry peppers, drained
- 1 can (2 oz.) anchovy fillets
- 1 large tomato, seeded and finely chopped
- 1 cup pimiento-stuffed olives, finely chopped
- 1 cup ripe olives, finely chopped
- 3 Tbsp. olive oil, divided
- ¼ cup grated Parmesan cheese
- 2 Tbsp. seasoned bread crumbs
- 1 tsp. capers, drained
- 1 Tbsp. minced fresh parsley or 1 tsp. dried parsley flakes
- 1 tsp. garlic powder
- ½ tsp. pepper
- ½ tsp. dried basil

1. Preheat oven to 350°. Cut tops off peppers and remove seeds; set aside. Drain and chop anchovies, reserving oil. In a large bowl, combine tomato, olives, 1 Tbsp. olive oil, Parmesan cheese, anchovies, anchovy oil, bread crumbs, capers, parsley and seasonings. Spoon into peppers.

2. Place in a greased 13x9-in. baking dish. Drizzle with the remaining 2 Tbsp. olive oil. Bake until tops are light golden brown, about 40 minutes.

FREEZE OPTION: *Cover and freeze cooled peppers in a greased 13x9-in. baking dish. To use, partially thaw in the refrigerator overnight. Remove from the refrigerator 30 minutes before baking. Preheat oven to 350°. Reheat peppers, covered, until heated through, 20-30 minutes.*

1 APPETIZER: *49 cal., 3g fat (0 sat. fat), 2mg chol., 612mg sod., 4g carb. (1g sugars, 1g fiber), 2g pro.*

BUTTERY HERB CHRISTMAS TREE

Your guests will be so impressed with this pull-apart treat shaped like a festive evergreen. Each roll is tender, flaky and flavored with a homemade herb butter that's sure to make mouths water. If you like, add decorations to the tree using seasonings or veggies.
—Kathryn Pollock, Tropic, UT

PREP: 45 min. + rising • **BAKE:** 15 min.
MAKES: 1 tree (17 rolls)

- 1 pkg. (¼ oz.) active dry yeast
- 2 Tbsp. warm water (105° to 115°)
- ½ cup warm 2% milk (105° to 115°)
- ¼ cup butter, softened
- 1 large egg, room temperature
- 2 Tbsp. sugar
- 1 tsp. salt
- 2½ to 3 cups all-purpose flour

HERB BUTTER
- ¼ cup butter, softened
- 1 small garlic clove, minced
- ½ tsp. dried basil
- ½ tsp. dried oregano
- ¼ tsp. dried minced onion
    Dash cayenne pepper
- 1 Tbsp. water
- 1 tsp. sesame seeds

1. In a large bowl, dissolve yeast in warm water. Add the milk, butter, egg, sugar, salt and 1½ cups flour. Beat until smooth. Stir in enough remaining flour to form a firm dough.

2. Turn dough onto a lightly floured surface; knead until smooth and elastic, 6-8 minutes. Place in a greased bowl, turning once to grease the top. Cover and let rise in a warm place until doubled, about 1 hour.

3. Punch dough down. Turn onto a lightly floured surface. Roll out dough to ⅛-in. thickness; cut out into seventeen 3½-in. circles.

4. For herb butter, combine the butter, garlic, basil, oregano, onion and cayenne. Set aside 1 tsp. herb butter. Spread the remaining herb butter over dough circles to within ½ in. of edges. Using the dull edge of a table knife, make an off-center crease in each roll. Fold along crease.

5. To form tree, place 1 roll near the top center of a parchment-lined 15x10x1-in. baking pan. Arrange 14 rolls overlapping slightly, forming a tree. Use water to moisten dough where they overlap.

6. For trunks, place the remaining rolls on the bottom of the tree. Cover and let rise until doubled, about 40 minutes.

7. In microwave, melt reserved butter mixture. Brush over rolls; sprinkle with sesame seeds. Bake at 350° until golden brown, 15-20 minutes. Serve warm.

1 ROLL: *130 cal., 6g fat (4g sat. fat), 27mg chol., 185mg sod., 16g carb. (2g sugars, 1g fiber), 3g pro.*

GRANDMA'S FAVORITE CHRISTMAS RECIPES

Over the river and through the woods takes you to
grandmother's house—and her amazing holiday cooking.
These mouthwatering recipes have a classic old-fashioned
appeal that makes them right at home on Grandma's table!

HONEY-MAPLE GLAZED HAM

My graham cracker-crusted ham gets a double coating of a simple honey-maple glaze. The first half melts into the ham while the second half forms a sweet caramelized topping.
—Alan Sproles, Knoxville, TN

PREP: 15 min. • **BAKE:** 2 hours
MAKES: 15 servings

- 1 spiral-sliced fully cooked bone-in ham (7 to 9 lbs.)
- ½ cup maple syrup
- ½ cup butter, softened
- ½ cup packed brown sugar
- ½ cup graham cracker crumbs
- ½ cup honey

1. Preheat oven to 325°. Line a roasting pan with heavy-duty foil. Place ham on a rack in prepared pan. Pour maple syrup over ham, separating slices. In a small bowl, beat butter, sugar, cracker crumbs and honey until blended; spread ¾ cup over ham.

2. Bake, uncovered, for 1½ hours. Spread the remaining butter mixture over ham. Bake until a thermometer reads 140°, basting occasionally with pan drippings, 30-45 minutes longer.

4 OZ. COOKED HAM: *335 cal., 12g fat (6g sat. fat), 109mg chol., 1180mg sod., 27g carb. (24g sugars, 0 fiber), 32g pro.*

PARSNIPS & TURNIPS AU GRATIN

You don't need potatoes to make a delicious au gratin dish! I sometimes opt to substitute rutabaga for the turnips. For many years it was a well-guarded recipe in my collection, but it's too good not to share.
—Priscilla Gilbert, Indian Harbour Beach, FL

PREP: 20 min. • **BAKE:** 15 min.
MAKES: 8 servings

- 1½ lbs. parsnips, peeled and sliced
- 1¼ lbs. turnips, peeled and sliced
- 1 can (10¾ oz.) reduced-fat reduced-sodium condensed cream of celery soup, undiluted
- 1 cup fat-free milk
- ½ tsp. pepper
- 1 cup shredded sharp cheddar cheese
- ½ cup panko bread crumbs
- 1 Tbsp. butter, melted

1. Place parsnips and turnips in a large saucepan; cover with water. Bring to a boil. Reduce heat; simmer, uncovered, until crisp-tender, 5-7 minutes.

2. Meanwhile, in a small saucepan, combine soup, milk and pepper. Bring to a boil; reduce heat to low. Stir in the shredded cheese until melted. Drain vegetables; transfer to an 11x7-in. baking dish coated with cooking spray. Pour sauce over vegetables.

3. Combine bread crumbs and butter; sprinkle over top. Bake, uncovered, at 400° until vegetables are tender and crumbs are golden brown, 15-20 minutes.

FREEZER OPTION: *Cool unbaked casserole; cover and freeze. To use, partially thaw in refrigerator overnight. Remove from refrigerator 30 minutes before baking. Preheat oven to 375°. Bake casserole as directed, increasing time as necessary to heat through and for a thermometer inserted in center to read 165°.*

¾ CUP: *189 cal., 7g fat (4g sat. fat), 21mg chol., 309mg sod., 27g carb. (9g sugars, 4g fiber), 7g pro.*
DIABETIC EXCHANGES: *1 starch, 1 high-fat meat, 1 vegetable.*

GRANDMA'S DIVINITY

Every year, my grandmother and I made divinity, just the two of us. I still make it to this day. It brings back so many good memories.
—Anne Clayborne, Walland, TN

PREP: 5 min. • **COOK:** 40 min. + standing
MAKES: 1½ lbs. (60 pieces)

    2 large egg whites
    3 cups sugar
    ⅔ cup water
    ½ cup light corn syrup
    1 tsp. vanilla extract
    1 cup chopped pecans

1. Place egg whites in the bowl of a stand mixer; let stand at room temperature for 30 minutes. Meanwhile, line three 15x10x1-in. pans with waxed paper.
2. In a large heavy saucepan, combine the sugar, water and corn syrup; bring to a boil, stirring constantly to dissolve sugar. Cook, without stirring, over medium heat until a candy thermometer reads 252° (hard-ball stage). Just before the temperature is reached, beat egg whites on medium speed until stiff peaks form.
3. Slowly add the hot sugar mixture in a thin stream over the egg whites, beating constantly and scraping sides of bowl occasionally. Add vanilla. Beat until the candy holds its shape, 5-6 minutes. (Do not overmix or the candy will get stiff and crumbly.) Immediately fold in pecans.
4. Quickly drop by heaping teaspoonfuls onto prepared pans. Let stand at room temperature until dry to the touch. Store layered with waxed paper in an airtight container at room temperature.
1 PIECE: *61 cal., 1g fat (0 sat. fat), 0 chol., 4mg sod., 13g carb. (12g sugars, 0 fiber), 0 pro.*

HOT COCOA FOR A CROWD

This is a simple, delicious and comforting hot cocoa with a hint of cinnamon. It has just the right amount of sweetness.
—Deborah Canaday, Manhattan, KS

PREP: 10 min. • **COOK:** 3 hours • **MAKES:** 12 servings

    5 cups nonfat dry milk powder
    ¾ cup sugar
    ¾ cup baking cocoa
    1 tsp. vanilla extract
    ¼ tsp. ground cinnamon
   11 cups water
       Optional: Miniature marshmallows and
       peppermint candy sticks

1. In a 5- or 6-qt. slow cooker, combine the milk powder, sugar, cocoa, vanilla and cinnamon; gradually whisk in water until smooth. Cover; cook on low 3-4 hours, until heated through.
2. If desired, top with marshmallows and use peppermint sticks for stirrers.
1 CUP: *164 cal., 1g fat (0 sat. fat), 5mg chol., 156mg sod., 31g carb. (28g sugars, 1g fiber), 11g pro.*
DIABETIC EXCHANGES: *1 starch, 1 fat-free milk.*

CRANBERRY AMBROSIA SALAD

My paternal grandmother used to make this for Christmas dinner. I'm not sure how many batches she made, as there were nearly 50 aunts, uncles and cousins in our family. I still make the recipe in memory of her, and it's still as good as I remember.
—*Janet Hurley, Shell Rock, IA*

PREP: 20 min. + chilling • **MAKES:** 9 servings

- 1 lb. fresh or frozen cranberries
- 1 can (20 oz.) crushed pineapple, drained
- 1 cup sugar
- 2 cups miniature marshmallows
- 1 cup heavy whipping cream, whipped
- ½ cup chopped pecans

1. In a food processor, cover and process the cranberries until coarsely chopped. Transfer to a large bowl; stir in pineapple and sugar. Cover and refrigerate overnight.
2. Just before serving, fold in the marshmallows, whipped cream and pecans. If desired, top with additional chopped pecans.
¾ CUP: 331 cal., 15g fat (7g sat. fat), 36mg chol., 17mg sod., 52g carb. (43g sugars, 3g fiber), 2g pro.

HOME SHOPPING? HOMEMADE!

Handmade gifts will please everyone on your list this year. Grandma might love a set of personalized wooden spoons created by her favorite family artist.

Start by lightly drawing your own designs on plain wooden utensils with a pencil. You can personalize the gift by labeling the handles with your loved one's name. Carefully use a hand-held wood-burning tool to burn the designs into the wood. Let the spoons cool completely and then erase the pencil marks.

Gather a collection of kitchen-friendly items, such as hot pads, oven mitts, pretty kitchen towels and recipe cards, and wrap them all up with a ribbon, with your one-of-a-kind spoons on top, for a beautiful Christmas gift.

GRANDMA PRUIT'S VINEGAR PIE

This historic pie has been in our family for many generations and is always served at our get-togethers.
—Suzette Pruit, Houston, TX

- -

PREP: 40 min. • **BAKE:** 1 hour + cooling
MAKES: 8 servings

- 2   **cups sugar**
- 3   **Tbsp. all-purpose flour**
- ¼   **to ½ tsp. ground nutmeg**
      Pastry for double-crust pie
- ½   **cup butter, cubed**
- ⅔   **cup white vinegar**
- 1   **qt. hot water**

1. Preheat oven to 450°. Whisk together sugar, flour and nutmeg; set aside. On a lightly floured surface, roll one-third of pie dough to a ⅛-in.-thick circle; cut into 2x1-in. strips. Layer a deep 12-in. enamel-coated cast-iron skillet or ovenproof casserole with half the strips; sprinkle with half the sugar mixture. Dot with half the butter. Repeat sugar and butter layers.
2. Roll remaining two-thirds of pie dough to a ⅛-in.-thick circle. Place over filling, pressing against the sides of skillet or casserole. Cut a slit in top. Add vinegar to hot water; slowly pour the vinegar mixture through slit. Liquid may bubble up through the crust; this is normal. To catch spills, line an oven rack with foil.
3. Bake until the crust is golden brown, about 1 hour. Cover edge loosely with foil during the last 15-20 minutes if needed to prevent overbrowning. Remove foil. Cool on a wire rack.
1 PIECE: *545 cal., 25g fat (13g sat. fat), 41mg chol., 316mg sod., 78g carb. (50g sugars, 0 fiber), 2g pro.*
PASTRY FOR DOUBLE-CRUST PIE (9 INCHES): *Combine 2¼ cups all-purpose flour and ¾ tsp. salt; cut in ¾ cup shortening until crumbly. Gradually add 4-6 Tbsp. 2% milk, tossing with a fork until dough holds together when pressed. Divide dough in half. Shape each into a disk; cover and refrigerate 1 hour or overnight.*

ONION-DATE BAKED BRIE

Many baked Brie recipes call for a fruity topping, but my family favors this savory version. I even use the onion-date mixture at the table as a relish.
—Allene Bary-Cooper, Wichita Falls, TX

- -

PREP: 35 min. • **BAKE:** 10 min.
MAKES: 8 servings

- 2   **large onions, sliced**
- 2   **Tbsp. olive oil**
- 2   **garlic cloves, minced**
- ¼   **tsp. ground ginger**
- ⅛   **tsp. salt**
- ⅛   **tsp. cayenne pepper**
- ½   **cup dry red wine or beef broth**
- ¼   **cup red wine vinegar, divided**
- 6   **oz. pitted dates, coarsely chopped**
- 1   **round (8 oz.) Brie cheese**
      Assorted crackers or French baguette slices
      Minced fresh thyme, optional

1. Preheat oven to 350°. In a large skillet, saute onions in oil until tender, 3-5 minutes. Add the garlic, ginger, salt and cayenne; cook 1 minute longer. Stir in wine and 2 Tbsp. vinegar. Bring to a boil; cook until liquid is almost evaporated, about 5 minutes. Cool slightly.
2. Place chopped dates, ¾ cup of the onion mixture and the remaining 2 Tbsp. vinegar in a food processor; cover and process until finely chopped.
3. Place Brie on a baking sheet. Spoon the date mixture over Brie; top with the remaining onion mixture.
4. Bake until Brie is heated through, 10-15 minutes. Garnish with thyme, if desired. Serve cheese with crackers or baguette slices.
1 SERVING: *204 cal., 11g fat (5g sat. fat), 28mg chol., 217mg sod., 20g carb. (15g sugars, 2g fiber), 7g pro.*

CORN-STUFFED CROWN ROAST

My mother always made this elegant entree for company dinners and special family celebrations.
—Dorothy Swanson, St. Louis, MO

- -

PREP: 20 min. • **BAKE:** 3 hours + standing
MAKES: 12 servings

- 1   pork crown roast (about 7 lbs. and 12 ribs)
- ½   tsp. pepper, divided
- 1   cup butter, cubed
- 1   cup chopped celery
- 1   cup chopped onion
- 6   cups crushed cornbread stuffing
- 2   cups frozen corn, thawed
- 2   jars (4½ oz. each) sliced mushrooms, undrained
- 1   tsp. salt
- 1   tsp. poultry seasoning

1. Preheat oven to 350°. Place roast on a rack in a large shallow roasting pan. Sprinkle with ¼ tsp. pepper. Cover rib ends with foil. Bake, uncovered, for 1½ hours.
2. Melt the butter in a Dutch oven over medium heat. Cook and stir celery and onion until tender, 3-5 minutes. Stir in the stuffing, corn, mushrooms, salt, poultry seasoning and remaining pepper. Carefully spoon 1-3 cups of the stuffing into the center of the roast. Place the remaining stuffing in a greased 2-qt. baking dish. Refrigerate until ready to use.
3. Bake the roast until a thermometer inserted in stuffing reads 140°, 1 hour. Cover and bake the extra stuffing until browned, 30-40 minutes. Transfer to a serving platter. Let stand for 15 minutes. Remove foil. Cut between ribs to serve.
1 SERVING: *545 cal., 30g fat (15g sat. fat), 124mg chol., 826mg sod., 30g carb. (3g sugars, 3g fiber), 38g pro.*

MERRY CHRISTMAS TEA

This sweet-tart tea has plenty of refreshing pomegranate flavor. Serve warm mugs to holiday guests coming in from the cold.
—Taste of Home *Test Kitchen*

- -

TAKES: 25 min. • **MAKES:** 9 servings (2¼ qt.)

- ⅓   cup minced fresh gingerroot
- 2   cinnamon sticks (3 in.), crushed
- 8   cups pomegranate juice
- 2   cups water
- 12 individual Raspberry Zinger tea bags
- ⅓   cup honey
     Optional: Pomegranate seeds and orange wedges

1. Place ginger and cinnamon sticks on a double thickness of cheesecloth. Bring up corners of cloth; tie with string to form a bag. Set aside.
2. Place pomegranate juice and water in a large saucepan. Bring to a boil. Remove from the heat. Add tea bags and spice bag; cover and steep for 8 minutes. Discard tea bags and spice bag; stir in honey. Serve warm. If desired, serve with pomegranate seeds, orange wedges and additional cinnamon sticks.
1 CUP: *163 cal., 0 fat (0 sat. fat), 0 chol., 27mg sod., 41g carb. (41g sugars, 0 fiber), 1g pro.*

GRANDMA'S ONION SQUARES

My grandma brought this recipe with her when she emigrated from Italy as a young wife and mother. It is still a family favorite.
—*Janet Eddy, Stockton, CA*

PREP: 40 min. • **BAKE:** 35 min. • **MAKES:** 9 servings

- 2 Tbsp. olive oil
- 2 cups sliced onions
- 1 tsp. salt, divided
- ¼ tsp. pepper
- 2 cups all-purpose flour
- 3 tsp. baking powder
- 5 Tbsp. shortening
- ⅔ cup 2% milk
- 1 large egg, room temperature
- ¾ cup sour cream

1. Preheat oven to 400°. In a large skillet, heat oil over medium heat. Add onions; cook and stir until softened, 8-10 minutes. Reduce heat to medium-low; cook until deep golden brown, 30-40 minutes, stirring occasionally. Stir in ½ tsp. salt and the pepper.
2. Meanwhile, in a large bowl, combine flour, baking powder and remaining ½ tsp. salt. Cut in shortening until mixture resembles coarse crumbs. Stir in milk just until moistened. Press into a greased 9-in. square baking pan; top with onions.
3. Combine egg and sour cream; spread over the onion layer. Bake until golden brown, 35-40 minutes. Cut into squares. Serve warm.
1 PIECE: 256 cal., 15g fat (5g sat. fat), 27mg chol., 447mg sod., 25g carb. (3g sugars, 1g fiber), 5g pro.

CAPTURING CHRISTMAS WITH POTPOURRI

There is something about fragrances during the holidays that transports me back to childhood. This scent reminds me of times decorating cookies and other treats at my grandmother's house. Don't let all of the water evaporate—just add more as it gets low. You can store the potpourri in the refrigerator in a glass jar and reuse for a couple days.
—*Cathy Arkle, Studio City, CA*

TAKES: 5 min.

- 10 whole cloves
- 6 whole allspice
- 6 cardamom pods
- 5 whole star anise
- 3 slices fresh gingerroot
- 3 pieces orange, lemon or lime peel
- 2 cinnamon sticks (3 in.)

Place cloves, allspice, cardamom, star anise, ginger, orange peel and cinnamon sticks on a double thickness of cheesecloth. Bring up corners of cloth; tie with a string to form a bag. Set aside. Fill Dutch oven or large stockpot two-thirds of the way full with water. Add spice bag. Bring to a boil; reduce heat and simmer, replenishing water as necessary.

SUGAR PLUM BREAD

I grew up with my Grandma Mitchell's plum bread. We slathered it with butter and ate it with cottage cheese and fresh fruit for a simple breakfast. It always makes an appearance at the holidays!
—Emily Tyra, Lake Ann, MI

PREP: 15 min. + standing
BAKE: 40 min. + cooling
MAKES: 1 loaf (12 slices)

- 1 cup pitted dried plums (prunes), coarsely chopped
- ¾ cup water
- 2 Tbsp. plus ¾ cup sugar, divided
- 2 Tbsp. shortening
- 1 large egg, room temperature
- 2 cups all-purpose flour
- 2 tsp. baking powder
- 1 tsp. baking soda
- ½ tsp. salt
- 2 Tbsp. coarse sugar

1. Preheat oven to 350°. In a small saucepan, combine dried plums, water and 2 Tbsp. sugar. Bring to a simmer over medium heat for 1 minute. Remove from heat; let stand until plums are plumped, about 10 minutes. Drain plums, reserving fruit and liquid. Measure liquid, adding enough water to yield ½ cup.
2. Cream shortening and the remaining ¾ cup sugar until light and fluffy, about 4 minutes. Beat in egg. In another bowl, whisk together flour, baking powder, baking soda and salt. Add to creamed mixture alternately with cooking liquid; fold in the cooled dried plums (batter will be thick).

3. Transfer batter to a greased 8x4-in. loaf pan. Sprinkle with coarse sugar. Bake until a toothpick inserted in center comes out with moist crumbs, 40-45 minutes. Cool in pan 10 minutes before removing to a wire rack to cool completely.
1 PIECE: *202 cal., 3g fat (1g sat. fat), 16mg chol., 291mg sod., 41g carb. (21g sugars, 1g fiber), 3g pro.*

Holiday Helper
If dried plums (prunes) aren't to your liking, try using dried apricots instead. Add a little lemon zest to some softened butter and slather on top!

APPLE CAKE WITH BUTTERMILK SAUCE

Apple cider pound cake is topped with simply spiced fresh apples and drizzled with vanilla buttermilk sauce for this easy apple cake.
—Sarita Gelner, Waunakee, WI

PREP: 40 min. • **BAKE:** 50 min. + cooling
MAKES: 12 servings

1½ cups apple cider or juice
APPLE TOPPING
  2 cups chopped peeled tart apples
  3 Tbsp. sugar
  1 Tbsp. orange juice
  ½ tsp. ground cinnamon
  ½ tsp. ground cloves
CAKE
  ½ cup butter, melted
  ¾ cup sugar
  2 large eggs, room temperature
1½ tsp. vanilla extract
1¼ cups cake flour
  1 tsp. baking powder
  ¼ tsp. salt
  ½ cup sour cream
BUTTERMILK SAUCE
  ¾ cup sugar
  6 Tbsp. butter, cubed
  ⅓ cup buttermilk
  2 tsp. light corn syrup
  ¼ tsp. baking soda
  ¼ tsp. vanilla extract

1. In a small saucepan, bring cider a boil; cook until liquid is reduced to about ¼ cup, 15-20 minutes. Remove from the heat and cool.
2. Preheat oven to 350°. In a large bowl, combine apples, sugar, orange juice, cinnamon and cloves; toss to coat. For cake batter, in a large bowl, beat butter, sugar, eggs, vanilla extract and cooled cider reduction until well blended. In another bowl, whisk cake flour, baking powder and salt; add to butter mixture alternately with sour cream, beating after each addition just until combined.
3. Transfer cake batter to a greased 8-in. springform pan; place on a baking sheet. Spoon apple mixture over batter. Bake until a toothpick inserted in the center comes out clean, 50-60 minutes. Cool 15 minutes on a wire rack.

4. For sauce, in a small saucepan combine sugar, butter, buttermilk, corn syrup and baking soda. Cook and stir over medium heat until bubbly, 4-6 minutes. Remove from the heat; stir in vanilla. Pour the sauce over warm cake. Serve warm. Refrigerate leftovers.
1 PIECE: *345 cal., 16g fat (10g sat. fat), 69mg chol., 255mg sod., 48g carb. (35g sugars, 1g fiber), 3g pro.*

SUGARED DATE BALLS

When I was a youngster, Mom always baked these tender old-fashioned cookies dotted with chewy dates and crunchy walnuts. Much to the delight of my family, I have continued her delicious tradition.
—Sandra Vautrain, Sugar Land, TX

PREP: 15 min. • **BAKE:** 25 min./batch
MAKES: about 2½ dozen

  ½ cup butter, softened
  ⅓ cup confectioners' sugar
  1 Tbsp. 2% milk
  1 tsp. vanilla extract
1¼ cups all-purpose flour
  ¼ tsp. salt
  ⅔ cup chopped dates
  ½ cup chopped nuts
    Additional confectioners' sugar

1. Preheat oven to 325°. In a bowl, cream butter and sugar. Beat in milk and vanilla. Combine flour and salt; gradually add to creamed mixture. Stir in dates and nuts.
2. Roll dough into 1-in. balls. Place 2 in. apart on ungreased baking sheets. Bake until the bottoms are lightly browned, 22-25 minutes. Roll warm cookies in confectioners' sugar; cool on wire racks.
1 DATE BALL: *74 cal., 4g fat (2g sat. fat), 8mg chol., 44mg sod., 8g carb. (3g sugars, 1g fiber), 1g pro.*

CORNISH HENS WITH WILD RICE & CELERY

Stuffed with a succulent combination of wild rice, mushrooms and dried cranberries, these golden hens are sure to become a special-occasion entree in your home. They're a wonderful change of pace from traditional turkey.
—Nancy Horsburgh, Everett, ON

PREP: 25 min. • **BAKE:** 50 min.
MAKES: 10 servings

- 2   Tbsp. butter
- ½   cup chopped celery
- ¼   cup sliced fresh mushrooms
- 2   pkg. (6.2 oz. each) fast-cooking long grain and wild rice mix
- 2   cans (14½ oz. each) reduced-sodium chicken broth
- ½   cup water
- ⅔   cup sliced water chestnuts, drained and chopped
- ½   cup dried cranberries
- ½   cup chopped green onions
- 2   Tbsp. reduced-sodium soy sauce
- 5   Cornish game hens (20 to 24 oz. each)

1. Preheat oven to 375°. In a large saucepan coated with cooking spray, melt butter over medium heat. Add celery and mushrooms; cook until tender. Stir in rice; cook 1 minute longer. Stir in contents of rice seasoning packets, broth and water. Bring to a boil. Reduce heat; simmer, covered, until rice is tender, 5-6 minutes. Stir in water chestnuts, cranberries, onions and soy sauce. Stuff hens with the rice mixture, or refrigerate and reheat it to serve with roasted hens.

2. Place the hens on a rack in a shallow roasting pan. Bake until the juices run clear and a thermometer reads 170°, 50-60 minutes. Cut each hen in half lengthwise to serve.

1 SERVING: *257 cal., 7g fat (3g sat. fat), 123mg chol., 564mg sod., 20g carb. (5g sugars, 1g fiber), 29g pro.* **DIABETIC EXCHANGES:** *4 lean meat, 1½ starch, ½ fat.*

CREAMED SPINACH & PEARL ONIONS

When I was a culinary student, this creamy side dish wowed me, and I don't even like spinach. This side is a keeper!
—Chelsea Puchel, Pickens, SC

TAKES: 25 min. • **MAKES:** 8 servings

- ¼   cup butter, cubed
- 1   pkg. (14.4 oz.) frozen pearl onions, thawed and drained
- 2   cups heavy whipping cream
- ½   cup grated Parmesan cheese
- ½   tsp. salt
- ¼   tsp. pepper
- 10 oz. fresh baby spinach (about 13 cups)

1. In a large cast-iron or other heavy skillet, heat butter over medium heat. Add pearl onions; cook and stir until tender, 6-8 minutes. Stir in cream. Bring to a boil; cook until liquid is reduced by half, 6-8 minutes.

2. Stir in cheese, salt and pepper. Add spinach; cook, covered, until spinach is wilted, 3-5 minutes, stirring occasionally.

½ CUP: *307 cal., 30g fat (18g sat. fat), 102mg chol., 328mg sod., 8g carb. (4g sugars, 1g fiber), 5g pro.*

3-IN-1 CHEESE BALL

Three incredible cheese balls with the flavors of pesto, horseradish-bacon and Gorgonzola make for a dazzling display at any holiday get-together.
—Taste of Home *Test Kitchen*

- -

PREP: 30 min. + chilling
MAKES: 3 large cheese balls
(about 1 cup each)

  2 **pkg. (8 oz. each) cream cheese, softened**
  1 **cup grated Parmesan cheese**
  2 **garlic cloves, minced**

PESTO CHEESE BALL

  2 **Tbsp. prepared pesto**
  2 **Tbsp. minced fresh basil**

HORSERADISH-BACON CHEESE BALL

  2 **Tbsp. prepared horseradish**
  ½ **cup crumbled cooked bacon**
  1 **green onion, finely chopped**

GORGONZOLA-CRANBERRY CHEESE BALL

  ⅓ **cup crumbled Gorgonzola cheese**
  ⅓ **cup dried cranberries**
  ½ **cup chopped walnuts, toasted**

FOR SERVING

      Optional (for decoration): Dried cranberries, miniature pretzels, cooked bacon, basil leaves and green onion
      Assorted crackers

1. In a large bowl, beat cream cheese, Parmesan cheese and garlic until blended. Divide mixture into 3 portions; place each in a small bowl.

2. For Pesto Cheese Ball: Beat pesto into 1 portion of cheese mixture. Stir in basil. Shape into a ball.

3. For Horseradish-Bacon Cheese Ball: Beat horseradish into second portion of cheese mixture. Stir in bacon and green onion. Shape into 1 large or 3 mini balls.

4. For Gorgonzola-Cranberry Cheese Ball: Beat Gorgonzola cheese into third portion of cheese mixture. Stir in cranberries. Shape into a ball; roll in walnuts to coat.

5. Cover and refrigerate at least 1 hour or until firm. Decorate as desired. Serve with crackers.

2 TBSP.: 94 cal., 9g fat (4g sat. fat), 24mg chol., 157mg sod., 1g carb. (1g sugars, 0 fiber), 3g pro.

QUICK CHRISTMAS EVE ORANGE ROLLS

This recipe is so dependable—I make it a lot during the holidays because it's quick and delicious. And there are never any leftovers!
—Angela Sheridan, Opdyke, IL

PREP: 15 min. • **COOK:** 40 min.
MAKES: 12 servings

- 1 pkg. (8 oz.) cream cheese, softened
- ¼ cup orange marmalade
- 2 Tbsp. orange juice
- ½ cup chopped pecans

DOUGH
- 3½ cups biscuit/baking mix
- 2 Tbsp. sugar
- 1 pkg. (¼ oz.) quick-rise yeast
- 1 cup warm water
- 2 Tbsp. butter, melted

GLAZE
- ½ cup confectioners' sugar
- ¼ cup orange marmalade, warmed

1. In a small bowl, beat cream cheese, orange marmalade and orange juice until blended; stir in pecans. Set aside.

2. In a large bowl, combine baking mix, sugar and yeast. Stir in warm water to form a soft dough. Turn dough onto a lightly floured surface; knead until smooth and elastic, about 5 minutes. Cover and let rest 10 minutes.

3. Roll dough into an 11x8-in. rectangle. Spread cream cheese mixture to within ½ in. of edges. Roll up jelly-roll style, starting with a long side; pinch seam to seal. Cut into 12 slices. Place in a greased 13x9-in. baking dish, cut side down. Cover with a kitchen towel. Let rise in a warm place until doubled, about 1 hour.

4. Preheat oven to 350°. Brush tops of rolls with melted butter. Bake until golden brown, 35-40 minutes. Cool slightly in pan on a wire rack.

5. For glaze, stir together confectioners' sugar and marmalade; drizzle over the warm rolls.

1 ROLL: *311 cal., 15g fat (6g sat. fat), 24mg chol., 445mg sod., 42g carb. (17g sugars, 2g fiber), 5g pro.*

MOM-MOM BESSIE'S COCONUT MOLASSES PIE

I am the proud keeper of my husband's grandmother's handwritten recipe book. Mom-Mom Bessie was one of the best cooks I knew, and we think of her every time we make this pie. The flavor combination of coconut and molasses is a family favorite.
—Susan Bickta, Kutztown, PA

PREP: 10 min. • **BAKE:** 55 min. + cooling
MAKES: 8 servings

- 1 cup packed light brown sugar
- 1 cup sour cream
- ½ cup dark corn syrup
- ½ cup dark molasses
- 2 large eggs, room temperature, lightly beaten
- ¼ cup 2% milk
- 2 Tbsp. all-purpose flour
- ¼ tsp. baking soda
- 1½ cups sweetened shredded coconut
- 1 frozen deep-dish pie crust (9 in.)
  Whipped cream, optional

1. Preheat oven to 350°. In a large bowl, combine the first 8 ingredients. Stir in coconut. Pour into crust; cover edges loosely with foil.

2. Bake until center is set, 45-55 minutes. Remove foil; cool pie on a wire rack. If desired, serve with whipped cream.

1 PIECE: *486 cal., 19g fat (10g sat. fat), 54mg chol., 243mg sod., 80g carb. (66g sugars, 1g fiber), 5g pro.*

Holiday Helper

If you're not fond of the taste of molasses, use ½ cup additional dark corn syrup in place of the molasses.

ROLLS, BISCUITS & MORE

Bring the aroma of homemade bread and rolls to your kitchen this season. From classic to modern, sweet to savory, these baked beauties will round out your menu and bring cheer to your table.

SEEDED HONEY WHEAT BREAD

I usually double this recipe because my family loves the poppy and sunflower seed bread so much they ask for seconds. Bread bakers will appreciate its perfect shape and soft texture.
—*Rachel Preus, Marshall, MI*

PREP: 45 min. + rising • **BAKE:** 25 min. + cooling
MAKES: 2 loaves (12 pieces each)

    1   cup whole wheat flour
    2   pkg. (¼ oz. each) quick-rise yeast
    1   tsp. salt
 3½ to 4 cups all-purpose flour
 1½   cups water
    ¼   cup butter, cubed
    ¼   cup honey
    ⅓   cup flaxseed
    ¼   cup unsalted sunflower kernels
    1   Tbsp. poppy seeds
    1   large egg

1. In a large bowl, combine whole wheat flour, yeast, salt and 1 cup all-purpose flour; set aside. In a small saucepan, heat water, butter and honey to 120°-130°. Add to dry ingredients. Stir in flax, sunflower kernels, poppy seeds and enough of the remaining flour to form a stiff dough.

2. Turn dough onto a floured surface; knead until smooth and elastic, 6-8 minutes. Cover and let rest 10 minutes. Punch down dough; divide in half. Shape into loaves. Place in 2 greased 8x4-in. loaf pans, seam side down. Cover and let rise in a warm place until doubled, about 15 minutes.

3. Preheat oven to 350°. In a small bowl, beat egg; brush over loaves. Bake until golden brown, 25-30 minutes. Remove from pans to wire racks to cool.

1 PIECE: *138 cal., 4g fat (2g sat. fat), 13mg chol., 118mg sod., 22g carb. (3g sugars, 2g fiber), 4g pro.*

GARLIC KNOTTED ROLLS

Using frozen yeast dough is an easy way to make homemade rolls. These cute knots add a special touch to any menu.
—*Kathy Harding, Richmond, MO*

PREP: 15 min. + rising • **BAKE:** 15 min. • **MAKES:** 10 rolls

    1   loaf (1 lb.) frozen bread dough, thawed
 1½   tsp. dried minced onion
    3   Tbsp. butter
    4   garlic cloves, minced
    ⅛   tsp. salt
    1   large egg, beaten
        Poppy seeds, optional

1. Pat out dough on a work surface; sprinkle with minced onion and knead until combined. Divide dough in half. Shape each half into 5 balls. To form knots, roll each ball into a 10-in. rope; tie into a knot. Tuck ends under. Place rolls 2 in. apart on a greased baking sheet.

2. In a small skillet over medium heat, melt butter. Add garlic and salt; cook and stir 1-2 minutes. Brush over rolls. Cover and let rise until doubled, about 30 minutes.

3. Preheat oven to 375°. Brush tops with egg; if desired, sprinkle with poppy seeds. Bake until golden brown, 15-20 minutes.

1 ROLL: *168 cal., 6g fat (2g sat. fat), 30mg chol., 315mg sod., 22g carb. (2g sugars, 2g fiber), 5g pro.*

MAPLE & BACON SWIRL BREAD

Swirled with maple syrup, raisins, bacon and brown sugar, this craveworthy bread is one they'll remember. An added bonus is that the dough is easy to work with and roll out. Try it as part of a Christmas morning brunch or enjoy it with a cup of coffee after dinner.
—Alicia Rooker, Milwaukee, WI

PREP: 50 min. + rising
BAKE: 35 min. + cooling
MAKES: 2 loaves (12 pieces each)

- 2 pkg. (¼ oz. each) active dry yeast
- ½ cup warm water (110° to 115°)
- 5 cups all-purpose flour
- ¾ cup sugar
- ½ tsp. salt
- ½ cup cold butter
- ½ cup sour cream
- 2 large eggs, lightly beaten, room temperature
- 2 large egg yolks, lightly beaten, room temperature
- 1 tsp. vanilla extract

FILLING
- 2 Tbsp. butter, melted
- 2 Tbsp. maple syrup
- 1 tsp. maple flavoring
- ½ cup packed brown sugar
- 8 bacon strips, cooked and crumbled
- ¼ cup raisins

1. In a small bowl, dissolve yeast in warm water. In a large bowl, mix flour, sugar and salt; cut in butter until crumbly. Add the sour cream, eggs, egg yolks, vanilla and yeast mixture; stir to form a soft dough (the dough will be sticky). Turn onto a floured surface; knead until smooth and elastic, 6-8 minutes. Do not let rise. Divide in half. Roll out the dough into two 12-in. squares; cover.

2. In a small bowl, combine melted butter, maple syrup and flavoring. Spread over each square to within ½ in. of edges. Sprinkle with brown sugar, bacon and raisins. Roll up each square jelly-roll style; pinch seams to seal.

3. Place on a parchment-lined rimmed baking sheet. Cover dough and let rise until nearly doubled, about 45 minutes. Preheat oven to 350°. Bake loaves until golden brown, 35-40 minutes. Remove from pan to a wire rack to cool.

1 PIECE: *225 cal., 8g fat (4g sat. fat), 48mg chol., 147mg sod., 34g carb. (13g sugars, 1g fiber), 5g pro.*

HERB BISCUIT LOAF

These buttery, golden rolls will make any meal special—from Thanksgiving dinner to a weekday supper. My husband loves their wonderful herb flavor.
—Amy Smith, Maplewood, MN

PREP: 15 min. • **BAKE:** 30 min.
MAKES: 20 servings

- ¼ cup butter, melted
- ½ tsp. dried minced onion
- ½ tsp. dried basil
- ¼ to ½ tsp. caraway seeds
- ⅛ tsp. garlic powder
- 2 tubes (12 oz. each) buttermilk biscuits

Preheat oven to 350°. In a shallow bowl, combine first 5 ingredients. Dip biscuits in butter mixture; fold in half and place in rows in a greased 8-in. square baking pan. Drizzle with remaining butter mixture. Bake until golden brown, 27-30 minutes.

1 BISCUIT: *121 cal., 6g fat (3g sat. fat), 6mg chol., 298mg sod., 15g carb. (2g sugars, 0 fiber), 2g pro.*

BISCUITS WITH SOUTHERN CHEESE SPREAD

Hosting a holiday tea party? Include a savory option to balance out the menu with these bread and butter pickle biscuits and cheese spread. They're perfect for snacking, too, so you might want to make more than one batch. They disappear surprisingly fast!
—Colleen Delawder, Herndon, VA

- -

PREP: 25 min. • **BAKE:** 10 min.
MAKES: 15 biscuits and 1⅓ cup spread

- 2¼ cups all-purpose flour
- 2 Tbsp. sugar
- 4 tsp. baking powder
- ¼ tsp. salt
- ½ cup cold unsalted butter
- ½ cup buttermilk
- ¼ cup finely chopped bread and butter pickle slices

CHEESE SPREAD
- 1 cup shredded cheddar cheese
- ⅓ cup mayonnaise
- 2 Tbsp. finely chopped bread and butter pickle slices
- ½ tsp. mustard seed
- ¼ tsp. pepper

1. Preheat oven to 450°. In a large bowl, whisk flour, sugar, baking powder and salt. Cut in the butter until mixture resembles coarse crumbs. Add the buttermilk and pickles; stir just until moistened.
2. Turn onto a lightly floured surface; knead gently 8-10 times. Pat or roll to ½-in. thickness; cut dough with a floured 2-in. biscuit cutter. Place 2 in. apart on a parchment-lined baking sheet. Bake until golden brown, 8-10 minutes.
3. Meanwhile, combine cheese spread ingredients. Serve with biscuits.

1 BISCUIT WITH ABOUT 1 TBSP. SPREAD: *200 cal., 12g fat (6g sat. fat), 24mg chol., 292mg sod., 18g carb. (3g sugars, 1g fiber), 4g pro.*

POPPY SEED BREAD WITH ORANGE GLAZE

My neighbor gave me this recipe, and I love that it makes two loaves. We usually eat one and then give the other away or freeze it for later. The citrusy glaze complements the bread perfectly.
—Heather Frese, Albany, MO

- -

PREP: 20 min. • **BAKE:** 55 min. + cooling
MAKES: 2 loaves (16 pieces each)

- 3 cups all-purpose flour
- 2¼ cups sugar
- 3 tsp. baking powder
- 1½ tsp. salt
- 3 large eggs, room temperature
- 1½ cups 2% milk
- 1 cup canola oil
- 1 Tbsp. plus 1½ tsp. poppy seeds
- 1½ tsp. each butter flavoring, almond extract and vanilla extract

GLAZE
- ¾ cup confectioners' sugar
- ¼ cup orange juice
- ½ tsp. each butter flavoring, almond extract and vanilla extract

1. Preheat oven to 350°. In a large bowl, combine the flour, sugar, baking powder and salt. In a small bowl, whisk the eggs, milk, oil, poppy seeds, butter flavoring and extracts. Stir into dry ingredients just until moistened.
2. Transfer to 2 greased and floured 9x5-in. loaf pans. Bake until a toothpick inserted in the center comes out clean, 55-60 minutes. Cool loaves for 10 minutes before removing from pans to wire racks. Combine glaze ingredients; drizzle over warm loaves.

1 PIECE: *190 cal., 8g fat (1g sat. fat), 21mg chol., 160mg sod., 27g carb. (18g sugars, 0 fiber), 2g pro.*

MOCHA CINNAMON ROLLS

I love cinnamon rolls and anything that's coffee flavored. So it seemed only natural to pair them in one delicious mashup. Enjoy them as a dessert, snack or breakfast treat.
—Victoria Mitchel, Gettysburg, PA

PREP: 45 min. + rising • **BAKE:** 25 min.
MAKES: 1 dozen

- 1 pkg. (¼ oz.) active dry yeast
- 1 cup warm 2% milk (110° to 115°)
- ¼ cup sugar
- ¼ cup butter, melted
- 2 Tbsp. instant coffee granules
- 1 large egg yolk, room temperature
- 1½ tsp. vanilla extract
- ¾ tsp. salt
- ½ tsp. ground nutmeg
- 2½ to 3 cups all-purpose flour

FILLING
- ¾ cup chopped pecans
- ⅔ cup semisweet chocolate chips
- ¼ cup sugar
- 2 Tbsp. instant coffee granules
- ½ tsp. ground cinnamon
- ¼ cup butter, softened
- ¼ cup butter, melted

FROSTING
- 1 oz. cream cheese, softened
- 1 cup confectioners' sugar
- 3 Tbsp. heavy whipping cream
- ¾ tsp. instant coffee granules
- ⅛ tsp. vanilla extract

1. In a large bowl, dissolve yeast in warm milk. Add sugar, butter, coffee granules, egg yolk, vanilla, salt, nutmeg and 2 cups flour. Beat on medium speed until smooth. Stir in enough remaining flour to form a soft dough (dough will be sticky).
2. Turn onto a floured surface; knead until smooth and elastic, 6-8 minutes. Place in a greased bowl, turning once to grease top. Cover and let rise in a warm place until doubled, about 1 hour. Place pecans, chocolate chips, sugar, instant coffee and cinnamon in a food processor; process until finely chopped. Punch dough down; turn onto a floured surface. Roll out into an 18x12-in. rectangle; spread dough with softened butter. Sprinkle pecan mixture over dough to within ½ in. of edges.
3. Roll up jelly-roll style, starting with a long side; pinch seam to seal. Cut roll into 12 slices. Place rolls, cut side down, in a greased 13x9-in. baking pan. Cover and let rise until doubled, about 1 hour.
4. Preheat oven to 350°. Drizzle rolls with melted butter. Bake until golden brown, 22-28 minutes. Place pan on a wire rack. In a small bowl, beat frosting ingredients until smooth. Spread frosting over rolls. Serve warm.
1 ROLL: *406 cal., 23g fat (11g sat. fat), 55mg chol., 259mg sod., 48g carb. (25g sugars, 2g fiber), 5g pro.*

GOLDEN SWEET ONION CORNBREAD

Put your cast-iron skillet to good use with this hearty cornbread. You'll be pleased with the results, especially if this is your first time baking bread in a skillet.
—Taste of Home *Test Kitchen*

PREP: 35 min. • **BAKE:** 20 min. + standing • **MAKES:** 8 servings

- 2 Tbsp. butter
- 1 large sweet onion, halved and thinly sliced
- 4 tsp. chopped seeded jalapeno pepper
- ½ tsp. chili powder, divided
- 2 Tbsp. brown sugar, divided
- 1½ cups all-purpose flour
- 1 cup yellow cornmeal
- 3 Tbsp. sugar
- 2 tsp. baking powder
- ½ tsp. kosher salt
- ½ tsp. baking soda
- 1¼ cups buttermilk
- 2 large eggs, room temperature, lightly beaten
- ¼ cup butter, melted
- ¾ cup shredded cheddar cheese
- 1 can (4 oz.) chopped green chiles

CRANBERRY BUTTER
- ½ cup whole-berry cranberry sauce
- ½ tsp. grated lime zest
- ½ cup butter, softened

1. In a 10-in. cast-iron skillet, melt 2 Tbsp. butter; tilt to coat bottom and sides. Add onion, jalapeno and ¼ tsp. chili powder; cook over medium-low heat until onion is lightly browned and tender. Stir in 1 Tbsp. brown sugar until dissolved; set aside.
2. In a large bowl, combine flour, cornmeal, sugar, baking powder, salt, baking soda, and remaining chili powder and brown sugar. In a small bowl, whisk buttermilk, eggs and melted butter. Stir into dry ingredients just until moistened. Fold in cheese and chiles.
3. Pour batter over onion mixture in skillet. Bake at 425° for 20-25 minutes or until golden brown. Meanwhile, in a small saucepan, cook cranberry sauce and lime zest over low heat until heated through. Cool completely.
4. Let cornbread stand for 10 minutes. Invert onto a serving platter; cut into wedges. Pour cranberry mixture over softened butter; serve with cornbread.
1 PIECE WITH 1 TBSP. BUTTER AND 1 TBSP. CRANBERRY MIXTURE: *468 cal., 25g fat (16g sat. fat), 118mg chol., 626mg sod., 52g carb. (17g sugars, 3g fiber), 10g pro.*

GARLIC POTATO BISCUITS

The beauty of biscuits is that you can enjoy the aroma of oven-fresh bread with less work than yeast breads.
—Diane Hixon, Niceville, FL

PREP: 25 min. • **BAKE:** 10 min. • **MAKES:** 15 biscuits

- 1 large potato (½ lb.), peeled and diced
- 3 to 4 garlic cloves, peeled
- ⅓ cup butter, softened
- 1 tsp. salt
- ¼ tsp. pepper
- 2 cups all-purpose flour
- 3 tsp. baking powder
- ⅓ cup 2% milk

1. Place potato and garlic in a saucepan; cover with water. Bring to a boil. Reduce heat; cover and simmer until tender. Drain. Add butter, salt and pepper to potato and garlic; mash. In a large bowl, combine flour and baking powder; stir in potato mixture until mixture resembles coarse crumbs. Add milk and stir well.
2. Turn dough onto a lightly floured surface. Roll out to ½-in. thickness. Cut with a floured 2-in. biscuit cutter. Place 1 in. apart on an ungreased baking sheet. Bake at 450° until golden brown, 10-12 minutes. Serve warm.
1 BISCUIT: *120 cal., 4g fat (3g sat. fat), 12mg chol., 283mg sod., 18g carb. (1g sugars, 1g fiber), 2g pro.*

PEAR, RICOTTA & ROSEMARY CORN MUFFINS

The sweetness of pear and golden raisins with the rosemary and ricotta makes these muffins perfect for a brunch party or family dinners. Indulge yourself by spreading a pat of butter over the scrumptious muffins while they're warm.

—Joseph Sciascia, San Mateo, CA

- -

PREP: 30 min. • **BAKE:** 20 min.
MAKES: 1 dozen

- ¼ cup golden raisins
- ¼ cup orange juice
- 2 Tbsp. butter
- 1 Tbsp. minced fresh rosemary or 1 tsp. dried rosemary, crushed
- 1 cup all-purpose flour
- 1 cup cornmeal
- ½ cup sugar
- 3 tsp. baking powder
- ¼ tsp. salt
- 2 large eggs, room temperature
- 1 cup whole-milk ricotta cheese
- 1 Tbsp. grated lemon zest
- 2 cups chopped peeled ripe pears

1. Preheat oven to 400°. In a microwave-safe bowl, combine raisins, orange juice, butter and rosemary; microwave, covered, on high 1 minute.

2. In a large bowl, whisk flour, cornmeal, sugar, baking powder and salt. In another bowl, whisk eggs, ricotta and lemon zest until blended. Add to flour mixture; stir just until moistened. Fold in the raisin mixture. Gently stir in pears (batter will be thick).

3. Divide batter among 12 greased muffin cups. Bake until a toothpick inserted in center comes out clean, 18-22 minutes. Cool 5 minutes before removing from pan to a wire rack. Serve warm.

1 MUFFIN: *203 cal., 5g fat (3g sat. fat), 44mg chol., 223mg sod., 34g carb. (14g sugars, 2g fiber), 6g pro.*
DIABETIC EXCHANGES: *2 starch, 1 fat.*

GARLIC FONTINA BREAD

With its golden brown color and soft texture, this bread is a must at any family meal. It's a modified version of a traditional white bread recipe my brother gave me. Try it as garlic bread toast with your favorite Italian meal. It's also great for grilled cheese sandwiches or simply enjoyed on its own.

—Cindy Ryan, St. Johns, MI

- -

PREP: 30 min. + rising
BAKE: 30 min. + cooling
MAKES: 2 loaves (16 pieces each)

- 2 pkg. (¼ oz. each) active dry yeast
- 2 cups warm water (110° to 115°)
- 3 Tbsp. sugar
- 2 Tbsp. shortening
- 1 Tbsp. garlic powder
- 2 tsp. salt
- 5 to 5½ cups all-purpose flour
- 1½ cups plus 2 Tbsp. shredded fontina cheese, divided
- 1½ tsp. canola oil

1. In a large bowl, dissolve yeast in warm water. Add the sugar, shortening, garlic powder, salt and 3 cups flour. Beat until smooth. Stir in enough remaining flour to form a firm dough. Stir in 1½ cups cheese.

2. Turn onto a floured surface; knead until smooth and elastic, 6-8 minutes. Place in a greased bowl, turning once to grease the top. Cover and let rise in a warm place until doubled, about 1 hour.

3. Punch dough down. Shape into 2 loaves. Place in 2 greased 9x5-in. loaf pans. Cover and let rise in a warm place until doubled, about 30 minutes. Brush with the oil and sprinkle with remaining cheese.

4. Bake at 375° for 30-35 minutes or until golden brown. Cool on a wire rack.

1 PIECE: *119 cal., 4g fat (2g sat. fat), 10mg chol., 215mg sod., 17g carb. (2g sugars, 1g fiber), 4g pro.*

KRIS KRINGLE STAR BREAD

(*PICTURED ON P. 154*)

*I make this recipe every holiday season.
Its pretty shape is unexpected and fun.*
—Evelyn Fisher, Haines, OR

PREP: 30 min. + rising • **BAKE:** 25 min.
MAKES: 2 breads (18 pieces each)

FILLING

- 2 cups chopped walnuts or hazelnuts
- 1 cup chopped maraschino cherries, patted dry
- ⅔ cup honey
- ½ cup sugar

BREAD

- 2 pkg. (¼ oz. each) active dry yeast
- 1 cup warm water (110° to 115°)
- ½ cup butter, softened
- ½ cup sugar
- 2 large eggs, room temperature
- 1 tsp. salt
- 4½ to 5 cups all-purpose flour
  Confectioners' sugar icing

1. In a small bowl, combine the filling ingredients; set aside. In a small bowl, dissolve yeast in water.
In a large bowl, combine butter, sugar, eggs, salt, yeast mixture and 2 cups flour; beat until smooth. Stir in enough remaining flour to form a soft dough.
2. Turn onto a floured surface; knead until smooth and elastic, 6-8 minutes. Place in a greased bowl, turning once to grease the top. Cover and let rise in a warm place until doubled, about 1 hour.
3. Punch dough down. Divide in half; roll each half into a 14-in. circle. Transfer to 2 greased baking sheets. Cut five 4-in.-long slits into each circle equal distance apart. Set aside half of filling for garnish; spoon remaining filling into the center of each section.
4. Fold the 2 outer edges of each section over each other to enclose filling, forming star points. Pinch edges together to seal. Cover and let rise in a warm place until doubled, 30 minutes.
5. Preheat the oven to 350°. Bake until golden brown, 20-25 minutes. Drizzle with confectioners' sugar icing. Spoon reserved filling into centers.
1 PIECE: *155 cal., 5g fat (1g sat. fat), 10mg chol., 74mg sod., 26g carb., (12g sugars, 1g fiber), 3g pro.*

JUMBO JALAPENO CHEDDAR ROLLS

Add some excitement to your Christmas or New Year's spread with these colorful rolls. The cheddar and jalapeno flavors are mild, but everyone loves the zesty taste.
—Linda Foreman, Locust Grove, OK

PREP: 35 min. + rising • **BAKE:** 20 min.
MAKES: 1 dozen

- 2 pkg. (¼ oz. each) active dry yeast
- 2 Tbsp. sugar
- 2 cups warm 2% milk (110° to 115°)
- 2 large eggs, room temperature
- 2 tsp. salt
- 6½ to 7½ cups all-purpose flour
- 2 cups shredded cheddar cheese
- ¼ cup chopped seeded jalapeno pepper

EGG WASH

- 1 large egg
- 2 tsp. water

1. In a large bowl, dissolve the yeast and sugar in warm milk. Add the eggs, salt and 4 cups flour. Beat on medium speed for 3 minutes. Add cheese and jalapeno. Stir in enough of the remaining flour to form a firm dough.
2. Turn onto a floured surface; knead until smooth and elastic, 6-8 minutes. Place in a greased bowl, turning once to grease the top. Cover and let rise in a warm place until doubled, about 1 hour.
3. Punch dough down. Turn onto a lightly floured surface; divide into 12 pieces. Shape each into a roll. Place 3 in. apart on lightly greased baking sheets. Cover and let rise until doubled, about 30 minutes.
4. Combine egg and water; brush over rolls. Bake at 375° until golden brown, 16-20 minutes. Remove from pans to wire racks. Serve warm.
1 ROLL: *368 cal., 9g fat (5g sat. fat), 77mg chol., 542mg sod., 57g carb. (5g sugars, 2g fiber), 14g pro.*

CARAWAY RYE DINNER ROLLS

Caraway seeds give these rye dinner rolls a delicate nutty flavor. Denser than most, the onion-infused buns are ideal for dipping in hearty holiday stews or slicing in half to make sandwiches.
—Deborah Maki, Kamloops, BC

- -

PREP: 35 min. + rising • **BAKE:** 15 min.
MAKES: 1½ dozen

- 1¼ cups rye flour
- ½ cup wheat germ
- 2 Tbsp. caraway seeds
- 1 pkg. (¼ oz.) active dry yeast
- 1 tsp. salt
- 3 cups all-purpose flour
- 1 cup 2% milk
- ½ cup water
- 3 Tbsp. butter
- 2 Tbsp. honey
- ⅓ cup finely chopped onion

EGG WASH
- 1 large egg
- 2 tsp. water

1. In a large bowl, mix first 5 ingredients and 1 cup all-purpose flour. In a small saucepan, heat milk, water, butter and honey to 120°-130°. Add to the dry ingredients; beat on medium speed for 3 minutes. Stir in onion and enough of the remaining all-purpose flour to form a soft dough (dough will be sticky).
2. Turn dough onto a floured surface; knead until smooth and elastic, about 6-8 minutes. Place in a greased bowl, turning once to grease the top. Cover and let dough rise in a warm place until doubled, about 1 hour.
3. Punch down dough. Turn onto a lightly floured surface; divide and shape into 18 balls. Place 2 in. apart on greased baking sheets. Cover with a kitchen towel; let rise in a warm place until almost doubled, about 45 minutes.
4. Preheat oven to 400°. For egg wash, in a small bowl, whisk egg and water; brush over rolls. Bake until lightly browned, 11-14 minutes. Remove to wire racks to cool.
1 ROLL: *152 cal., 3g fat (2g sat. fat), 17mg chol., 158mg sod., 26g carb. (3g sugars, 2g fiber), 5g pro.*

LEFSE

Lefse is a soft Scandinavian flatbread made with potatoes. We traditionally make these delicious treats during the holiday season and top them with butter and sugar or jelly, then roll them up. It's hard to eat just one.
—Donna Goutermont, Sequim, WA

- -

PREP: 1 hour • **COOK:** 5 min./batch
MAKES: 12 servings

- 2 lbs. potatoes, peeled and cubed
- ⅓ cup heavy whipping cream, warmed
- ¼ cup shortening or butter, softened
- 1 tsp. sugar
- ¾ tsp. salt
- 2 cups all-purpose flour

1. Place potatoes in a large saucepan; add water to cover. Bring to a boil. Reduce the heat; simmer, covered, until tender, 10-12 minutes. Drain. Press through a potato ricer or strainer into a large bowl.

Stir in cream, shortening, sugar and salt. Cool completely.
2. Preheat griddle over medium-high heat. Stir flour into potato mixture. Turn onto a lightly floured surface; knead until smooth and combined, 6-8 times. Divide into 12 portions. Roll each portion between 2 sheets of waxed paper into an 8-in. circle.
3. Place on griddle; cook until lightly browned, 2-3 minutes on each side. Remove to a platter; cover loosely with a kitchen towel. Repeat with remaining portions. When cool, stack lefse between pieces of waxed paper or paper towels and store in an airtight container.
1 PIECE: *180 cal., 7g fat (3g sat. fat), 8mg chol., 151mg sod., 27g carb. (1g sugars, 1g fiber), 3g pro.*

CHAI-SPICED STAR BREAD

My chai star bread is great for potlucks and parties because it looks beautiful and is easy to share. Prepare the dough ahead of time, refrigerate, then pop it into the oven before serving. Try using this recipe with other fruits, too, such as persimmons or apples.
—Elizabeth Ding, El Cerrito, CA

- -

PREP: 45 min. + rising
BAKE: 20 min. + cooling
MAKES: 16 servings

  2 tsp. active dry yeast
  ½ cup warm water (110° to 115°)
  ½ cup warm 2% milk (110° to 115°)
  ¼ cup sugar
  2¾ to 3¼ cups all-purpose flour
FILLING
  5 Tbsp. butter, softened
  ¾ cup packed brown sugar
  2 tsp. vanilla extract
  1 tsp. ground ginger
  1 tsp. ground cinnamon
  ½ tsp. ground nutmeg
  ½ tsp. ground allspice
  ¼ tsp. ground cloves
  1 medium Bartlett pear, peeled
     and chopped
  1 large egg, beaten

1. In a small bowl, dissolve yeast in warm water. In a large bowl, combine milk, sugar, yeast mixture and 1½ cups flour; beat on medium speed until smooth. Stir in enough remaining flour to form a soft dough (dough will be sticky).

2. Turn onto a floured surface; knead until smooth and elastic, 6-8 minutes. Place in a greased bowl, turning once to grease top. Cover and let rise in a warm place until doubled, about 1 hour.

3. Punch down dough. Turn onto a lightly floured surface; divide into 4 portions. Roll each into a 12-in. circle. Place 1 circle on a parchment-lined 14-in. pizza pan. For filling, combine butter, brown sugar, vanilla and spices. Spread circle with a third of the filling. Repeat twice, layering dough and filling; top with pears. Top with the final portion of dough.

4. Place a 2½-in. round cutter on top of dough in center of circle (do not press down). With a sharp knife, make 16 evenly spaced cuts from round cutter to edge of dough, forming a starburst. Remove cutter; grasp 2 strips and rotate twice outward. Pinch ends together. Repeat with the remaining strips. Cover with a kitchen towel; let rise until almost doubled, about 30 minutes.

5. Preheat oven to 375°. Brush dough with beaten egg. Bake until golden brown, 20-25 minutes. Cool bread completely on a wire rack.

1 PIECE: *178 cal., 4g fat (3g sat. fat), 13mg chol., 37mg sod., 32g carb. (15g sugars, 1g fiber), 3g pro.*

OLIVE FOCACCIA

After adding my own special touches to a basic focaccia recipe, including sun-dried tomatoes, olives and roasted sweet red peppers, the bread was simply delectable. The flavorful, chewy loaf makes a wonderful accompaniment to nearly any meal.
—Dee Froemel, Hayward, WI

- -

PREP: 30 min. + rising • **BAKE:** 15 min.
MAKES: 1 loaf (8 pieces)

  1⅛ tsp. active dry yeast
  ½ cup warm water (110° to 115°)
  1 Tbsp. sugar
  1 Tbsp. Italian seasoning
  ¼ tsp. salt
  ¼ tsp. pepper
  1⅓ to 1⅔ cups all-purpose flour
  2 Tbsp. oil-packed sun-dried
     tomatoes, chopped
  2 Tbsp. roasted sweet red peppers,
     drained and chopped
  2 Tbsp. sliced ripe olives, drained
  5 Greek olives, sliced
  5 sliced green olives with pimientos,
     drained
  2 Tbsp. minced fresh parsley
  1 Tbsp. olive oil
  1 tsp. kosher salt
  1 tsp. shredded Parmesan cheese
  1 tsp. shredded Romano cheese

1. In a large bowl, dissolve yeast in warm water. Add the sugar, Italian seasoning, salt, pepper and 1 cup of flour. Beat until smooth. Stir in enough of the remaining flour to form a firm dough. Stir in the tomatoes, peppers, olives and parsley.

2. Turn onto a floured surface; knead until smooth and elastic, 6-8 minutes. Place in a greased bowl, turning once to grease the top. Cover and let rise in a warm place until doubled, about 50 minutes.

3. Punch dough down. Shape into a 9-in. circle on a greased baking sheet. Cover and let rise in a warm place until doubled, about 25 minutes.

4. With fingertips, make several dimples over the top of the dough. Brush with oil. Sprinkle with kosher salt and cheeses.

5. Bake at 400° until golden brown, 14-18 minutes. Remove to a wire rack.

1 PIECE: *118 cal., 3g fat (0 sat. fat), 0 chol., 418mg sod., 19g carb. (2g sugars, 1g fiber), 3g pro.*

SAVORY COCKTAIL SCONES

Scones are one of my favorite comfort foods, and I wanted to make a savory version with roasted garlic butter. The addition of bacon seemed natural. Their small size makes them fun for cocktail parties; they also work for brunch buffets.
—Donna-Marie Ryan, Topsfield, MA

PREP: 55 min. • **BAKE:** 15 min.
MAKES: 16 scones and about ⅔ cup butter

- 1 whole garlic bulb
- 2 tsp. olive oil
- ½ cup butter, softened

SCONES
- 2 bacon strips, chopped
- ⅓ cup chopped onion
- 2 cups all-purpose flour
- 3 tsp. baking powder
- ½ tsp. baking soda
- ½ tsp. salt
- ½ cup cold butter
- 1 large egg, room temperature
- ½ cup sherry
- ⅓ cup heavy whipping cream
- ¼ cup 2% milk

1. Remove papery outer skin from garlic (do not peel or separate cloves). Cut top off of garlic bulb. Brush with oil. Wrap bulb in heavy-duty foil. Bake at 400° for 40-45 minutes or until softened. Cool 10-15 minutes. Squeeze softened garlic into a small bowl; mash with a fork. Stir in butter; set aside.

2. In a small skillet, cook bacon over medium heat until crisp. Remove to paper towels with a slotted spoon; drain, reserving 1 Tbsp. drippings. In the same skillet, cook and stir onion in drippings until softened. Reduce heat to medium-low; cook, stirring occasionally, until onions are deep golden brown, about 30 minutes. Set aside.

3. In a large bowl, combine the flour, baking powder, baking soda and salt. Cut in butter until mixture resembles coarse crumbs. Whisk egg, sherry and cream; stir into crumb mixture just until moistened. Fold in onion and bacon.

4. Turn onto a floured surface; knead 10 times. Pat into a 10x5-in. rectangle. Using a floured knife, cut into eight 2½-in. squares; cut each square diagonally in half.

5. Place scones on a parchment-lined baking sheet; brush with milk. Bake at 400° until golden brown, 12-15 minutes. Serve warm, with garlic butter.

1 SCONE WITH ABOUT 2 TSP. BUTTER: *204 cal., 15g fat (9g sat. fat), 52mg chol., 297mg sod., 13g carb. (1g sugars, 1g fiber), 3g pro.*

brown sugar mixture. Roll up each rectangle jelly-roll style, starting with a short side; pinch seams to seal. Place in greased 9x5-in. loaf pans, seam side down. Cover with kitchen towels; let rise in a warm place until doubled, about 30 minutes.

4. Bake at 350° until golden brown, 50-60 minutes. Cool 10 minutes before removing from pans to wire racks to cool.

1 PIECE: *202 cal., 5g fat (1g sat. fat), 15mg chol., 130mg sod., 36g carb. (10g sugars, 3g fiber), 5g pro.*

WELSH CAKES

My grandfather was Welsh and he liked to make Welsh cakes on the griddle. Our whole family loves them. Sometimes he would make them for Christmas and wrap them up in little bundles for each family. It's a special memory I will always cherish.
—Wendy Masters, East Garafraxa, ON

- -

PREP: 20 min. • **COOK:** 5 min./batch
MAKES: about 4½ dozen

 3½ cups all-purpose flour
 1 cup sugar
 1½ tsp. baking powder
 1 tsp. salt
 ½ tsp. baking soda
 1 cup cold butter, cubed
 ¾ cup 2% milk
 1 large egg, beaten
 1¼ cups dried currants or raisins

1. In a large bowl, whisk the flour, sugar, baking powder, salt and baking soda. Cut in butter until mixture resembles coarse crumbs. Add milk and egg; stir just until moistened. Fold in currants.

2. Pat or roll dough to ¼-in. thickness; cut with a floured 2-in. biscuit cutter. Preheat griddle over medium heat. In batches, place cakes onto griddle; cook until tops puff and bottoms are golden brown, 1-2 minutes. Turn; cook until second side is golden brown. Cool on wire racks.

1 PIECE: *87 cal., 4g fat (2g sat. fat), 13mg chol., 99mg sod., 13g carb. (6g sugars, 0 fiber), 1g pro.*

SWIRLED PUMPKIN YEAST BREAD

I call this my hostess gift bread since it yields two loaves—one to keep and one to give. It's fantastic for any occasion. Swirls of cinnamon sugar make every slice so good.
—Shirley Runkle, St. Paris, OH

- -

PREP: 45 min. + rising
BAKE: 50 min. + cooling
MAKES: 2 loaves (16 pieces each)

 3 cups whole wheat flour
 2 cups quick-cooking oats
 ⅔ cup packed brown sugar
 2 pkg. (¼ oz. each) active dry yeast
 2½ tsp. pumpkin pie spice
 1½ tsp. salt
 1 tsp. sugar
 4½ to 5 cups bread flour
 1½ cups warm water (120° to 130°)
 1 cup canned pumpkin
 ⅓ cup canola oil
 ⅓ cup unsweetened applesauce
 2 large eggs, room temperature
 ½ cup raisins

FILLING
 ½ cup packed brown sugar
 1 tsp. ground cinnamon
 ¼ cup butter, softened

1. In a large bowl, mix first 7 ingredients and 2 cups of bread flour. In a small saucepan, heat water, pumpkin, oil and applesauce to 120°-130°. Add to dry ingredients; beat on medium speed for 2 minutes. Add the eggs; beat on high for 2 minutes. Stir in the raisins and enough remaining bread flour to form a firm dough.

2. Turn the dough onto a floured surface; knead 6-8 minutes or until smooth and elastic. Place dough in a greased bowl, turning once to grease the top. Cover; let rise in a warm place until doubled, about 1 hour.

3. Mix brown sugar and cinnamon. Punch down dough. Turn onto a lightly floured surface; divide in half. Roll each portion into an 18x9-in. rectangle. Spread each with 2 Tbsp. butter to within ½ in. of edges and sprinkle with ¼ cup of the

CHRISTMAS LIGHTS

Eating healthy doesn't mean sacrificing taste or fulfillment, especially during the holidays. Look here for a temptingly delicious lineup of special occasion recipes that are so full of flavor, no one will realize they're eating light!

EASY & ELEGANT TENDERLOIN ROAST

I love the simplicity of this recipe. A blend of olive oil, garlic, salt and pepper is all it takes to amp up the flavor of a juicy tenderloin. Just pop it into the oven and you've got an impressive main dish to feed a crowd. You'll relish the extra time you'll have to spend with family instead of fussing in the kitchen.
—Mary Kandell, Huron, OH

PREP: 10 min. • **BAKE:** 45 min. + standing • **MAKES:** 12 servings

- 1 beef tenderloin (5 lbs.)
- 2 Tbsp. olive oil
- 4 garlic cloves, minced
- 2 tsp. sea salt
- 1½ tsp. coarsely ground pepper

1. Preheat oven to 425°. Place beef roast on a rack in a shallow roasting pan. In a small bowl, mix the oil, garlic, salt and pepper; rub over roast.
2. Roast until meat reaches desired doneness (for medium-rare, a thermometer should read 135°; medium, 140°; medium-well, 145°), 45-65 minutes. Remove from oven; tent with foil. Let stand 15 minutes before slicing.
5 OZ. COOKED BEEF: *294 cal., 13g fat (5g sat. fat), 82mg chol., 394mg sod., 1g carb. (0 sugars, 0 fiber), 40g pro.*
DIABETIC EXCHANGES: *5 lean meat, ½ fat.*

GOUDA MIXED POTATO MASH

Can't decide what type of spuds to serve? Make both by preparing this casserole featuring Yukon Gold and sweet potatoes. The Gouda cheese is an unexpected twist.
—Shelby Goddard, Baton Rouge, LA

PREP: 20 min. • **COOK:** 15 min. • **MAKES:** 12 servings

- 6 medium Yukon Gold potatoes, peeled and cubed
- 2 medium sweet potatoes, peeled and cubed
- ½ cup 2% milk
- 1 cup shredded Gouda cheese
- 1 tsp. paprika
- ½ tsp. salt
- ½ tsp. pepper

1. Place Yukon Gold and sweet potatoes in a Dutch oven; add water to cover. Bring to a boil. Reduce heat; cook, uncovered, 10-15 minutes or until tender. Drain; return to pan.
2. Mash potatoes, gradually adding milk. Stir in cheese, paprika, salt and pepper.
⅔ CUP: *178 cal., 3g fat (2g sat. fat), 12mg chol., 189mg sod., 33g carb. (6g sugars, 3g fiber), 6g pro.*
DIABETIC EXCHANGES: *2 starch, ½ fat.*

ROASTED ARTICHOKES WITH LEMON AIOLI

Petals of savory artichoke leaves are so delicious dipped into a creamy lemon aioli. It may seem intimidating to roast whole artichokes, but the steps couldn't be easier—and the earthy, comforting flavor is a definite payoff.
—Taste of Home *Test Kitchen*

PREP: 20 min. • **BAKE:** 50 min.
MAKES: 4 servings

- 4 medium artichokes
- 2 Tbsp. olive oil
- ½ medium lemon
- ½ tsp. salt
- ¼ tsp. pepper

AIOLI
- ¼ cup mayonnaise
- ¼ cup plain Greek yogurt
- ½ tsp. minced fresh garlic
- ¼ tsp. grated lemon zest
  Dash pepper

1. Preheat oven to 400°. Using a sharp knife, cut 1 in. from top of each artichoke. Using kitchen scissors, cut off the tips of the outer leaves. Cut each artichoke lengthwise in half. With a spoon, carefully scrape and remove the fuzzy centers of halved artichokes.
2. Drizzle oil into a 15x10x1-in. baking pan. Rub cut surfaces of artichokes with lemon half; sprinkle with salt and pepper. Place artichokes in pan, cut side down. Squeeze lemon juice over artichokes. Cover pan with foil; bake on a lower oven rack until tender and a leaf near the center pulls out easily, 50-55 minutes.
3. Meanwhile, mix aioli ingredients; refrigerate until serving. Serve aioli with artichokes.
2 HALVES WITH 2 TBSP. AIOLI: *233 cal., 19g fat (3g sat. fat), 5mg chol., 446mg sod., 16g carb. (2g sugars, 7g fiber), 4g pro.*

Holiday Helper

To clean an artichoke, rinse under cold water. Use a soft kitchen brush to gently remove the light film produced as it grows, which can give artichokes a bitter taste.

TZATZIKI SHRIMP CUCUMBER ROUNDS

I created these appetizers with what I had on hand one night, and now they're one of my husband's favorites. The garlicky sauce, bacon-wrapped shrimp and burst of cool cuke flavor make them irresistible.
—Shannon Trelease, East Hampton, NY

PREP: 25 min. • **COOK:** 10 min./batch
MAKES: 2 dozen

- ¼ cup reduced-fat plain yogurt
- 2 Tbsp. finely chopped peeled cucumber
- ⅛ tsp. garlic salt
- ⅛ tsp. dill weed
- 6 bacon strips
- 24 uncooked shrimp (31-40 per lb.), peeled and deveined
- 1 to 2 Tbsp. canola oil
- 2 medium cucumbers, cut into ¼-in. slices

1. In a small bowl, combine the yogurt, chopped cucumber, garlic salt and dill; set aside.
2. Cut each bacon strip in half widthwise and then lengthwise. Wrap a piece of bacon around each shrimp. Secure with toothpicks.
3. In a large nonstick skillet, heat oil over medium heat; cook shrimp in batches for 3-4 minutes on each side or until bacon is crisp.
4. Spoon a rounded ½ tsp. of the yogurt sauce onto each cucumber slice; top each with shrimp.
1 APPETIZER: *30 cal., 2g fat (0 sat. fat), 18mg chol., 64mg sod., 1g carb. (0 sugars, 0 fiber), 3g pro.*

SALMON WITH HORSERADISH PISTACHIO CRUST

Impress everyone at your table with this elegant but easy salmon. Feel free to switch up the ingredients to suit your tastes. You can substitute scallions for the shallots or try almonds or pecans instead of pistachios. The nutty coating also plays well with pork and chicken.
—Linda Press Wolfe, Cross River, NY

TAKES: 30 min. • **MAKES:** 6 servings

- 6   salmon fillets (4 oz. each)
- ⅓   cup sour cream
- ⅔   cup dry bread crumbs
- ⅔   cup chopped pistachios
- ½   cup minced shallots
- 2   Tbsp. olive oil
- 1   to 2 Tbsp. prepared horseradish
- 1   Tbsp. snipped fresh dill or
     1 tsp. dill weed
- ½   tsp. grated lemon or orange zest
- ¼   tsp. crushed red pepper flakes
- 1   garlic clove, minced

Preheat oven to 350°. Place salmon, skin side down, in an ungreased 15x10x1-in. baking pan. Spread sour cream over each fillet. Combine remaining ingredients. Pat crumb-nut mixture onto tops of salmon fillets, pressing to help coating adhere. Bake until fish just begins to flake easily with a fork, 12-15 minutes.

1 SALMON FILLET: *376 cal., 25g fat (5g sat. fat), 60mg chol., 219mg sod., 15g carb. (3g sugars, 2g fiber), 24g pro.*
DIABETIC EXCHANGES: *3 lean meat, 2 fat.*

> ### Holiday Helper
> Any nuts may be used instead of the pistachios. Some of our favorites are almonds and pecans.

BUTTERNUT SQUASH PANZANELLA SALAD

This colorful salad is easy to make—and it's even easier if you use precut chunks of butternut squash. You can use pecans in place of the almonds or watercress instead of the arugula or spinach.
—Nancy Buchanan, Costa Mesa, CA

PREP: 25 min. • **BAKE:** 20 min.
MAKES: 8 servings

- 6   cups cubed day-old French bread
     (bite-sized cubes)
- 3   Tbsp. olive oil
- ½   tsp. chili powder
- ¼   tsp. salt

SALAD
- 4   cups cubed peeled butternut squash
     (1½-in. cubes)
- 1½ cups sliced fresh mushrooms
- ½   cup olive oil, divided
- ½   tsp. salt, divided
- ½   tsp. pepper, divided
- 6   cups fresh arugula or fresh
     baby spinach
- 6   Tbsp. sherry vinegar
- 3   shallots, thinly sliced
- ½   cup salted roasted almonds
- 6   Tbsp. crumbled goat cheese

1. Preheat oven to 400°. Toss bread with oil, chili powder and salt. Spread evenly in an ungreased 15x10x1-in. baking pan. Bake until golden brown, about 5 minutes. Transfer to a large bowl; cool.
2. In another large bowl, combine squash and mushrooms. Add 2 Tbsp. oil, ¼ tsp. salt and ¼ tsp. pepper; toss to coat. Transfer to a greased 15x10x1-in. baking pan. Roast until tender, 20-25 minutes, stirring occasionally.
3. Add arugula and squash mixture to toasted bread. In a small bowl, whisk together vinegar, shallots and remaining oil, salt and pepper. Drizzle over salad; toss gently to combine. Top with almonds and goat cheese. Serve immediately.
¾ CUP: *361 cal., 26g fat (4g sat. fat), 7mg chol., 435mg sod., 29g carb. (5g sugars, 4g fiber), 7g pro.*

PEAR & POMEGRANATE LAMB TAGINE

Pomegranate, pear and orange go together so well that I decided to use them all in a Middle Eastern-themed tagine with lamb. This tastes delicious served over couscous, polenta, or cauliflower mashed with some feta cheese.
—Arlene Erlbach, Morton Grove, IL

PREP: 20 min. • **COOK:** 6 hours
MAKES: 4 servings

2½ lbs. lamb shanks
2   large pears, finely chopped
3   cups thinly sliced shallots
½   cup orange juice, divided
½   cup pomegranate juice, divided
1   Tbsp. honey
1½ tsp. ground cinnamon
1   tsp. salt
1   tsp. ground allspice
1   tsp. ground cardamom
¼   cup pomegranate seeds
¼   cup minced fresh parsley
    Cooked couscous, optional

1. Place lamb in a 5- or 6-qt. oval slow cooker. Add pears and shallots. Combine ¼ cup orange juice, ¼ cup pomegranate juice, honey and seasonings; add to slow cooker.
2. Cook, covered, on low until meat is tender, 6-8 hours. Remove lamb to a rimmed serving platter; keep warm. Stir remaining orange and pomegranate juices into cooking liquid; pour over lamb. Sprinkle with pomegranate seeds and parsley. If desired, serve over couscous.

½ LAMB SHANK WITH 1 CUP SHALLOT MIXTURE: *438 cal., 13g fat (5g sat. fat), 99mg chol., 680mg sod., 52g carb. (28g sugars, 5g fiber), 31g pro.*

> ### Holiday Helper
> Anjou pears are a smart choice for this recipe and are usually available from November through late spring.

ROASTED ASPARAGUS & TOMATOES

I have a habit of buying too much asparagus when I can get it, but I don't ever let it go to waste! I toss the crisp spears with cherry tomatoes and goat cheese for this side. Be sure to use high-quality goat cheese—it makes all the difference.
—Holly Battiste, Barrington, NJ

TAKES: 30 min. • **MAKES:** 4 servings

1   lb. fresh asparagus, trimmed
1   cup grape tomatoes
¼   cup coarsely chopped walnuts
1   Tbsp. olive oil
¼   tsp. dried oregano
¼   tsp. salt
¼   tsp. pepper
2   Tbsp. crumbled goat cheese
1   Tbsp. minced fresh basil

1. Preheat oven to 400°. Place asparagus, grape tomatoes and walnuts in a greased 15x10x1-in. baking pan. Mix oil, oregano, salt and pepper; add to asparagus mixture and toss to coat.
2. Roast until asparagus is crisp-tender, 15-20 minutes, turning the vegetables occasionally. Sprinkle with cheese. Top with basil before serving.
1 SERVING: *108 cal., 9g fat (2g sat. fat), 4mg chol., 173mg sod., 5g carb. (2g sugars, 2g fiber), 4g pro.*
DIABETIC EXCHANGES: *2 fat, 1 vegetable.*

MANGO GLACE WITH PINEAPPLE POMEGRANATE SALSA

I came up with these chilled bites on a 100-degree day, but they're refreshing any time of year. Citrusy fruits brighten the dark, cold days of winter. Very ripe fruit eliminates the need for added sugar.
—Jodi Taffel, Altadena, CA

PREP: 45 min. + freezing • **MAKES:** 1 dozen

- 4 medium ripe mangoes, peeled and chopped
- 1 fresh ripe pineapple, peeled and cut into ½-in. pieces
- 2 Tbsp. lime juice

SALSA
- 1 cup finely chopped fresh pineapple
- 2 Tbsp. pomegranate seeds
- 1 Tbsp. minced fresh mint

1. Combine mangoes, pineapple and lime juice in a blender. Cover and process until smooth. Strain through a fine-mesh strainer into a large bowl. Pour into 1¾-in. silicone ice cube trays. Freeze until firm, 8 hours or overnight.
2. Combine salsa ingredients; cover and refrigerate overnight.
3. Remove cubes from freezer 10 minutes before serving. Run a small spatula around the edge of each fruit cube to loosen; remove from trays. Serve with salsa.

1 CUBE WITH 4 TSP. SALSA: *114 cal., 1g fat (0 sat. fat), 0 chol., 2mg sod., 29g carb. (24g sugars, 3g fiber), 1g pro.*

HOW TO SEED A POMEGRANATE

Here's the simplest way to extract those tart little gems inside a pomegranate.

Cut the pomegranate in half along its middle. Hold it cut side down over a bowl of water, then, using a large spoon, give it a hearty smack on the skin. Keep smacking until all the seed pods—known as arils—fall from the white membrane into the bowl. Discard the skin and the membrane. Drain the water, reserving the arils. You can eat them whole, seeds and all.

ROSEMARY TURKEY BREAST

I season turkey with a blend of rosemary, garlic and paprika. I rub the mixture directly on the meat under the skin, so I can remove the skin before serving and not lose any of the flavor. The result is an entree that's lower in fat yet delicious. It makes the perfect centerpiece for holiday meals.
—Dorothy Pritchett, Wills Point, TX

PREP: 10 min. • **BAKE:** 1½ hours + standing
MAKES: 15 servings

- 2 Tbsp. olive oil
- 8 to 10 garlic cloves, peeled
- 3 Tbsp. chopped fresh rosemary or 3 tsp. dried rosemary, crushed
- 1 tsp. salt
- 1 tsp. paprika
- ½ tsp. coarsely ground pepper
- 1 bone-in turkey breast (5 lbs.)

1. In a food processor, combine the oil, garlic, rosemary, salt, paprika and pepper; process until garlic is coarsely chopped.
2. With your fingers, carefully loosen skin from both sides of turkey breast. Spread half the garlic mixture over the meat under the skin. Smooth skin over meat and secure to underside of breast with toothpicks. Spread remaining garlic mixture over turkey skin.
3. Place the turkey breast on a rack in a shallow roasting pan. Bake turkey breast, uncovered, at 325° until a thermometer reads 165°, 1½-2 hours. (Cover loosely with foil if the turkey browns too quickly.) Let stand for 15 minutes before slicing. Discard toothpicks.

4 OZ. COOKED TURKEY: *148 cal., 3g fat (0 sat. fat), 78mg chol., 207mg sod., 1g carb. (0 sugars, 0 fiber), 29g pro.*
DIABETIC EXCHANGES: *4 lean meat.*

SLOW-COOKER TEQUILA POACHED PEARS

If you're looking for a unique dessert, try this one. Tequila is deliciously refreshing paired with fresh pears and mint. Bring out this creative dinner finale when you want to impress guests.
—Nancy Heishman, Las Vegas, NV

PREP: 20 min. • **COOK:** 4 hours
MAKES: 8 servings

- 2 cups water
- 1 can (11.3 oz.) pear nectar
- 1 cup tequila
- ½ cup sugar
- 2 Tbsp. lime juice
- 2 tsp. grated lime zest
- 1 cinnamon stick (3 in.)
- ¼ tsp. ground nutmeg
- 8 whole Anjou pears, peeled
  Sweetened whipped cream, optional
  Fresh mint leaves

1. In a large saucepan, combine first 8 ingredients. Bring mixture to a boil over medium-high heat; boil 2 minutes, stirring constantly.
2. Place pears in a 4- or 5-qt. slow cooker; add liquid. Cook, covered, on low until tender, 4-5 hours. Remove cinnamon stick and discard. Pour 3 cups cooking liquid into a small saucepan. Bring to a boil; cook, uncovered, until liquid is reduced to 1 cup, about 20 minutes.
3. Halve pears lengthwise and core them. Serve with sauce, whipped cream if desired, and mint leaves.

1 PEAR WITH 2 TBSP. SAUCE: *155 cal., 0 fat (0 sat. fat), 0 chol., 3mg sod., 40g carb. (30g sugars, 6g fiber), 1g pro.*

HONEY-MUSTARD BRUSSELS SPROUTS SALAD

Even if you dislike Brussels sprouts, you'll love this salad. The dressing is tasty and pairs nicely with the apples, grapes and walnuts. Add whatever cheese, nuts or fruit you prefer.
—Sheila Sturrock, Coldwater, ON

- -

TAKES: 25 min. • **MAKES:** 10 servings

- 1 lb. fresh Brussels sprouts, trimmed and shredded
- 2 medium tart apples, chopped
- 1 medium red onion, chopped
- 1 small sweet orange pepper, chopped
- ½ cup chopped walnuts
- ½ cup green grapes, sliced
- ½ cup shredded cheddar cheese
- 3 bacon strips, cooked and crumbled
- ¼ cup olive oil
- 2 Tbsp. red wine vinegar
- 2 Tbsp. honey mustard
- 1 garlic clove, minced
- ¼ tsp. salt
- ¼ tsp. pepper

In a large bowl, combine the first 8 ingredients. In a small bowl, whisk the remaining ingredients; pour over salad. Toss to coat.
1 CUP: *170 cal., 12g fat (3g sat. fat), 8mg chol., 177mg sod., 13g carb. (7g sugars, 3g fiber), 5g pro.*
DIABETIC EXCHANGES: *2 fat, 1 starch.*

ALMOND-PECAN DATE TRUFFLES

My daughter and I came across a date candy recipe when she was learning about ancient Egypt. We changed some of the spices and nuts to suit our taste. My mom always made a coconut date ball for Christmas. The truffles remind me of past Christmases and are ideal when you're in need of something quick yet festive on a holiday tray.
—Lori Daniels, Beverly, WV

- -

PREP: 20 min. + chilling • **MAKES:** about 1½ dozen

- ⅓ cup apple juice
- 1 pkg. (8 oz.) chopped dates
- 1 cup finely chopped pecans, toasted
- 1¼ tsp. ground cinnamon
- ¼ tsp. ground nutmeg
- 1 cup ground almonds, toasted

1. In a microwave, warm apple juice. Stir in dates; let stand 5 minutes to soften, stirring occasionally. Remove dates from apple juice; discard liquid. Transfer dates to bowl of a food processor fitted with the blade attachment; process until smooth. Add pecans and spices; pulse just until combined (mixture will be thick).
2. Shape mixture into 1-in. balls; place on a waxed paper-lined baking sheet. Refrigerate, covered, 30-60 minutes.
3. Roll date balls in almonds.
1 DATE BALL: *109 cal., 7g fat (1g sat. fat), 0 chol., 0 sod., 12g carb. (9g sugars, 2g fiber), 2g pro.*

Holiday Helper

To toast nuts, bake in a shallow pan in a 350° oven for 5-10 minutes or cook in a skillet over low heat until lightly browned, stirring occasionally.

AUTUMN BISQUE

I like cozy comfort soups that have a creamy texture—without the cream. This one's full of good stuff such as rutabagas, leeks, fresh herbs and almond milk.
—Merry Graham, Newhall, CA

PREP: 25 min. • **COOK:** 50 min.
MAKES: 12 servings (3 qt.)

- ¼ cup dairy-free spreadable margarine
- 2 tsp. minced fresh chives
- 2 tsp. minced fresh parsley
- ½ tsp. grated lemon zest

BISQUE

- 2 Tbsp. olive oil
- 2 large rutabagas, peeled and cubed (about 9 cups)
- 1 large celery root, peeled and cubed (about 3 cups)
- 3 medium leeks (white portion only), chopped (about 2 cups)
- 1 large carrot, cubed (about ⅔ cup)
- 3 garlic cloves, minced
- 7 cups vegetable stock
- 2 tsp. minced fresh thyme
- 1½ tsp. minced fresh rosemary
- 1 tsp. salt
- ½ tsp. coarsely ground pepper
- 2 cups almond milk
- 2 Tbsp. minced fresh chives

1. Mix first 4 ingredients. Using a melon baller or 1-tsp. measuring spoon, shape mixture into 12 balls. Freeze balls on a waxed paper-lined baking sheet until firm. Transfer to a freezer container; freeze up to 2 months.

2. In a 6-qt. stock pot, heat the oil over medium heat; saute rutabagas, celery root, leeks and carrot for 8 minutes. Add garlic; cook and stir for 2 minutes. Stir in stock, herbs, salt and pepper; bring to a boil. Reduce heat; simmer, covered, until vegetables are tender, 30-35 minutes.

3. Puree soup using an immersion blender. Or cool slightly and puree in batches in a blender; return to pan. Stir in milk; heat through. Remove herbed margarine from freezer 15 minutes before serving. Top servings with chives and margarine.

1 CUP: *146 cal., 7g fat (2g sat. fat), 0 chol., 672mg sod., 20g carb. (9g sugars, 5g fiber), 3g pro.*
DIABETIC EXCHANGES: *1 starch, 1 fat.*

ORANGE-GLAZED PORK LOIN

Here's one of the best pork recipes I've ever tried. My family looks forward to this roast, and guests always ask for the recipe. The flavorful rub and a glaze spiked with orange juice are also outstanding on pork chops.
—Lynnette Miete, Alna, ME

PREP: 10 min.
BAKE: 1 hour 20 min. + standing
MAKES: 16 servings

- 1 tsp. salt
- 1 garlic clove, minced
- 2 to 3 fresh thyme sprigs or ¼ tsp. dried thyme
- ¼ tsp. ground ginger
- ¼ tsp. pepper
- 1 boneless pork loin roast (5 lbs.)

GLAZE

- 1 cup orange juice
- ¼ cup packed brown sugar
- 1 Tbsp. Dijon mustard
- ⅓ cup cold water
- 1 Tbsp. cornstarch

1. Preheat oven to 350°. Combine first 5 ingredients; rub over roast. Place fat side up on a rack in a shallow roasting pan. Bake, uncovered, for 1 hour.

2. Meanwhile, in a saucepan over medium heat, combine orange juice, brown sugar and mustard. In a small bowl, mix water and cornstarch until smooth. Add to the orange juice mixture. Bring to a boil; cook and stir 2 minutes. Reserve 1 cup glaze for serving; brush half of remaining glaze over pork roast.

3. Bake pork until a thermometer reads 145°, 20-40 minutes longer, brushing occasionally with remaining glaze. Let stand 10 minutes before slicing. Reheat reserved glaze; serve with roast.

4 OZ. COOKED PORK WITH 1 TBSP. GLAZE: *199 cal., 7g fat (2g sat. fat), 71mg chol., 212mg sod., 6g carb. (5g sugars, 0 fiber), 28g pro.*
DIABETIC EXCHANGES: *4 lean meat, ½ starch.*

DIPPED & DRIZZLED COOKIES

*Christmas cookies fresh from the oven are divine,
but those that are dipped or drizzled are twice as fine!
Pour a glass of milk and grab a stack of napkins—
these treasures are worth every ooey, gooey bite.*

HAZELNUT-ESPRESSO SANDWICH COOKIES

The inspiration for this cute cookie came from my sister's description of a hazelnut cookie she tried in Italy. She declared my version to be a wonderful approximation. My kids like to help fill them.
—Cindy Beberman, Orland Park, IL

PREP: 45 min. + chilling
BAKE: 10 min./batch + cooling
MAKES: 3 dozen

- 1 cup butter, softened
- 1¼ cups sugar
- 1 large egg, room temperature
- 1 large egg yolk, room temperature
- 4 tsp. instant espresso granules
- 2 tsp. vanilla extract
- 2½ cups all-purpose flour
- ½ tsp. salt
- ½ tsp. baking powder
- 1 cup finely ground hazelnuts

FILLING
- 1¾ cups semisweet chocolate chips, divided
- 1¼ cups milk chocolate chips
- 1 cup heavy whipping cream

1. In a large bowl, cream butter and sugar until light and fluffy, 5-7 minutes. Beat in the egg, yolk, espresso granules and vanilla. Combine flour, salt and baking powder; gradually add to the creamed mixture and mix well. Stir in hazelnuts.

2. Divide dough into thirds; flatten each portion into a circle. Wrap separately and refrigerate for 1 hour or until easy to handle.

3. On a lightly floured surface, roll out 1 portion of dough to ⅛-in. thickness. Cut with a floured 1½-in. cookie cutter; place ½ in. apart on ungreased baking sheets. Repeat with remaining dough; chill and reroll scraps.

4. Bake at 375° for 6-8 minutes or until the edges begin to brown. Remove to wire racks to cool.

5. For filling, place ¾ cup semisweet chocolate chips and the milk chocolate chips in a small bowl. In a small saucepan, bring cream just to a boil. Pour over the chocolate; whisk until smooth. Refrigerate until the filling reaches spreading consistency, about 1½ hours, stirring occasionally.

6. Spread filling over the bottoms of half of the cookies; top with remaining cookies. In a microwave, melt the remaining 1 cup semisweet chips; stir until smooth. Drizzle over cookies. Let stand until set. Store in an airtight container in the refrigerator.

1 SANDWICH COOKIE: *214 cal., 13g fat (7g sat. fat), 35mg chol., 85mg sod., 23g carb. (15g sugars, 1g fiber), 2g pro.*

SNOW-CAPPED MOCHA FUDGE DROPS

Everyone loves seeing chocolate on a cookie tray. My version is fudgy with a hint of mocha. If you're serving these at the holidays, add red and green colored sugar or sprinkles for a festive touch.
—Patricia Harmon, Baden, PA

- -

PREP: 40 min.
BAKE: 10 min./batch + cooling
MAKES: about 3½ dozen

- 1 cup semisweet chocolate chips, divided
- ½ cup butter, cubed
- 1 Tbsp. instant coffee granules or espresso powder
- ¾ cup sugar
- ¾ cup packed brown sugar
- 2 large eggs, room temperature
- 2 tsp. vanilla extract
- 2 cups all-purpose flour
- ¼ cup baking cocoa
- ½ tsp. baking powder
- ¼ tsp. salt
- ½ cup chopped pecans or walnuts
- 10 oz. white candy coating, melted
  White edible glitter and/or red and green colored sugar

1. Preheat the oven to 350°. In a large microwave-safe bowl, microwave ½ cup chocolate chips and the butter until the butter is melted; stir until the chocolate is melted. Stir in coffee granules; cool slightly.

2. Whisk in sugars. Whisk in eggs, 1 at a time, and vanilla until blended. In a small bowl, whisk flour, cocoa, baking powder and salt; stir into chocolate mixture. Stir in the pecans and the remaining ½ cup chocolate chips.

3. Drop dough by tablespoonfuls 1 in. apart onto ungreased baking sheets. Bake until set, 8-10 minutes. Cool on pans for 2 minutes. Remove to wire racks to cool completely.

4. Dip tops of cookies into melted candy coating; sprinkle with glitter and/or colored sugar. Let stand until set.

1 COOKIE: *131 cal., 6g fat (4g sat. fat), 15mg chol., 43mg sod., 19g carb. (13g sugars, 1g fiber), 1g pro.*

COCONUT KEY LIME THUMBPRINTS

Here's the cookie I created for the Las Vegas World Food Championships in 2013. It's similar to a shortbread thumbprint, but with more personality.
—Amy Freeze, Avon Park, FL

- -

PREP: 40 min. + cooling
BAKE: 15 min./batch + cooling
MAKES: about 2½ dozen

- 2 Tbsp. cornstarch
- ⅔ cup Key lime juice
- ¾ cup sugar
- 2 large egg yolks

COOKIES
- 1 cup butter, softened
- ½ cup confectioners' sugar
- ⅛ tsp. salt
- 1 tsp. vanilla extract
- ½ tsp. coconut extract
- 2 cups all-purpose flour
- 2 large egg whites
- 2 tsp. water
- 2½ cups sweetened shredded coconut

DRIZZLE
- 4 oz. white baking chocolate, chopped
- 1 Tbsp. shortening

1. For lime curd, in a small saucepan, whisk cornstarch and lime juice until smooth. Whisk in sugar and egg yolks; cook and stir over medium heat until boiling. Transfer to a bowl; cool slightly. Press plastic wrap onto surface of curd; refrigerate until cold.

2. Preheat oven to 400°. Cream butter, confectioners' sugar and salt until light and fluffy, 5-7 minutes. Beat in extracts. Gradually beat in flour.

3. In a small bowl, whisk together egg whites and water. Place coconut in a separate bowl. Shape dough into 1¼-in. balls. Dip balls in egg whites, then roll in coconut, coating well. Place 2 in. apart on parchment-lined baking sheets. Press a deep indentation in the center of each with the handle of a wooden spoon. Bake until edges are golden brown, 12-14 minutes.

4. Reshape indentations as needed. Cool on pans 5 minutes. Remove to wire racks to cool completely.

5. Fill each cookie with about 1½ tsp. curd. In a microwave, melt the white chocolate and shortening; stir until smooth. Drizzle over cookies.

1 COOKIE: *182 cal., 11g fat (7g sat. fat), 29mg chol., 76mg sod., 21g carb. (13g sugars, 1g fiber), 2g pro.*

CASHEW GINGER COOKIE TWISTS

Here's a fun cookie for a party or cookie exchange. After the white chocolate sets, you can dip the other side of the twists into melted dark chocolate and sprinkle with orange zest or finely chopped cashews.
—Carole Holt, St. Paul, MN

PREP: 55 min. + chilling
BAKE: 10 min./batch + cooling
MAKES: 40 cookies

- ¾ cup butter, softened
- ⅓ cup confectioners' sugar
- 1½ tsp. grated orange zest
- ¼ tsp. ground ginger
- 1 large egg, room temperature
- ¾ tsp. vanilla extract
- 2 cups all-purpose flour, divided
- ½ cup honey-roasted cashews
- 1½ cups white baking chips
- 1 Tbsp. shortening
- ⅓ cup finely chopped crystallized ginger

1. Beat first 4 ingredients until blended; beat in egg and vanilla. Place ¼ cup flour and cashews in a food processor; pulse until cashews are ground. Add the remaining 1¾ cups flour; pulse to blend. Gradually beat the flour mixture into butter mixture.
2. Divide dough in half; shape each into a 10-in.-long log. Wrap and refrigerate until firm, about 1 hour.
3. Preheat oven to 375°. Unwrap and cut each log into twenty ½-in. slices. Roll each slice into an 8-in. rope; shape each rope into a pretzel. Place pretzels 2 in. apart on ungreased baking sheets.
4. Bake until the edges are light brown, 8-10 minutes. Cool on pans 2 minutes. Remove to wire racks to cool completely.
5. In a microwave, melt baking chips and shortening; stir until smooth. Dip tops of cookies in baking chips; sprinkle with crystallized ginger. Let stand until set.
1 COOKIE: *113 cal., 7g fat (4g sat. fat), 15mg chol., 42mg sod., 12g carb. (6g sugars, 0 fiber), 1g pro.*

JAMAICAN CHOCOLATE COOKIES WITH CARAMEL CREME

I made these for an office party cookie contest—and not a crumb was left on the platter! Sweet potatoes are the secret ingredient. Canned sweet potatoes will work, too, if you're short on time.
—Noelle Myers, Grand Forks, ND

PREP: 45 min. + standing
BAKE: 10 min./batch + cooling
MAKES: about 2½ dozen sandwich cookies

- 1 pkg. (11½ oz.) semisweet chocolate chunks, divided
- ½ cup butter, softened
- ½ cup confectioners' sugar
- ½ cup mashed sweet potatoes
- 1 tsp. minced fresh gingerroot
- ½ tsp. vanilla extract
- 1¼ cups all-purpose flour
- ¼ cup cornstarch
- 2 Tbsp. baking cocoa
- 1½ tsp. baking powder
- ¼ tsp. baking soda
- ¼ tsp. plus ⅛ tsp. salt, divided
- ⅔ cup whipped cream cheese
- ⅓ cup dulce de leche
- 2 Tbsp. sweetened condensed milk
- ⅛ tsp. ground cinnamon
- ⅛ tsp. ground allspice

1. Preheat oven to 375°. In a microwave, melt ⅔ cup chocolate chunks; stir until smooth. Cool slightly. In a large bowl, cream butter and confectioners' sugar until light and fluffy, 5-7 minutes. Beat in the sweet potatoes, cooled chocolate, ginger and vanilla. In another bowl, whisk the flour, cornstarch, baking cocoa, baking powder, baking soda and ¼ tsp. salt; gradually beat into the creamed mixture.
2. Shape dough into ¾-in. balls; place 2½ in. apart on parchment-lined baking sheets. Flatten slightly with bottom of a glass dipped in confectioners' sugar. Bake until edges are firm, 8-10 minutes. Remove cookies from pans to wire racks to cool completely.
3. Meanwhile, whisk cream cheese, dulce de leche, sweetened condensed milk, cinnamon, allspice and remaining ⅛ tsp. salt until smooth. Spread filling on bottoms of half of the cookies; cover with the remaining cookies.
4. For chocolate coating, microwave remaining chocolate chunks; stir until smooth. Dip cookies halfway into the chocolate; let stand until set. Store between pieces of waxed paper in an airtight container in the refrigerator.
1 SANDWICH COOKIE: *134 cal., 7g fat (5g sat. fat), 12mg chol., 103mg sod., 17g carb. (10g sugars, 1g fiber), 2g pro.*

FRUITCAKE COOKIES WITH RUM GLAZE

These gems are like fruitcake—only better! If you choose to omit the rum, you may wish to increase the rum extract for flavor.
—Sheila Joan Suhan, Scottdale, PA

PREP: 45 min. + cooling
BAKE: 15 min./batch + cooling
MAKES: about 4 dozen

- 1 cup golden raisins
- ¾ cup dried cherries
- ½ cup diced dried apricots
- ¾ cup water
- ¼ cup rum or additional water
- ¾ cup chopped pecans
- ⅓ cup diced crystallized ginger
- ⅓ cup diced candied orange peel
- 1 cup butter, softened
- 2 cups sugar, divided
- 2 large eggs, room temperature
- 1½ tsp. rum extract
- 3½ cups all-purpose flour
- 1 tsp. baking soda
- ½ tsp. salt

GLAZE
- 3 cups confectioners' sugar
- 3 to 5 Tbsp. 2% milk
- 3 Tbsp. rum or additional milk

1. Place first 5 ingredients in a small saucepan; bring to a boil. Reduce heat; simmer, uncovered, until liquid is almost absorbed, 12-15 minutes. Cool completely. Stir in pecans, ginger and orange peel.
2. Cream butter and 1½ cups sugar until light and fluffy, 5-7 minutes. Beat in eggs and extract. Whisk together flour, baking soda and salt; gradually beat into creamed mixture. Stir in fruit mixture.
3. Place the remaining ½ cup sugar in a shallow bowl. Shape 2 Tbsp. of dough into balls; toss in sugar to coat lightly. Place 2 in. apart on parchment-lined baking sheets.

4. Bake at 350° until golden brown and just set, 11-13 minutes. Remove from pans to wire racks; cool completely.
5. Mix glaze ingredients. Drizzle glaze over cooled cookies.
1 COOKIE: 176 cal., 5g fat (3g sat. fat), 18mg chol., 92mg sod., 31g carb. (21g sugars, 1g fiber), 2g pro.

Holiday Helper

If you don't have parchment, you can bake these cookies on greased baking sheets. But be sure to use a metal spatula when removing them because they'll stick just a bit.

DOUBLE-DRIZZLED BISCOTTI

Semisweet and white chocolate drizzles give these a pretty look. The baking time is shorter than with other biscotti recipes, so they're a little softer.
—Cheryl Ludemann, Boonville, NY

PREP: 25 min. • **BAKE:** 30 min. + cooling
MAKES: about 3 dozen

- ¾ cup butter, softened
- 1 cup sugar
- 3 large eggs, room temperature
- 1 tsp. almond extract
- 1 tsp. vanilla extract
- 3 cups all-purpose flour
- 2 Tbsp. aniseed
- 1½ tsp. baking powder
- ¼ tsp. salt
- 1 cup chopped walnuts
- ⅓ cup semisweet chocolate chips
- 2 tsp. shortening, divided
- ⅓ cup white baking chips

1. Preheat oven to 350°. In a large bowl, cream butter and sugar until light and fluffy, 5-7 minutes. Beat in the eggs and extracts. In a small bowl, whisk the flour, aniseed, baking powder and salt; gradually beat into the creamed mixture. Stir in the walnuts.
2. Divide dough in half. On an ungreased baking sheet, shape each half into a 14x2-in. rectangle. Bake 15-20 minutes or until firm to the touch.
3. Cool on pans on wire racks until cool enough to handle. Transfer the baked rectangles to a cutting board. Using a serrated knife, cut diagonally into ½-in. slices. Place on ungreased baking sheets, cut side down. Bake 6-7 minutes on each side or until golden brown. Remove from pans to wire racks to cool completely.
4. In a microwave, melt semisweet chips and 1 tsp. shortening; stir until smooth. Drizzle over biscotti. In a microwave, melt white chips and remaining shortening; stir until smooth. Drizzle over biscotti.
1 COOKIE: *126 cal., 7g fat (3g sat. fat), 25mg chol., 61mg sod., 14g carb. (7g sugars, 1g fiber), 2g pro.*

SNOWY MOUNTAIN COOKIES

I was excited to bake these with my mom after coming home from studying abroad in Germany. The cookies remind me of the Swabian Alps I could see from my room there. Be careful not to overheat the white chocolate; it will lose that attractive shine.
—Stephanie Bouley, North Smithfield, RI

PREP: 20 min. + chilling
BAKE: 10 min./batch. + cooling
MAKES: about 7 dozen

- 1¼ cups butter, softened
- 1 cup sugar
- 2 large eggs, room temperature
- 1 Tbsp. vanilla extract
- 4 cups all-purpose flour
- 1 tsp. salt
- 1 pkg. (10 oz.) miniature semisweet chocolate chips
- 1 cup finely chopped walnuts, optional
- 1 pkg. (10 to 12 oz.) white baking chips
  White nonpareils

1. Cream butter and sugar until light and fluffy, 5-7 minutes. Beat in eggs and vanilla. In another bowl, whisk flour and salt; gradually beat into the creamed mixture. Add chocolate chips and, if desired, walnuts; mix well. Divide dough in half. Shape each into a disk; wrap and refrigerate until firm enough to roll, about 30 minutes.
2. Preheat oven to 325°. On a lightly floured surface, roll each portion of dough to ¼-in. thickness. Cut with a floured 2-in. triangle-shaped cookie cutter. Place 2 in. apart on ungreased baking sheets. Bake until edges begin to brown, 10-12 minutes. Cool on pans 2 minutes. Remove to wire racks to cool completely.
3. Meanwhile, in a microwave, melt the white baking chips; stir until smooth. Dip cookie tops in melted chips; sprinkle with nonpareils. Let stand until set.
1 COOKIE: *99 cal., 5g fat (3g sat. fat), 13mg chol., 56mg sod., 12g carb. (7g sugars, 0 fiber), 1g pro.*

RED VELVET PEPPERMINT THUMBPRINTS

I love red velvet cookies and cakes. In this pretty thumbprint, I added my favorite holiday ingredient: peppermint. It's a fun seasonal twist!
—*Priscilla Yee, Concord, CA*

- -

PREP: 30 min.
BAKE: 10 min./batch + cooling
MAKES: about 4 dozen

1	cup butter, softened
1	cup sugar
1	large egg, room temperature
4	tsp. red food coloring
1	tsp. peppermint extract
2½	cups all-purpose flour
3	Tbsp. baking cocoa
1	tsp. baking powder
¼	tsp. salt
2	cups white baking chips
2	tsp. canola oil
¼	cup crushed peppermint candies

1. Preheat oven to 350°. In a large bowl, cream butter and sugar until light and fluffy, 5-7 minutes. Beat in egg, food coloring and extract. In another bowl, whisk flour, cocoa, baking powder and salt; gradually beat into creamed mixture.
2. Shape dough into 1-in. balls. Place 1 in. apart on ungreased baking sheets. Press a deep indentation in the center of each with the end of a wooden spoon handle.
3. Bake 9-11 minutes or until set. Remove cookies from pans to wire racks to cool completely.
4. In a microwave, melt baking chips with the oil; stir until smooth. Spoon a scant teaspoon filling into each cookie. Drizzle tops with remaining mixture. Sprinkle with peppermint candies. Let stand until set.
1 COOKIE: *118 cal., 7g fat (4g sat. fat), 16mg chol., 63mg sod., 14g carb. (9g sugars, 0 fiber), 1g pro.*

DOUBLE-DIPPED SHORTBREAD COOKIES

My mom and her friend did a lot of cookie swaps together. They were always finding new recipes to share, including this one. There's something about a dipped cookie that makes it seem so special, so we usually save these for the holidays.
—*Ginger King, Big Bear Lake, CA*

- -

PREP: 15 min. + chilling
BAKE: 10 min./batch + cooling
MAKES: about 2½ dozen

¾	cup butter, softened
1½	cups confectioners' sugar
3	oz. semisweet chocolate, melted and cooled
1	tsp. vanilla extract
1½	cups all-purpose flour
2	tsp. baking cocoa
⅛	tsp. salt
3	oz. semisweet chocolate, chopped
¼	cup heavy whipping cream
4	oz. white baking chocolate, chopped

1. Cream butter and confectioners' sugar until light and fluffy, 5-7 minutes. Beat in melted chocolate and the vanilla. In another bowl, whisk flour, cocoa and salt; gradually beat into the creamed mixture. Shape rounded tablespoonfuls of dough into 2-in.-long logs. Place 2 in. apart on ungreased baking sheets. Refrigerate, covered, for 1 hour.
2. Preheat oven to 350°. Bake cookies until edges are set, 8-10 minutes. Cool on pans 2 minutes. Remove to wire racks to cool completely.
3. In a microwave, melt semisweet chocolate with cream; stir until smooth. Dip each cookie halfway into chocolate; allow excess to drip off. Place on waxed paper. In the microwave, melt white chocolate; stir until smooth. Drizzle cookies with melted white chocolate. Let stand until set.
1 COOKIE: *137 cal., 8g fat (5g sat. fat), 14mg chol., 47mg sod., 14g carb. (9g sugars, 0 fiber), 1g pro.*

CHOCOLATE ALMOND CRESCENTS

If you like chocolate-covered almonds, you're in for a treat, cookie-style. These buttery crescents make a thoughtful gift.
—*Vicki Raatz, Waterloo, WI*

PREP: 20 min. + chilling • **BAKE:** 10 min./batch + cooling
MAKES: 6 dozen

1¼ cups butter, softened
⅔ cup sugar
2 cups finely chopped almonds
1½ tsp. vanilla extract
2 cups all-purpose flour
½ cup baking cocoa
⅛ tsp. salt
1¼ cups semisweet chocolate chips, melted
1 to 2 Tbsp. confectioners' sugar
Sweetened shredded coconut, optional

1. In a large bowl, cream butter and sugar until light and fluffy, 5-7 minutes. Beat in almonds and vanilla. In another bowl, whisk flour, cocoa and salt; gradually beat into the creamed mixture. Refrigerate, covered, 2 hours or until firm enough to shape.
2. Preheat oven to 350°. Shape 2 tsp. of dough into 2-in.-long logs. Form each log into a crescent. Place crescents 2 in. apart on ungreased baking sheets. Bake 10-12 minutes or until set. Remove from pans to wire racks to cool completely.
3. Dip cookies halfway into melted chocolate, allowing excess to drip off. Place on waxed paper. If desired, sprinkle with coconut. Let stand until set. Cover dipped ends of cookies with waxed paper; dust undipped ends with confectioners' sugar. Store between pieces of waxed paper in airtight containers.
1 COOKIE: *85 cal., 6g fat (3g sat. fat), 8mg chol., 27mg sod., 7g carb. (4g sugars, 1g fiber), 1g pro.*

PISTACHIO SHORTBREAD SANDWICHES

I tasted these melt-in-your-mouth morsels at a Christmas party some years ago, and I have since tweaked the recipe to include pistachios. The cookies disappear so quickly at parties, you just might have to watch the plate—and check the kids' pockets!
—Lorraine Caland, Shuniah, ON

PREP: 20 min.
BAKE: 20 min./batch + cooling
MAKES: about 1½ dozen

- 1¼ cups unsalted butter, softened
- 1 cup sugar
- 1 tsp. vanilla extract
- 2 cups all-purpose flour
- ½ tsp. salt
- 2 cups ground pistachios
  Confectioners' sugar
- ⅔ cup apricot preserves

GLAZE (OPTIONAL)
- 1½ cups confectioners' sugar
- 4 tsp. lemon juice

1. Cream butter and sugar until light and fluffy, 5-7 minutes. Beat in vanilla. In another bowl, whisk flour and salt; gradually beat into the creamed mixture. Stir in pistachios.
2. Preheat oven to 300°. On a surface sprinkled with confectioners' sugar, roll dough to ¼-in. thickness. Cut with a 2½-in. fluted round cookie cutter dusted with confectioners' sugar. Place cookies 1 in. apart on ungreased baking sheets. Bake until the edges begin to brown, 18-20 minutes. Cool on pans 5 minutes. Remove to wire racks to cool completely.
3. Spread preserves on bottoms of half of the cookies; cover with remaining cookies. If desired, combine confectioners' sugar and lemon juice until smooth. Drizzle over cool cookies.
1 SANDWICH COOKIE: *314 cal., 19g fat (9g sat. fat), 34mg chol., 131mg sod., 33g carb. (17g sugars, 2g fiber), 5g pro.*

PEANUT BUTTER SPRITZ FINGERS

We love these cookies because they satisfy the need for chocolate and for something crunchy, sweet and nutty, all in just one bite!
—Irma Lowery, Reedsburg, WI

PREP: 25 min. + chilling
BAKE: 10 min./batch + standing
MAKES: about 4½ dozen

- ½ cup butter, softened
- ½ cup creamy peanut butter
- ½ cup sugar
- ½ cup packed brown sugar
- 1 large egg, room temperature
- 1 tsp. vanilla extract
- 1½ cups all-purpose flour
- ¾ tsp. baking soda
- ½ tsp. baking powder
- ¼ tsp. salt
- 3 milk chocolate candy bars (4 oz. each), chopped
- 1 cup finely chopped unsalted peanuts

1. In a large bowl, cream butter, peanut butter and sugars until light and fluffy, 5-7 minutes. Beat in egg and vanilla. In another bowl, combine the flour, baking soda, baking powder and salt; gradually add to creamed mixture and mix well. Cover dough and refrigerate 30 minutes or until easy to handle.
2. Using a cookie press fitted with a star disk, press dough into long strips, 2 in. apart, onto ungreased baking sheets. Cut each strip into 2-in. pieces (do not separate pieces).
3. Bake at 350° for 7-9 minutes or until cookies are golden brown. Remove to wire racks to cool.
4. In a microwave, melt candy bars; stir until smooth. Dip 1 end of each cookie into chocolate; allow excess to drip off. Coat with peanuts. Place on waxed paper; let stand until set.
1 COOKIE: *85 cal., 5g fat (2g sat. fat), 9mg chol., 65mg sod., 9g carb. (5g sugars, 0 fiber), 2g pro.*

CHOCOLATE COCONUT NEAPOLITANS

These yummy striped cookies with a chocolaty twist are easy and fun to make, but they do need some time in the freezer.
—Lena Marie Brownell, Rockland, MA

PREP: 30 min. + freezing
BAKE: 15 min./batch • **MAKES:** 5½ dozen

- 1 cup butter, softened
- 1½ cups sugar
- 1 large egg, room temperature
- 1 tsp. vanilla extract
- 2½ cups all-purpose flour
- 1½ tsp. baking powder
- ½ tsp. salt
- 1 tsp. almond extract
- 4 drops red food coloring
- ½ cup sweetened shredded coconut, finely chopped
- 4½ tsp. chocolate syrup
- ½ cup semisweet chocolate chips
- 1½ tsp. shortening

1. Line a 9x5-in. loaf pan with waxed paper; set aside. In a large bowl, cream butter and sugar until light and fluffy, 5-7 minutes. Beat in the egg and vanilla. Combine the flour, baking powder and salt; gradually add to creamed mixture and mix well.

2. Divide dough into thirds. Add almond extract and red food coloring to 1 portion; spread evenly into prepared pan. Add the coconut to second portion; spread evenly over first layer. Add chocolate syrup to the third portion; spread over second layer. Cover with foil; freeze for 4 hours or overnight.

3. Unwrap loaf and cut in half lengthwise. Cut each portion widthwise into ¼-in. slices. Place 2 in. apart on ungreased baking sheets. Bake at 350° until the edges are lightly browned, 12-14 minutes. Remove to wire racks to cool.

4. In a microwave, melt chocolate chips and shortening; stir until smooth. Dip 1 end of each cookie into chocolate; allow excess to drip off. Place on waxed paper; let stand until set.

1 COOKIE: *72 cal., 4g fat (2g sat. fat), 11mg chol., 58mg sod., 10g carb. (6g sugars, 0 fiber), 1g pro.*

CHOCOLATE-DIPPED ORANGE COOKIES

These tender cookies will make a pretty addition to your cookie platter—and the combination of cream cheese, orange, chocolate and almonds makes them irresistible.
—Linda Call, Falun, KS

PREP: 40 min. • **BAKE:** 20 min./batch + cooling
MAKES: about 6 dozen

- 1 cup butter, softened
- 1 pkg. (8 oz.) cream cheese, softened
- 1 cup sugar
- ½ tsp. salt
- 2 Tbsp. grated orange zest
- ½ tsp. vanilla extract
- 2½ cups all-purpose flour
- 1 cup finely chopped blanched almonds

GLAZE
- 5 oz. semisweet chocolate, chopped
- 3 Tbsp. butter
- ¼ cup finely chopped blanched almonds

1. Preheat oven to 325°. In a large bowl, beat butter, cream cheese, sugar and salt until blended. Beat in orange zest and vanilla. Gradually beat in flour. Stir in almonds.
2. Shape dough into 1-in. balls; place 2 in. apart on ungreased baking sheets. Flatten with bottom of a glass dipped in sugar. Bake until firm, 20-25 minutes. Remove from pans to wire racks to cool completely.
3. For glaze, in a microwave, melt chocolate and butter; stir until smooth. Dip each cookie halfway in chocolate; allow excess to drip off. Sprinkle with almonds. Place on waxed paper; let stand until set.
1 COOKIE: *81 cal., 6g fat (3g sat. fat), 12mg chol., 57mg sod., 7g carb. (3g sugars, 0 fiber), 1g pro.*

RED VELVET CAKE BITES

Add something a little different to your cookie tray this year. We love red velvet for these bites, but any cake mix flavor can work. I've rolled chopped macadamia nuts into pineapple cake and dipped them into white chocolate. Whatever you do, have fun!
—Anne Powers, Munford, AL

PREP: 45 min. + chilling • **BAKE:** 25 min. + cooling • **MAKES:** 5 dozen

- 1 pkg. red velvet cake mix (regular size)
- 1 can (16 oz.) cream cheese frosting
- 1 lb. each white, milk chocolate and dark chocolate candy coating

1. Prepare and bake cake mix according to package directions, using a 13x9-in. baking pan. Cool completely.
2. Crumble the cake into a large bowl. Add frosting; beat well. Refrigerate until easy to handle, about 1 hour. Shape into 1½-in. balls; transfer to waxed paper-lined baking sheets. Refrigerate at least 1 hour.
3. In a microwave, melt white candy coating; stir until smooth. Dip 20 cake balls into coating; allow excess to drip off. Return to baking sheets; let stand until set. Repeat with milk chocolate and dark chocolate coatings and remaining cake balls. If desired, drizzle with additional candy coating. Store in airtight containers.
FREEZE OPTION: *Freeze uncoated cake balls in freezer containers, layered between waxed paper. To use, thaw in covered containers. Dip into coatings as directed.*
1 CAKE BALL: *206 cal., 11g fat (7g sat. fat), 11mg chol., 79mg sod., 28g carb. (24g sugars, 0 fiber), 1g pro.*

CHAI CHOCOLATE CHIP SHORTBREAD

I've always loved the taste of chai tea, so I decided to try to incorporate it into one of my recipes. Everyone who samples my shortbread can't believe how delicious it is.
—*Paula Marchesi, Lenhartsville, PA*

- -

PREP: 35 min. + chilling • **BAKE:** 15 min./batch + cooling
MAKES: 4 dozen

1¾	cups all-purpose flour
½	cup sugar
⅓	cup cornstarch
¼	cup vanilla chai tea latte mix
1	cup cold butter, cubed
½	tsp. vanilla extract
¾	cup finely chopped almonds
⅓	cup miniature semisweet chocolate chips
4	oz. semisweet chocolate, melted

1. Place flour, sugar, cornstarch and latte mix in a food processor; pulse until blended. Add butter and vanilla; pulse until butter is the size of peas. Add the almonds and chocolate chips; pulse until blended.
2. Transfer to a lightly floured surface; knead until dough forms a ball. Divide dough into 6 portions; wrap separately. Refrigerate at least 30 minutes or until firm enough to roll.
3. Preheat oven to 375°. On a lightly floured surface, roll each portion of dough into a 5-in. circle. Cut into 8 wedges. Place 2 in. apart on ungreased baking sheets.
4. Bake 15-18 minutes or until edges begin to brown. Cool for 1 minute before removing from pans to wire racks. Drizzle with melted chocolate; let stand until set. Store in airtight containers.
1 COOKIE: *97 cal., 6g fat (3g sat. fat), 10mg chol., 36mg sod., 9g carb. (4g sugars, 1g fiber), 1g pro.*

VIENNESE COOKIES

When I worked at a medical clinic, I became known as the cookie lady because of my love for baking. A Swedish friend gave me this recipe; I often triple or quadruple it so I have plenty to share.
—*Beverly Stirrat, Mission, BC*

- -

PREP: 35 min. + chilling • **BAKE:** 10 min./batch + cooling
MAKES: about 3 dozen

1¼	cups butter, softened
⅔	cup sugar
2¼	cups all-purpose flour
1⅔	cups ground almonds
1	cup apricot preserves
2	cups semisweet chocolate chips
2	Tbsp. shortening

1. In a large bowl, cream butter and sugar until light and fluffy, 5-7 minutes. Combine flour and ground almonds; gradually add to creamed mixture and mix well. Cover and refrigerate 1 hour.
2. Preheat oven to 350°. On a lightly floured surface, roll dough to ¼-in. thickness. Cut with a floured 2¼-in. round cookie cutter. Place 2 in. apart on ungreased baking sheets. Bake 7-9 minutes or until the edges are lightly browned. Remove to wire racks to cool completely.
3. Spread jam on the bottoms of half of the cookies; top with remaining cookies. In a microwave, melt chocolate chips and shortening; stir until smooth. Dip half of each sandwich cookie into chocolate mixture; allow excess to drip off. Place on waxed paper until set. Store in an airtight container.
1 SERVING: *186 cal., 11g fat (6g sat. fat), 16mg chol., 47mg sod., 21g carb. (12g sugars, 1g fiber), 2g pro.*

CHOCOLATE LEBKUCHEN

Having lived in Germany, I try to keep my German cooking as authentic as possible. These lovely lebkuchen are a culinary Christmas custom.
—Cathy Lemmon, Quinlan, TX

PREP: 1 hour + cooling
BAKE: 15 min. + cooling
MAKES: about 1½ dozen

1 cup plus 2 Tbsp. all-purpose flour
¼ cup sugar
   Dash salt
⅓ cup cold butter, cubed
3 Tbsp. water
1 tsp. vanilla extract

TOPPING
¼ cup butter, softened
¼ cup sugar
1 large egg, room temperature
1 Tbsp. canola oil
⅔ cup quick-cooking oats
½ cup all-purpose flour
⅓ cup ground almonds
⅓ cup ground hazelnuts
¼ cup baking cocoa
1 tsp. baking powder
½ tsp. ground cinnamon
¼ tsp. each ground cloves, cardamom
   and allspice
¼ cup finely chopped candied
   lemon peel
¼ cup finely chopped candied
   orange peel

GLAZE
6 oz. semisweet chocolate, chopped
2 oz. unsweetened chocolate, chopped
¼ cup butter, cubed

1. Preheat oven to 325°. In a small bowl, combine flour, sugar and salt; cut in the butter until mixture resembles coarse crumbs. Combine water and vanilla; gradually add to crumb mixture, tossing with a fork until dough forms a ball.

2. On a lightly floured surface, roll out dough to ¹⁄₁₆-in. thickness. Cut with a floured 2½-in. round cookie cutter. Place on ungreased baking sheets. Bake until set, 8-10 minutes. Remove from pans to wire racks to cool.

3. For topping, in a small bowl, cream the butter and sugar until light and fluffy, 5-7 minutes. Beat in egg and oil. Combine the oats, flour, nuts, cocoa, baking powder and spices; gradually add to the creamed mixture and mix well. Fold in the candied citrus peels.

4. Drop 1 rounded Tbsp. topping onto each cookie; gently press down. Place 2 in. apart on ungreased baking sheets. Bake at 325° until set, 13-16 minutes. Remove from pans to wire racks to cool.

5. In a microwave-safe bowl, melt the chocolate and butter; stir until smooth. Dip each cookie halfway in chocolate; allow excess to drip off. Place on waxed paper; let stand until set. Store in airtight containers.

1 COOKIE: *238 cal., 14g fat (8g sat. fat), 32mg chol., 122mg sod., 27g carb. (15g sugars, 2g fiber), 4g pro.*

CRANBERRY COOKIES WITH BROWNED BUTTER GLAZE

I won a baking contest with these chunky glazed cookies that are so easy, even novice bakers can pull them off. What makes them special? Fresh cranberries.
—Laurie Cornett, Charlevoix, MI

PREP: 40 min.
BAKE: 10 min./batch + cooling
MAKES: about 4½ dozen

½	cup butter, softened
1	cup sugar
¾	cup packed brown sugar
1	large egg, room temperature
2	Tbsp. orange juice
3	cups all-purpose flour
1	tsp. baking powder
½	tsp. salt
¼	tsp. baking soda
¼	cup 2% milk
2½	cups coarsely chopped fresh cranberries
1	cup white baking chips
1	cup chopped pecans or walnuts

GLAZE

⅓	cup butter, cubed
2	cups confectioners' sugar
1½	tsp. vanilla extract
3	to 4 Tbsp. water

1. Preheat oven to 375°. In a large bowl, cream together butter and sugars until light and fluffy, 5-7 minutes. Beat in egg and orange juice. In another bowl, whisk flour, baking powder, salt and baking soda; add to creamed mixture alternately with milk. Stir in the cranberries, baking chips and pecans.

2. Drop dough by level tablespoonfuls 1 in. apart onto greased baking sheets. Bake 10-12 minutes or until light brown. Remove from pans to wire racks to cool completely.

3. For glaze, in a small heavy saucepan, melt butter over medium heat. Heat 5-7 minutes or until golden brown, stirring constantly. Remove from heat. Stir in confectioners' sugar, vanilla and enough water to reach a drizzling consistency. Drizzle over cookies. Let stand until set.

1 COOKIE: 130 cal., 5g fat (3g sat. fat), 12mg chol., 66mg sod., 19g carb. (13g sugars, 1g fiber), 1g pro.

APRICOT-FILLED SANDWICH COOKIES

I bake these delightful cookies every year for Christmas. When I bring a big tray of homemade treats to share with the faculty at school, these bites are always the first to disappear. I've even had requests to make them for wedding receptions.
—Deb Lyon, Bangor, PA

PREP: 40 min.
BAKE: 10 min./batch + cooling
MAKES: about 4 dozen

1	cup butter, softened
1	cup sugar
2	large eggs, room temperature
3	cups all-purpose flour
⅔	cup finely chopped walnuts

FILLING

2	cups dried apricots
¾	cup water
¼	cup sugar
½	tsp. ground cinnamon

TOPPING

½	cup semisweet chocolate chips
½	tsp. shortening
4	tsp. confectioners' sugar

1. Preheat oven to 350°. Cream the butter and 1 cup sugar until light and fluffy, 5-7 minutes. Beat in the eggs. Combine the flour and walnuts; gradually beat into the creamed mixture.

2. Shape dough into 1½-in.-thick logs. Cut logs crosswise into ¼-in. slices. Place slices 2 in. apart on ungreased baking sheets. Bake until the bottoms begin to brown, 10-12 minutes. Cool cookies completely on pans on wire racks.

3. Meanwhile, for filling, combine apricots and water in a large saucepan. Bring to a boil. Cook and stir until the apricots are tender, about 10 minutes. Drain; cool to room temperature. Pulse ¼ cup granulated sugar, cinnamon and apricots in a blender or food processor until smooth. Spread over bottoms of half of the cookies; cover with remaining cookies.

4. For topping, melt chocolate chips and shortening in a microwave; stir until smooth. Drizzle over cookies. Sprinkle with confectioners' sugar.

1 SANDWICH COOKIE: 119 cal., 6g fat (3g sat. fat), 18mg chol., 34mg sod., 16g carb. (9g sugars, 1g fiber), 2g pro.

MINT-FILLED COOKIES

I tuck a peppermint patty inside these bites for a surprise. They will melt in your mouth.
—Karen Nielson, St. George, UT

PREP: 30 min. + chilling
BAKE: 10 min./batch + cooling
MAKES: 40 cookies

- 1 cup butter, softened
- 4 oz. cream cheese, softened
- 1 cup sugar
- ½ cup packed brown sugar
- 2 large eggs, room temperature
- 1 Tbsp. 2% milk
- 1 tsp. vanilla extract
- 4 cups all-purpose flour
- 1 tsp. baking soda
- ½ tsp. salt
- 40 chocolate-covered peppermint patties (1½ in.), unwrapped
- ¾ cup semisweet chocolate chips
- 1 Tbsp. shortening

1. In a large bowl, cream butter, cream cheese and sugars until light and fluffy, 5-7 minutes. Beat in eggs, milk and vanilla. In another bowl, whisk together flour, baking soda and salt; gradually beat into the butter mixture.

2. Divide dough in half; shape each into a disk. Wrap in waxed paper and refrigerate 30 minutes or until firm enough to roll.

3. Preheat oven to 400°. On a lightly floured surface, roll each portion of dough to ¼-in. thickness. Cut with a floured 3-in. round cookie cutter. Place a mint patty in the center of each circle; fold dough over patty. Pinch to seal seams. Place on greased baking sheets, seam side down.

4. Bake 8-10 minutes or until cookies are golden brown. Remove from pans to wire racks to cool completely.

5. In a microwave, melt chocolate chips and shortening; stir until smooth. Drizzle over cookies. Refrigerate until set. Store in an airtight container in the refrigerator.

FREEZE OPTION: *Transfer unrolled disks to a freezer container; freeze. To use, thaw dough in refrigerator until soft enough to roll. Prepare, bake and decorate cookies as directed.*

1 COOKIE: *208 cal., 8g fat (5g sat. fat), 24mg chol., 117mg sod., 33g carb. (21g sugars, 1g fiber), 2g pro.*

CUCCIDATI

The compliments make these worth the effort. It's the best recipe I've found!
—Carolyn Fafinski, Dunkirk, NY

PREP: 30 min. + chilling
BAKE: 10 min./batch + cooling
MAKES: about 5 dozen

- 2 cups raisins
- ¾ lb. pitted dates
- ¾ cup sugar
- 2 small navel oranges, peeled and quartered
- ⅓ lb. dried figs
- ⅓ cup chopped walnuts
- ¼ cup water

DOUGH
- 1 cup shortening
- 1 cup sugar
- 2 large eggs, room temperature
- ¼ cup 2% milk
- 2 tsp. vanilla extract
- 3½ cups all-purpose flour
- 1 tsp. salt
- 1 tsp. baking powder
- 1 tsp. baking soda

GLAZE
- 2 cups confectioners' sugar
- 2 to 3 Tbsp. 2% milk

1. Place the first 7 ingredients in a food processor; cover and process until finely chopped. Set aside.

2. In a large bowl, cream shortening and sugar until light and fluffy, 5-7 minutes. Beat in the eggs, milk and vanilla. Combine flour, salt, baking powder and baking soda; gradually add to the creamed mixture and mix well. Divide dough into 4 portions; cover and refrigerate for 1 hour.

3. Roll out each portion between 2 sheets of waxed paper into a 16x6-in. rectangle. Spread 1 cup filling lengthwise down the center of each. Starting at a long side, fold dough over filling; fold the other side over the top. Pinch seams and edges to seal. Cut each rectangle diagonally into 1-in. strips. Place seam side down on parchment-lined baking sheets.

4. Bake at 400° for 10-14 minutes or until the edges are golden brown. Cool for 10 minutes before removing from pans to wire racks to cool completely.

5. Combine confectioners' sugar and enough milk to achieve the desired consistency; drizzle over cool cookies. Store in an airtight container.

1 COOKIE: *132 cal., 4g fat (1g sat. fat), 7mg chol., 67mg sod., 24g carb. (17g sugars, 1g fiber), 1g pro.*

CHOCOLATE-DIPPED CRANBERRY COOKIES

These pretty pink cookies always turn out so tender. They are the hit of my holiday!
—Barbara Nowakowski,
North Tonawanda, NY

PREP: 25 min.
BAKE: 15 min./batch + cooling
MAKES: 3½ dozen

- 1 cup shortening
- 1 cup sugar
- 1 large egg, room temperature
- 1 tsp. vanilla extract
- 2 cups all-purpose flour
- 1 tsp. baking powder
- ½ tsp. salt
- 2 cups coarsely chopped fresh or frozen cranberries
- 2 cups semisweet chocolate chips
- 2 Tbsp. shortening
- 1¼ cups chopped walnuts, optional

1. Preheat oven to 350°. In a large bowl, cream shortening and sugar until light and fluffy. Beat in egg and vanilla. Combine flour, baking powder and salt; gradually add to the creamed mixture and mix well. Using paper towels, lightly pat chopped cranberries dry; stir into dough.

2. Drop dough by rounded teaspoonfuls 2 in. apart onto baking sheets coated with cooking spray. Bake until lightly browned, 11-13 minutes. Remove cookies to wire racks to cool.

3. In a microwave, melt chocolate chips and shortening; stir until smooth. Dip each cookie halfway into the chocolate; place on waxed paper. Sprinkle with walnuts if desired. Let stand until set.

FREEZE OPTION: *Drop cookie dough by rounded teaspoonfuls onto baking sheets; cover and freeze until firm. Transfer cookie dough balls to a freezer container. May be frozen for up to 3 months. To use, bake frozen cookie dough as directed, increasing time by 3-4 minutes. Proceed with recipe as directed.*

1 COOKIE: *130 cal., 8g fat (3g sat. fat), 5mg chol., 40mg sod., 15g carb. (9g sugars, 1g fiber), 1g pro.*

BARKS, BRITTLES & CANDIES

These tempting sweets make the perfect holiday gift for co-workers, neighbors and friends—whether right next door or thousands of miles away. Easy to make and easy to ship, these delicious morsels are Christmas perfection.

CRANBERRY MACADAMIA BARK

This nutty, fruity bark makes a welcome gift. I fill special Christmas tins with it for family and friends.
—*Pamela Galiardi, San Jose, CA*

PREP: 10 min. + chilling • **COOK:** 5 min. • **MAKES:** about 1¼ lbs.

1 lb. white candy coating, coarsely chopped
1 jar (3 oz.) macadamia nuts
½ cup dried cranberries

1. Line a baking sheet with parchment or waxed paper. In a microwave, melt candy coating; stir until smooth. Stir in macadamia nuts and cranberries.
2. Spread onto prepared pan. Refrigerate until firm. Break into pieces.
1 OZ.: 163 cal., 10g fat (6g sat. fat), 0 chol., 15mg sod., 20g carb. (19g sugars, 1g fiber), 0 pro.

¾-Liter Mold Jars

+

Elastic Ribbons

+

Reindeer Gift Tags

=

Berry Basket with Lid

+

Color Twist Wool

+

Gift Labels
ENJOY!
ENJOY!

=

7-in. Holiday Loaf Pans

+

Red & White Ribbon

+

Gift Tags
MADE with LOVE

=

REINDEER GAMES

COUNTRY CHRISTMAS

COMFORT & JOY

CUTE PACKAGING IDEAS

Homemade edible gifts deserve creative packaging that strikes a festive note and doesn't hide the goodies! Embellish simple boxes and containers for a special holiday delivery that makes spirits bright.

PECAN CHERRY BARK

I just love to make chocolates at Christmastime. This popular candy combines pecans, chocolate and cherries. It's crunchy, sweet and just plain yummy.
—Sue Kauffman, Columbia City, IN

PREP: 25 min. + chilling
COOK: 10 min. + cooling
MAKES: about 4 lbs.

- ¼ cup butter, cubed
- ½ cup packed brown sugar
  Dash ground nutmeg
  Dash ground cinnamon
- 1¾ cups chopped pecans
- 1 lb. dark chocolate candy coating, coarsely chopped
- 3 Tbsp. shortening, divided
- 1 lb. milk chocolate candy coating, coarsely chopped
- 1 lb. white candy coating, coarsely chopped
- 1¾ cups dried cherries or cranberries

1. In a large skillet, melt butter over medium heat. Stir in brown sugar and spices; bring to a boil. Cook and stir until sugar is completely dissolved, about 3 minutes. Stir in pecans until coated. Spread onto foil to cool.
2. Line two 15x10x1-in. pans with parchment or waxed paper. In a microwave, melt dark chocolate candy coating and 1 Tbsp. shortening, stirring until smooth. Divide between prepared pans, spreading to desired thickness. Refrigerate just until set, but not firm.
3. In microwave, melt milk chocolate candy coating and 1 Tbsp. shortening, stirring to blend; spread over the dark chocolate layer. Refrigerate until set, but not firm.
4. Repeat with the white candy coating and remaining 1 Tbsp. shortening; spread over top. Sprinkle with cherries and candied pecans, pressing to adhere. Refrigerate until firm. Break into pieces.
1 OZ.: *165 cal., 10g fat (6g sat. fat), 2mg chol., 7mg sod., 20g carb. (18g sugars, 1g fiber), 1g pro.*

CURRY-KISSED COCONUT FUDGE

If you love Thai flavors and love fudge, you'll adore this creamy coconut fudge sprinkled with a hint of sweet curry powder.
—Sarah Meuser, New Milford, CT

PREP: 25 min. + chilling
MAKES: about 4½ lbs. (117 pieces)

- 2 tsp. plus ¼ cup butter, divided
- 4 pkg. (10 to 12 oz. each) white baking chips
- 2 cans (14 oz. each) sweetened condensed milk
- 1½ tsp. coconut extract
- ½ tsp. sea salt
- ¼ tsp. curry powder

1. Line a 13x9-in. pan with foil or parchment; grease foil with 2 tsp. butter.
2. In a large heavy saucepan, cook and stir baking chips, milk and remaining ¼ cup butter over low heat until smooth. Remove from heat; stir in extract and salt.
3. Spread into prepared pan; sprinkle with curry powder. Refrigerate, covered, until firm, about 2 hours.
4. Using foil, lift fudge out of pan. Remove foil; cut fudge into 1-in. squares. Store in an airtight container in the refrigerator.
1 PIECE: *78 cal., 4g fat (3g sat. fat), 6mg chol., 29mg sod., 9g carb. (9g sugars, 0 fiber), 1g pro.*

OREOS & CANDY CANE CHOCOLATE BARK

There are incredible surprises in this festive bark, including dark chocolate, candy canes and cream-filled cookies. We keep a big supply ready for gift-giving.
—Robin Turner, Lake Elsinore, CA

PREP: 15 min. + chilling
MAKES: about 1½ lbs

- 2 pkg. (10 oz. each) dark chocolate chips
- 10 candy cane or chocolate mint creme Oreo cookies, split and chopped
- ⅓ cup white baking chips
- ⅛ tsp. peppermint extract
- 2 candy canes, crushed

1. Line a 15x10x1-in. baking pan with parchment. In the top of a double boiler or a metal bowl over hot water, melt dark chocolate; stir until smooth. Remove from heat. Stir in cookies; spread over the prepared pan.
2. Microwave white baking chips on high until melted, stirring every 30 seconds. Stir in extract. Drizzle over dark chocolate mixture; sprinkle with crushed candy canes. Let cool.
3. Refrigerate until set, about 1 hour. Break into pieces. Store in an airtight container.
1 OZ.: *158 cal., 9g fat (6g sat. fat), 1mg chol., 36mg sod., 21g carb. (18g sugars, 2g fiber), 2g pro.*

> ### Holiday Helper
> If the bark hardens too quickly, you may have trouble getting toppings to stick. Try popping the pan into a warm oven for a minute to soften the chocolate before adding toppings.

PEANUT BRITTLE BARS

Pairing the old-fashioned flavor of peanut brittle with yummy chocolate chips turns these bars into a satisfying treat and sought-after holiday gift. This is the perfect recipe for peanut candy bars.
—Kristin Gleason, St. John, KS

PREP: 15 min. • **BAKE:** 25 min. + cooling
MAKES: about 4 dozen

- 1½ cups all-purpose flour
- ½ cup whole wheat flour
- 1 cup packed brown sugar
- 1 tsp. baking soda
- ¼ tsp. salt
- 1 cup butter

TOPPING
- 2 cups salted peanuts
- 1 cup milk chocolate chips
- 1 jar (12¼ oz.) caramel ice cream topping
- 3 Tbsp. all-purpose flour

1. Preheat oven to 350°. In a large bowl, combine flours, brown sugar, baking soda and salt. Cut in butter until mixture resembles coarse crumbs. Pat into a greased 15x10x1-in. baking pan. Bake until golden brown, 10-12 minutes.
2. Sprinkle peanuts and chocolate chips over warm crust. Combine caramel topping and flour; drizzle over top. Bake until golden brown and bubbly, 12-16 minutes. Cool on a wire rack.
1 BAR: *142 cal., 8g fat (3g sat. fat), 11mg chol., 133mg sod., 17g carb. (11g sugars, 1g fiber), 3g pro.*

COFFEE BEAN BARK

Chopped coffee beans add a yummy crunch to this pretty two-toned bark. Coffee lovers won't be able to resist pieces of the chocolaty candy treat.
—Anne Addesso, Sheboygan, WI

- -

PREP: 15 min. + chilling • **COOK:** 5 min. • **MAKES:** about 1½ lbs.

　2　**cups semisweet chocolate chips**
　2　**tsp. instant coffee granules**
　⅔　**cup coarsely chopped coffee beans, divided**
　1　**pkg. (10 to 12 oz.) white baking chips**

1. Line a 15x10x1-in. pan with parchment or waxed paper. In a microwave-safe bowl, microwave chocolate chips and coffee granules on high for 45 seconds; stir. Continue microwaving in 15-second intervals until smooth, stirring after each interval. Stir in ⅓ cup coffee beans.
2. Spread into prepared pan. Refrigerate until set, but not hard, about 15 minutes.
3. In a microwave, melt white baking chips according to package directions. Stir in remaining ⅓ cup coffee beans; spread over chocolate layer. Refrigerate until firm. Break into pieces.
1 OZ.: *132 cal., 8g fat (5g sat. fat), 2mg chol., 13mg sod., 16g carb. (15g sugars, 1g fiber), 1g pro.*

CHOCOLATE ALMOND BRITTLE

Here in Kern County, there are thousands of acres of almond orchards. I like to experiment with recipes to try to come up with something new. This candy is the result of a lot of taste-testing (somebody had to do it!). I think it turned out rather well.
—Pat Parsons, Bakersfield, CA

- -

PREP: 15 min. + cooling • **MAKES:** about 1 lb.

　1　**cup sugar**
　½　**cup light corn syrup**
　⅛　**tsp. salt**
　1　**cup coarsely chopped almonds**
　1　**Tbsp. butter**
　1　**tsp. vanilla extract**
　1½　**tsp. baking soda**
　¾　**lb. dark or milk chocolate candy coating**

1. Grease a 15x10x1-in. metal baking pan; set aside. In a 1½-qt. microwave-safe bowl, combine the sugar, corn syrup and salt. Microwave, uncovered, on high for 2½ minutes. Stir in almonds; cook on high for 2½ minutes. Add the butter and vanilla; cook on high for 1 minute.
2. Stir in baking soda. As soon as the mixture foams, quickly pour onto prepared pan. Cool completely. Break into 2-in. pieces.
3. Melt chocolate coating in a microwave. Dip 1 side of brittle into chocolate and place on waxed paper to harden. Store in an airtight container.
2 OZ.: *483 cal., 22g fat (12g sat. fat), 4mg chol., 313mg sod., 73g carb. (62g sugars, 3g fiber), 4g pro.*

CHERRY DIVINITY

This light and airy confection is a treat any time of year and especially brightens up dessert platters at Christmas and for Valentine's Day. Replace the cherry gelatin with any flavor to suit your taste.
—Crystal Ralph-Haughn, Bartlesville, OK

PREP: 35 min. • **COOK:** 25 min. + standing
MAKES: 5 dozen

- 2 **large egg whites**
- 3 **cups sugar**
- ¾ **cup water**
- ¾ **cup light corn syrup**
- 1 **pkg. (3 oz.) cherry gelatin**
- 1 **cup chopped walnuts**

1. Place egg whites in the bowl of a large stand mixer; let stand at room temperature for 30 minutes. Meanwhile, line three 15x10x1-in. baking pans with waxed paper.
2. In a heavy saucepan, combine the sugar, water and corn syrup; cook and stir until sugar is dissolved and mixture comes to a boil. Cook over medium heat, without stirring, until a candy thermometer reads 250° (hard-ball stage).
3. Just before the temperature is reached, beat egg whites until foamy. Gradually beat in gelatin. Beat until stiff peaks form. With mixer running on high speed, carefully pour hot syrup in a slow, steady stream into the bowl. Beat just until candy loses its gloss and holds its shape, about 5 minutes. Immediately stir in walnuts.
4. Quickly drop by tablespoonfuls onto prepared pans. Let stand at room temperature overnight or until dry to the touch. Store in an airtight container at room temperature.
1 PIECE: *69 cal., 1g fat (0 sat. fat), 0 chol., 8mg sod., 15g carb. (12g sugars, 0 fiber), 1g pro.*

HAZELNUT TOFFEE

The Willamette Valley produces a lot of hazelnuts, so this recipe is truly representative of our area. I always make plenty of this delicious toffee to serve at Christmas and give as gifts.
—Earlene Ertelt, Woodburn, OR

PREP: 15 min. • **COOK:** 15 min. + standing
MAKES: 2 lbs.

- 1¾ **cups finely chopped hazelnuts**
- 1½ **cups sugar**
- ½ **cup water**
- ⅓ **cup light corn syrup**
- 1 **cup butter**
- ¼ **tsp. salt**
- ¼ **tsp. baking soda**
- ¼ **tsp. orange extract**
- 1 **cup semisweet chocolate chips**

1. Place hazelnuts in a greased 15x10x1-in. baking pan. Bake at 300° until toasted, about 15 minutes; set aside.
2. In a large heavy saucepan, combine sugar, water and corn syrup; bring to a boil over medium heat. Cover and boil for 2 minutes. Stir in butter; cook over medium heat, stirring occasionally, until a thermometer reads 300°-310° (hard-crack stage). Remove from heat; quickly stir in salt, baking soda, orange extract and 1¼ cups toasted hazelnuts.
3. Pour onto a greased baking sheet and spread to ¼-in. thickness. Sprinkle with chocolate chips. Let stand until chocolate is melted, about 5 minutes; spread chocolate over toffee. Sprinkle with remaining ½ cup hazelnuts. Let stand for 1 hour. Break into pieces.
1 OZ.: *163 cal., 11g fat (5g sat. fat), 15mg chol., 77mg sod., 17g carb. (15g sugars, 1g fiber), 1g pro.*

CINNAMON ALMOND BRITTLE

It simply wouldn't be Christmas at our house without this old-time favorite twist on peanut brittle. No one believes how easy it is to make!
—Lynette Kleinschmidt, Litchfield, MN

PREP: 15 min. • **COOK:** 20 min. + cooling
MAKES: about 2 lbs.

 1 tsp. plus 3 Tbsp. butter, cubed
 2 cups sugar
 ¾ cup light corn syrup
 ¼ cup water
 3 cups slivered almonds, toasted
 2 tsp. ground cinnamon
 ½ tsp. salt
 1½ tsp. baking soda
 1 tsp. vanilla extract

1. Preheat oven to 200°. Grease 2 baking sheets with 1 tsp. butter; place in oven to warm.
2. In a large heavy saucepan, combine sugar, corn syrup and water. Bring to a boil, stirring constantly to dissolve sugar. Using a pastry brush dipped in water, wash down the sides of the pan to eliminate sugar crystals. Cook, without stirring, over medium heat until a candy thermometer reads 240° (soft-ball stage). Stir in almonds, cinnamon, salt and remaining 3 Tbsp. butter; cook until thermometer reads 300° (hard-crack stage), stirring frequently and brushing sides of pan as needed.
3. Remove from heat; stir in baking soda and vanilla. Immediately pour onto prepared pans, spreading to ¼-in. thickness. Cool completely.
4. Break brittle into pieces. Store in an airtight container between layers of waxed paper.
1 OZ.: *142 cal., 6g fat (1g sat. fat), 3mg chol., 111mg sod., 21g carb. (19g sugars, 1g fiber), 2g pro.*

OLD-TIME BUTTER CRUNCH CANDY

Both my children and my grandchildren say the season wouldn't be the same without the big tray of candies and cookies I prepare. This one's the most popular part of that collection. We love the nutty pieces draped in chocolate.
—Mildred Duffy, Bella Vista, AR

PREP: 15 min. + cooling • **COOK:** 25 min. • **MAKES:** about 2 lbs.

- 1 cup butter
- 1¼ cup sugar
- 2 Tbsp. light corn syrup
- 2 Tbsp. water
- 2 cups finely chopped toasted almonds
- 8 milk chocolate candy bars (1.55 oz. each)

1. Line a 13x9-in. pan with foil; set aside. Using part of the butter, grease the sides of a large heavy saucepan. Add the remaining butter to the saucepan; melt over low heat. Add sugar, corn syrup and water. Cook and stir over medium heat until a candy thermometer reads 300° (hard-crack stage).
2. Remove from the heat and stir in almonds. Quickly pour into the prepared pan, spreading to cover bottom of pan. Cool completely. Carefully invert pan to remove candy in 1 piece; remove foil.
3. Melt half of the chocolate in a double boiler or microwave-safe bowl; spread over top of candy. Let cool. Turn candy over and repeat with remaining chocolate; cool.
4. Break into 2-in. pieces. Store in an airtight container.
2 OZ.: *375 cal., 26g fat (12g sat. fat), 35mg chol., 137mg sod., 34g carb. (29g sugars, 3g fiber), 5g pro.*

LIME-IN-THE-COCONUT ALMOND BARK

I love the combination of flavors in this tropical treat, and it takes mere minutes to make.
—Julie Beckwith, Crete, IL

TAKES: 25 min. • **MAKES:** about 1 lb.

- 1 pkg. (10 to 12 oz.) white baking chips
- 4 tsp. shortening
- 2 to 4 drops green food coloring, optional
- ½ cup sweetened shredded coconut, toasted
- ½ cup chopped almonds, toasted
- 4 tsp. grated lime zest

1. Line a 9-in. square baking pan with foil; set aside. In a microwave, melt chips and shortening; stir until smooth. Stir in food coloring if desired. Stir in the coconut, almonds and lime zest. Spread into prepared pan. Chill until firm, 10-15 minutes.
2. Break into small pieces. Store in an airtight container at room temperature.
1 OZ.: *143 cal., 10g fat (5g sat. fat), 2mg chol., 24mg sod., 13g carb. (12g sugars, 1g fiber), 2g pro.*

PISTACHIO CRANBERRY BARK

This bark makes a lovely holiday gift from the kitchen. Fill a plate or cup with candy, then gather up clear cellophane around it and tie with red and green ribbons.
—Susan Wacek, Pleasanton, CA

PREP: 20 min. + chilling • **MAKES:** about 1 lb.

- 2 cups semisweet chocolate chips
- 1 cup chopped pistachios, toasted, divided
- ¾ cup dried cranberries, divided
- 5 oz. white candy coating, melted

1. In a microwave-safe bowl, microwave chocolate chips until melted; stir until smooth. Stir in ¾ cup pistachios and half of the cranberries; spread onto a waxed paper-lined baking sheet. Drizzle with melted candy coating. Cut through layers with a knife to swirl.

2. Sprinkle with the remaining pistachios and cranberries. Refrigerate until firm.

3. Cut or break into pieces. Store in an airtight container in the refrigerator.

1 OZ.: 215 cal., 12g fat (6g sat. fat), 0 chol., 36mg sod., 28g carb. (24g sugars, 2g fiber), 3g pro.

Almond Cranberry Bark: Substitute slivered almonds for the pistachios.

Cherry Pretzel Bark: Substitute ½ cup each slivered almonds and crushed pretzels for the pistachios and chopped dried cherries for the cranberries.

Chocolate Peppermint Bark: Omit pistachios and cranberries. Stir ½ cup crushed peppermint candies into melted chocolate. Sprinkle swirled chocolate with another ½ cup crushed peppermint candies.

CHOCOLATE CARAMEL CANDY

This dazzling treat tastes like a Snickers bar but has homemade flavor beyond compare. When I entered it in a recipe contest at our harvest festival, it won five ribbons, including grand prize and the judges' special award.
—Jane Meek, Pahrump, NV

PREP: 45 min. + chilling
MAKES: about 8 dozen

- 2 tsp. butter
- 1 cup milk chocolate chips
- ¼ cup butterscotch chips
- ¼ cup creamy peanut butter

FILLING
- ¼ cup butter
- 1 cup sugar
- ¼ cup evaporated milk
- 1½ cups marshmallow creme
- ¼ cup creamy peanut butter
- 1 tsp. vanilla extract
- 1½ cups chopped salted peanuts

CARAMEL LAYER
- 1 pkg. (14 oz.) caramels
- ¼ cup heavy whipping cream

ICING
- 1 cup (6 oz.) milk chocolate chips
- ¼ cup butterscotch chips
- ¼ cup creamy peanut butter

1. Line a 13x9-in. pan with foil; grease foil with 2 tsp. butter and set aside.

2. In a small saucepan, combine milk chocolate chips, butterscotch chips and peanut butter; stir over low heat until melted and smooth. Spread into the prepared pan. Refrigerate until set.

3. For filling, in a small heavy saucepan, melt butter over medium heat. Add sugar and milk; bring to a gentle boil. Reduce heat to medium-low; cook and stir for 5 minutes. Remove from heat; stir in marshmallow creme, peanut butter and vanilla until smooth. Add peanuts. Spread over first layer. Refrigerate until set.

4. For caramel layer, in a small heavy saucepan, combine caramels and cream; stir over low heat until melted and smooth. Cook and stir 4 minutes. Spread over filling. Refrigerate until set.

5. For icing, in another saucepan, combine milk chocolate chips, butterscotch chips and peanut butter; stir over low heat until melted and smooth. Pour over the caramel layer. Refrigerate at least 4 hours or overnight.

6. Remove from the refrigerator 20 minutes before cutting. Remove from pan and cut into 1-in. squares. Store in an airtight container.

1 PIECE: 86 cal., 5g fat (2g sat. fat), 4mg chol., 41mg sod., 10g carb. (9g sugars, 0 fiber), 2g pro.

HOLIDAY WHITE CHOCOLATE FUDGE

When December arrives, friends and family eagerly await my creamy white fudge. It's a little something different from the traditional chocolate.
—Gioviana Buser, Riverside, CA

- -

PREP: 10 min. • **COOK:** 15 min. + chilling
MAKES: about 3 lbs. (117 pieces)

- 1½ tsp. plus ¾ cup butter, softened, divided
- 3 cups sugar
- 1 can (5 oz.) evaporated milk (about ⅔ cup)
- 1 pkg. (12 oz.) white baking chips
- 1 jar (7 oz.) marshmallow creme
- 1 tsp. vanilla extract

1. Line a 13x9-in. pan with foil; grease foil with 1½ tsp. butter.
2. In a heavy saucepan, combine sugar, milk and remaining ¾ cup butter; bring to a rapid boil over medium heat, stirring constantly. Boil 4 minutes, stirring constantly.
3. Remove from heat; stir in baking chips and marshmallow creme until melted. Stir in vanilla. Immediately spread into prepared pan. Refrigerate until firm, 1-2 hours.
4. Using foil, lift fudge out of pan. Remove foil; cut fudge into 1-in. squares. Store between layers of waxed paper in an airtight container.
1 PIECE: *54 cal., 2g fat (1g sat. fat), 4mg chol., 15mg sod., 8g carb. (8g sugars, 0 fiber), 0 pro.*

TIGER BUTTER BARK CANDY

Fans of tiger butter fudge will revel in this version that is similar to bark candy. The chocolate swirls are pretty, and the creamy peanut flavor is a treat for the taste buds.
—Philip Jones, Lubbock, TX

- -

PREP: 10 min. + chilling • **COOK:** 5 min. • **MAKES:** about 1¼ lbs.

- 1 lb. white candy coating, coarsely chopped
- ½ cup chunky peanut butter
- ½ cup semisweet chocolate chips
- ½ tsp. shortening

1. Line a 15x10x1-in. pan with parchment or waxed paper. In a microwave, melt candy coating and peanut butter; stir until smooth. Spread into prepared pan.
2. In microwave, melt chocolate chips and shortening, stirring to blend. Drizzle over top; cut through mixtures with a knife to swirl.
3. Refrigerate until firm. Break into pieces.
1 OZ.: *179 cal., 11g fat (7g sat. fat), 0 chol., 32mg sod., 20g carb. (18g sugars, 1g fiber), 2g pro.*

SPICED RUM-NUT BRITTLE

Seasoned with cayenne pepper and cinnamon, this spicy microwave brittle packs its own heat to warm up holiday visitors. It makes a great stocking stuffer!
—Terri McKitrick, Delafield, WI

- -

PREP: 25 min. + cooling • **MAKES:** about 1 lb.

1 cup sugar
½ cup light corn syrup
½ cup chopped cashews
½ cup chopped pecans
1 tsp. butter
½ tsp. ground cinnamon
¼ tsp. cayenne pepper
⅛ tsp. salt
  Pinch ground nutmeg
1 tsp. baking soda
½ tsp. rum extract
½ tsp. vanilla extract

1. Grease a 15x10x1-in. pan; set aside.
2. In a 2-qt. microwave-safe bowl, combine sugar and corn syrup. Microwave, uncovered, on high for 3 minutes; stir. Microwave 2½ minutes longer.
3. Stir in the cashews, pecans, butter, cinnamon, cayenne, salt and nutmeg. Microwave, uncovered, on high for 2 minutes or until mixture turns a light amber color (mixture will be very hot).
4. Quickly stir in baking soda and extracts until light and foamy. Immediately pour into prepared pan; spread with a metal spatula. Cool completely.
5. Break into pieces; store in an airtight container.

1 OZ.: *263 cal., 9g fat (2g sat. fat), 1mg chol., 267mg sod., 46g carb. (43g sugars, 1g fiber), 2g pro.*

BANANA CREAM CHOCOLATE TRUFFLES

This truffle recipe was created from ripe bananas and my imagination, and the outcome blew my family and friends away! I don't particularly like bananas, but I could eat these truffles all day long.
—Michele Lassuy, Orlando, FL

- -

PREP: 35 min. + freezing
MAKES: about 4 dozen

1 pkg. (14.3 oz.) Golden Oreo cookies
1 pkg. (8 oz.) cream cheese, softened
2 tsp. banana extract
⅓ cup mashed ripe banana
1 lb. milk chocolate candy coating, melted
  Dried banana chips, coarsely crushed

1. Pulse cookies in a food processor until fine crumbs form. In a bowl, beat cream cheese and extract until blended. Beat in banana. Stir in cookie crumbs. Freeze, covered, until firm enough to shape, about 2 hours.
2. Shape mixture into 1-in. balls. Dip cookie balls in candy coating; place on waxed paper-lined baking sheets. Top immediately with banana chips.
3. Refrigerate until set, about 30 minutes. Store in a covered container in the refrigerator.

1 TRUFFLE: *110 cal., 6g fat (4g sat. fat), 5mg chol., 45mg sod., 13g carb. (9g sugars, 0 fiber), 1g pro.*

Holiday Helper

To coat the truffles, we used 2 forks to dip and turn them in the chocolate coating. To crush the banana chips, place them in a zip-top plastic bag and pound them with a meat mallet or rolling pin until broken.

CRUNCH TIME GIFTS

*Even with all your careful planning, it inevitably happens—
you need a gift, and you need it fast! But fast can still be
thoughtful and handmade. All these crunchy, tasty treats
can be made in your kitchen in an afternoon.*

SESAME-GARLIC PUMPKIN SEEDS

This everything mix of pumpkin seeds with other seeds and seasoning is a fun treat. Pop the seeds left from your Halloween jack-o'-lantern in the freezer and use them at Christmas!
—Danielle Lee, West Palm Beach, FL

PREP: 10 min. • **BAKE:** 35 min. • **MAKES:** 2 cups

- 1 large egg white
- 1 Tbsp. canola oil
- 2 cups fresh pumpkin seeds
- 1 tsp. sesame seeds
- 1 tsp. poppy seeds
- 1 tsp. dried minced onion
- 1 tsp. dried minced garlic
- ¾ tsp. kosher salt
- ½ tsp. caraway seeds

Whisk egg white and oil until frothy. Add pumpkin seeds; toss to coat. Stir in sesame seeds, poppy seeds, onion, garlic, salt and caraway seeds. Spread in a single layer in a parchment-lined 15x10x1-in. baking pan. Bake at 325° for 35-40 minutes or until dry and golden brown, stirring every 10 minutes.

¼ CUP: 95 cal., 5g fat (1g sat. fat), 0 chol., 190mg sod., 9g carb. (0 sugars, 3g fiber), 4g pro. **DIABETIC EXCHANGES:** 1 fat, ½ starch.

GLUTEN-FREE ALMOND CRISPIES

Every bite of these cookies contains cinnamon and maple. Your whole family will love them.
—Jean Ecos, Hartland, WI

PREP: 20 min. • **BAKE:** 10 min./batch • **MAKES:** about 3 dozen

- ⅓ cup maple syrup
- ¼ cup canola oil
- 1 Tbsp. water
- 1 tsp. almond extract
- 1 cup brown rice flour
- ½ cup almond flour
- ¼ cup sugar
- 1 tsp. baking powder
- 1 tsp. ground cinnamon
- ⅛ tsp. salt
- ½ cup finely chopped almonds

1. Beat the syrup, oil, water and extract until well blended. Combine the flours, sugar, baking powder, cinnamon and salt; gradually beat into syrup mixture until blended. Stir in almonds.
2. Drop by rounded teaspoonfuls onto parchment-lined baking sheets; flatten slightly. Bake at 350° for 10-12 minutes or until bottoms are lightly browned. Cool for 1 minute before removing from pans to wire racks.

1 CRISPIE: 54 cal., 3g fat (0 sat. fat), 0 chol., 18mg sod., 6g carb. (3g sugars, 1g fiber), 1g pro. **DIABETIC EXCHANGES:** ½ starch, ½ fat.

CHOCOLATE PECAN PIE SNACK MIX

My crowd-pleasing party mix is buttery, chocolaty and nutty. The recipe yields a party-sized portion, but I recommend keeping it covered so it doesn't disappear before the event!
—Annette Niemiec, Scottsdale, AZ

TAKES: 30 min. • **MAKES:** 4 qt.

- 4 cups Rice Chex
- 4 cups Chocolate Chex
- 4 cups Honey Nut Chex
- 2 cups coarsely chopped pecans, toasted
- 1 cup packed brown sugar
- ½ cup butter, cubed
- ⅓ cup light corn syrup
- ½ tsp. baking soda
- 2 cups semisweet chocolate chips
- 2 Tbsp. shortening

1. In a large bowl, combine cereals and pecans. In a small microwave-safe bowl, combine brown sugar, butter and corn syrup. Microwave, uncovered, on high for 2 minutes, stirring once. Whisk in baking soda. Pour over the cereal mixture; toss to coat.

2. Cook in batches on high in a microwave-safe bowl for 3 minutes, stirring after every minute. Spread onto waxed paper-lined baking sheets to cool completely. In a microwave, melt chocolate chips and shortening; stir until smooth. Drizzle over the cereal mixture; refrigerate until set.

3. Break into pieces. Store in an airtight container at room temperature.

¾ **CUP:** *350 cal., 19g fat (7g sat. fat), 12mg chol., 223mg sod., 47g carb. (30g sugars, 3g fiber), 3g pro.*

FAMILY-FAVORITE CINNAMON CANDY

I have fond memories of standing at my grandmother's stove with my mom and my aunts, helping to make this cherished recipe. Now I share the tradition with my kids.
—Wendy Hagan, Oak Grove, LA

PREP: 10 min. • **COOK:** 40 min. + cooling
MAKES: 3½ lbs.

- 1 Tbsp. butter
- 3¾ cups sugar
- 1¼ cups light corn syrup
- 1 cup water
- 3 pkg. (6 oz. each) Red Hots
- ¼ cup confectioners' sugar

1. Grease two 15x10x1-in. pans with butter; set aside. In a large heavy saucepan, combine sugar, corn syrup and water. Bring to a boil over medium heat, stirring constantly to dissolve sugar. Add Red Hots; return to a boil, stirring carefully until Red Hots are melted, about 10 minutes. (Mixture will be very hot;

wear an oven mitt while stirring to prevent burns.) Cook, without stirring, until a candy thermometer reads 300° (hard-crack stage).

2. Remove from heat. Immediately divide mixture between the prepared pans; cool completely, about 1 hour.

3. Break candy into pieces. Place confectioners' sugar in a large resealable bag. In batches, add candy and toss to coat lightly.

1 **OZ.:** *115 cal., 0 fat (0 sat. fat), 1mg chol., 7mg sod., 29g carb. (27g sugars, 0 fiber), 0 pro.*

STRIPED CHOCOLATE POPCORN

Inspired by the chocolate popcorn at a candy shop, I decided to try something a little different for a bake sale. Sweet and salty and crunchy proved to be a recipe for success.
—Mary Schmittinger, Colgate, WI

PREP: 15 min. + standing • **MAKES:** 17 cups

- 12 cups popped popcorn
- 2 cups miniature pretzels
- 1 cup pecan halves, toasted
- ¼ cup butter, melted
- 4 oz. white candy coating, coarsely chopped
- 2 oz. milk chocolate candy coating, coarsely chopped

1. In a large bowl, combine the popcorn, pretzels and pecans. Drizzle with butter and toss; set aside.
2. In a microwave, melt white candy coating at 70% power for 1 minute; stir. Microwave at additional 10- to 20-second intervals, stirring until smooth. Drizzle over the popcorn mixture; toss to coat. Spread on foil-lined baking sheets.
3. In a microwave, melt the milk chocolate coating; stir until smooth. Drizzle over the popcorn mixture. Let stand in a cool place until chocolate is set. Store in an airtight container.
1 CUP: 177 cal., 12g fat (5g sat. fat), 7mg chol., 170mg sod., 16g carb. (7g sugars, 2g fiber), 2g pro.

Holiday Helper

For an even bigger timesaver, skip the first step and use two bags of microwave buttered popcorn. Think about other add-ins and flavor combinations—miniature marshmallows, or dark chocolate and almonds...the possibilities are endless!

CHEESE CRISPIES

For years I've taken these crispy, crunchy snacks to work. They get high marks from everybody in the teachers lounge. For extra convenience, the dough can be made up to two days in advance.
—Eileen Ball, Cornelius, NC

PREP: 15 min. + chilling • **BAKE:** 15 min./batch
MAKES: about 4½ dozen

- 1 cup unsalted butter, softened
- 2½ cups shredded extra-sharp cheddar cheese
- 2 cups all-purpose flour
- ¾ tsp. salt
- ½ tsp. cayenne pepper
- 2½ cups Rice Krispies
  Pecan halves, optional

1. Beat butter and cheese until blended. In another bowl, whisk flour, salt and cayenne; gradually beat into the cheese mixture. Stir in Rice Krispies. If necessary, turn onto a lightly floured surface and knead 4-6 times, forming a stiff dough.
2. Divide dough in half; shape each into a 7-in.-long roll. Wrap and refrigerate for 1 hour or overnight.
3. Preheat oven to 350°. Unwrap and cut dough crosswise into ¼-in. slices. Place 1 in. apart on parchment-lined baking sheets. If desired, top each slice with a pecan half. Bake until edges are golden brown, 14-16 minutes. Remove from pans to wire racks to cool.
1 CRACKER: 73 cal., 5g fat (3g sat. fat), 15mg chol., 73mg sod., 5g carb. (0 sugars, 0 fiber), 2g pro.

CHOCOLATE-DIPPED PHYLLO STICKS

These light, crunchy treats are wonderful with coffee or alongside sorbet or sherbet.
—Peggy Woodward, Shullsburg, WI

PREP: 30 min. • **BAKE:** 5 min.
MAKES: 20 sticks

- 4 sheets phyllo dough (14x9-in. size)
- 2 Tbsp. butter, melted
- 1 Tbsp. sugar
- ¼ tsp. ground cinnamon
  Cooking spray
- 2 oz. semisweet chocolate, finely chopped
- ½ tsp. shortening
- ½ oz. white baking chocolate, melted

1. Preheat oven to 425°. Place 1 sheet of phyllo dough on a work surface; brush with butter. Cover with a second sheet of phyllo; brush with butter. (Keep the remaining phyllo dough covered with plastic wrap and a damp towel to prevent it from drying out.) Cut phyllo lengthwise in half; cut each half crosswise into 5 rectangles (4½x2¾ in.). Tightly roll up each rectangle jelly-roll style, starting with a long side.
2. Mix sugar and cinnamon. Lightly coat sticks with cooking spray; sprinkle with 1½ tsp. sugar mixture. Place on an ungreased baking sheet. Bake until lightly browned, 3-5 minutes. Remove to a wire rack to cool. Repeat with the remaining phyllo, butter and cinnamon-sugar.
3. In a microwave, melt semisweet chocolate and shortening; stir until smooth. Dip 1 end of each baked phyllo stick into the chocolate; allow extra to drip off. Place on waxed paper; let stand until set. Drizzle with white chocolate.
1 PHYLLO STICK: *42 cal., 3g fat (2g sat. fat), 3mg chol., 19mg sod., 3g carb. (2g sugars, 0 fiber), 0 pro.*

TOFFEE TRIANGLES

These tempting triangles combine crunchy toffee and smooth semisweet chocolate. To make the holiday schedule lighter, make up the cookie mix, then dip into it to whip up batches of triangles as you need them!
—Jeanette Meidal, Savage, MN

PREP: 20 min. • **BAKE:** 15 min. + cooling
MAKES: 5 dozen

- 2 cups Quick Cookie Mix
- 1 cup packed brown sugar
- ⅓ cup butter, softened
- 1 tsp. vanilla extract
- 1 large egg, room temperature
- 1 cup semisweet chocolate chips
- ½ cup mixed nuts, chopped

1. Preheat oven to 350°. In a large bowl, beat the cookie mix, brown sugar, butter and vanilla until mixture resembles coarse crumbs. Add egg and mix well.
2. Spread batter into a greased 13x9-in. baking pan. Bake until lightly browned, 12-15 minutes.
3. Sprinkle with chocolate chips; let stand for 5 minutes. Spread chocolate over bars. Sprinkle with nuts. Let stand until chocolate is set. Cut into squares, then cut in half to form triangles. Store in an airtight container.
QUICK COOKIE MIX: *Beat 1½ cups softened butter, 3 tsp. salt and 2 tsp. baking powder until blended. Gradually add 6 cups flour; mix just until crumbly. Store in an airtight container in the refrigerator for up to 1 month. Makes: 8 cups.*
1 TRIANGLE: *66 cal., 4g fat (2g sat. fat), 9mg chol., 59mg sod., 8g carb. (5g sugars, 0 fiber), 1g pro.*

SPICY MIXED NUTS

Cumin and chili powder give extra oomph to classic homemade nut mix. It's perfect for holiday snacking and gift giving.
—Delores Hill, Helena, MT

PREP: 5 min. • **COOK:** 10 min. + cooling • **MAKES:** 3 cups

- 3 Tbsp. butter
- 1 can (15 to 16 oz.) mixed nuts
- ¼ tsp. Worcestershire sauce
- ½ tsp. salt
- ¼ tsp. paprika
- ¼ tsp. cayenne pepper
- ¼ tsp. chili powder
- ⅛ tsp. ground cumin

In a large skillet, melt butter over low heat. Add nuts and Worcestershire sauce; cook and stir 5-7 minutes. Drain on paper towels. Place nuts in a large bowl. Combine the remaining ingredients; sprinkle over nuts, tossing to coat. Cool. Store in an airtight container at room temperature.

¼ CUP: 225 cal., 19g fat (2g sat. fat), 0 chol., 232mg sod., 10g carb. (2g sugars, 3g fiber), 7g pro.

PEPPERMINT LIP SCRUB

If you're looking for another way to use holiday ingredients to whip up a quick and easy homemade gift, try using peppermint candy to make a festive smile smoother.

After all, even if you're diligent about applying lip balm in the winter, dry lips can be a painful reality in colder climates. Luckily, it couldn't be easier to make a three-ingredient lip scrub that makes a perfect stocking stuffer for friends and neighbors.

To make, place several peppermint candies or candy canes in a food processor, then pulse until finely ground. The candies should be roughly the consistency of sugar. In a bowl, add 1 Tbsp. white sugar and 1 Tbsp. coconut oil. Mix in 2 Tbsp. finely ground peppermint candy until well combined. Place in a small airtight jar. (Makes 6 applications.)

To finish, add a label and a tag with these instructions for how to use the scrub: Scoop out a small amount with your finger, then gently rub the mixture over your lips, focusing on dry areas. If there's extra left on your lips, you can rinse it away with water—but no one's to know if you lick the sweet mixture off!

CANDY SNACK MIX

This crunchy, salty-sweet mix disappears in a hurry when it's set out on snack tables.
—Mary Newsom, Grand Ridge, FL

TAKES: 15 min. • **MAKES:** 25 cups

1 pkg. (24 oz.) roasted peanuts
1 pkg. (19.6 oz.) Golden Grahams cereal
1 pkg. (15 oz.) raisins
½ cup butter, cubed
12 oz. white candy coating, coarsely chopped
2 cups creamy peanut butter
1 pkg. (2 lbs.) confectioners' sugar
2½ cups red and green milk chocolate M&M's

1. In a large bowl, combine the peanuts, cereal and raisins. In a microwave, melt the butter, candy coating and peanut butter; stir until smooth. Pour over the cereal mixture and toss to coat.
2. Working in batches, place sugar in a large bag; add the coated mixture. Close bag and shake to coat. Spread onto baking sheets; sprinkle with M&M's. When cool, store in airtight containers.
¾ CUP: *594 cal., 29g fat (10g sat. fat), 10mg chol., 443mg sod., 79g carb. (60g sugars, 4g fiber), 11g pro.*

> ### Holiday Helper
> You can find clear cellophane bags to hold your goodies at craft stores and gift stores. Then close the top and tie it with a ribbon, and tuck it into a stocking, a Mason jar or a coffee cup. Be sure to attach a tag listing all the ingredients, to help out any of your friends who might have food allergies.

CRUNCHY CHOCOLATE CLUSTERS

This easy candy has a south-of-the-border flavor with the combination of cinnamon, chocolate and coffee. Sweet, salty and crunchy, it's a great no-bake treat.
—Roxanne Chan, Albany, CA

TAKES: 25 min. • **MAKES:** ¾ lb. (12 pieces)

¾ cup coarsely crushed pretzels
¼ cup raisins
2 Tbsp. pine nuts, toasted
1⅓ cups semisweet chocolate chips
½ tsp. instant coffee granules
¼ tsp. ground cinnamon
¼ cup sour cream
Coarse sea salt

1. Place pretzels, raisins and pine nuts in a bowl. In a microwave, melt chocolate chips; stir until smooth. Stir in coffee granules, cinnamon and sour cream. To rewarm, microwave in additional 5- to 10-second intervals. Add to the pretzel mixture; toss until combined.
2. Drop mixture by heaping tablespoonfuls onto a waxed paper-lined baking sheet. Sprinkle with salt.
3. Refrigerate until set, about 10 minutes. Store in an airtight container in the refrigerator.
1 PIECE: *139 cal., 8g fat (4g sat. fat), 1mg chol., 86mg sod., 19g carb. (12g sugars, 1g fiber), 2g pro.*

BOURBON PECAN PRALINES

Like authentic pecan pralines found in New Orleans, these treats are sweet, crunchy and rich!
—Taste of Home *Test Kitchen*

- -

PREP: 15 min. • **COOK:** 25 min. + standing
MAKES: 1 lb. (about 16 pralines)

- ¼   **cup butter, cubed**
- ½   **cup sugar**
- ½   **cup packed brown sugar**
- ¾   **cup heavy whipping cream**
- 1   **cup pecan halves, toasted**
- ½   **cup chopped pecans, toasted**
- 1   **Tbsp. bourbon**

1. Grease 2 baking sheets; set aside. In a large heavy saucepan over medium heat, melt butter. Stir in sugars, then the cream; cook and stir until mixture comes to a boil. Cook, stirring occasionally, until a candy thermometer reads 236° (soft-ball stage), about 20 minutes.
2. Remove from the heat; stir in the pecan halves, chopped pecans and bourbon. Immediately drop by tablespoonfuls onto prepared baking sheets. Let stand until pralines are set and no longer glossy. Store in an airtight container.
1 PRALINE: *183 cal., 14g fat (5g sat. fat), 20mg chol., 28mg sod., 15g carb. (14g sugars, 1g fiber), 1g pro.*

CRUNCHY GRANOLA PRETZEL STICKS

I love this healthier portable snack that's sweet, crunchy and fun to make. If you don't have granola, use other cereals or nuts. You can even do bacon bits!
—Kelly Silvers, Edmond, OK

- -

PREP: 25 min. + standing • **MAKES:** 2 dozen

- 1   **pkg. (12 oz.) dark chocolate chips**
- 24 **pretzel rods**
- 1   **cup granola without raisins**

1. In a microwave, melt chocolate chips in a 2-cup glass measuring cup; stir until smooth. Pour into 1 side of a large shallow dish.
2. Roll each pretzel halfway into chocolate. Allow excess coating to drip off, then sprinkle pretzels with granola. Place on waxed paper until set. Store in an airtight container.
1 PRETZEL STICK: *121 cal., 5g fat (3g sat. fat), 0 chol., 210mg sod., 19g carb. (8g sugars, 2g fiber), 3g pro.*

CHOCOLATE-DIPPED APPLE RINGS

I always include these apple treats in my holiday packages. Sometimes I add a dash of cayenne pepper or chipotle powder to the cinnamon mixture.
—Laurie Bock, Lynden, WA

PREP: 30 min.
BAKE: 2 hours 20 min. + standing
MAKES: about 6 dozen

- 2 lbs. medium apples
- 1½ cups sugar
- 2 Tbsp. ground cinnamon
- 12 oz. semisweet chocolate, chopped
  Assorted sprinkles or small candies

1. Preheat oven to 225°. Core apples and cut crosswise into ⅛-in. slices. In a shallow bowl, mix sugar and cinnamon. Dip apple slices in sugar mixture to coat both sides; shake off excess. Arrange in a single layer on parchment-lined baking sheets.
2. Bake for 1½ hours. Turn slices over; bake 50-60 minutes longer or until the apples are dry and slightly shriveled. Remove from pans to wire racks to cool completely.
3. In top of a double boiler or a metal bowl over simmering water, melt chocolate; stir until smooth. Dip the apple slices in chocolate; allow excess to drip off. Place on parchment or waxed paper; decorate with sprinkles as desired. Let stand until set. Store in airtight containers.

1 DIPPED APPLE RING: *40 cal., 1g fat (1g sat. fat), 0 chol., 0 sod., 5g carb. (5g sugars, 0 fiber), 0 pro.*

POTATO CHIP CLUSTERS

Just three offbeat ingredients add up to one delectable no-bake treat. These super easy, sweet-and-salty candy clusters make for merry munching during holiday trips or parties. They also travel well in containers without melting or getting soft.
—Donna Brockett, Kingfisher, OK

PREP: 15 min. + chilling
MAKES: about 3 dozen

- 9 oz. white baking chocolate, chopped
- 2 cups coarsely crushed ridged potato chips
- ½ cup chopped pecans

In a large microwave-safe bowl, melt white chocolate. Stir in potato chips and pecans. Drop by tablespoonfuls onto waxed paper-lined baking sheets. Refrigerate until set.

1 SERVING: *33 cal., 3g fat (1g sat. fat), 0 chol., 19mg sod., 2g carb. (1g sugars, 0 fiber), 0 pro.*

Holiday Helper

Try shoestring potatoes or Fritos (yes, Fritos!) in place of the potato chips. For easy grab-and-go treats, drop straight into muffin liners.

Getting Ready for the Holidays

PARTY TIMELINE

This useful checklist will help you budget your time wisely and keep your party on schedule.

1 MONTH PRIOR:

- ☐ Choose date and time.
- ☐ Set budget.
- ☐ Determine guest list.

3 WEEKS PRIOR:

- ☐ Send out invitations (ask about any food allergies).
- ☐ Check to make sure you have enough chairs, linens, serving dishes and utensils. Rent or buy more if needed.
- ☐ Arrange for a helper (this would be a good thing to ask an older child or teenager to do).

2 WEEKS PRIOR:

- ☐ Plan the menu; create a master shopping list.
- ☐ Make a large grocery shopping trip to buy nonperishables and ingredients for freezer-friendly dishes. Prepare and freeze any dishes that can be made in advance.

1 WEEK PRIOR:

- ☐ Follow up with any guests who haven't responded.
- ☐ Clean the house thoroughly; put away breakable items.
- ☐ Stock the bar.
- ☐ Choose the music.

2 TO 3 DAYS PRIOR:

- ☐ Notify neighbors if cars will be parked on the street.
- ☐ Clean glassware, china and silverware. Clean and iron table linens.
- ☐ Think about the party space: Where will coats go? Where are the trash cans? How will people move around your house? Move furniture if necessary. Set up cleanup stations (salt, stain remover, club soda, clean cloths) to have at the ready.
- ☐ Put up decorations.
- ☐ Finish grocery shopping.

1 DAY PRIOR:

- ☐ Buy flowers.
- ☐ Finish as much of the cooking and prep work as possible.
- ☐ Do a quick cleanup of the house. Check the guest bathroom—empty trash and set out fresh hand towels.

DAY OF:

- ☐ Chill wine, set up the bar, and slice lemons and any other garnishes.
- ☐ Set the table and/or buffet.
- ☐ Finish any cooking.
- ☐ Set aside space for dirty dishes.
- ☐ Take out trash; have trash cans and extra garbage bags ready.

HOW TO SET THE TABLE

- The dinner plate is the center of the place setting; everything else is positioned around it. Arrange the flatware in the order in which it will be used.

- Forks go to the left of the plate. If you're serving a salad, place a small salad fork to the left of the dinner fork. Place the napkin under the forks or on the plate.

- The knife and spoons go to the right of the plate. Place the knife with the sharp edge toward the plate. The soupspoon goes outside of the teaspoon. If soup is to be served, set the bowl on the plate.

- The desert utensil—whether a fork or a spoon— can either be placed horizontally above the plate or be brought out when dessert is served.

- Smaller plates for salad or bread go above and to the left of the forks. Position the butter plate with the butter spreader across the plate.

- Cup and saucer go above the spoons with the handle to the right.

- Water and wine glasses go to the left of the coffee cup; the water glass goes on the left.

HOW MUCH FOOD & DRINK TO SERVE

Take the stress out of planning with our guide to how many drinks and how much food to stock, course by course. A good rule of thumb is to round up from these and err on the side of having too much—better to end up with a few leftovers than to leave your guests hungry.

APPETIZERS

On average, each guest will have about six appetizers (this number may double if you're having a cocktail-style event). Stock up on bulk items like nuts, pretzels and olives, both to supplement prepared appetizers and to set out before guests arrive.

Guests	Appetizers
5	30 appetizers
10	60 appetizers
20	120 appetizers

ENTREES AND SIDES

- Poultry, fish or meat: 6 oz. per serving
- Grains: 1½ oz. as a side dish, 2 oz. as a main dish casserole
- Potatoes: 5 oz.
- Vegetables: 4 oz.
- Beans: 2 oz.
- Pasta: 4 oz. (main dish)
- Bread such as buns, rolls or cornbread: 1 to 2 pieces

DESSERTS

Guests	Cake/Tart/Pastry	Creamy Dessert	Ice Cream
5	5 pieces	20 oz.	25 oz.
10	10 pieces	40 oz.	50 oz.
20	20 pieces	80 oz.	100 oz.

DRINKS

These guidelines are for parties that last two hours. Figure on 1 lb. of ice per guest.
(if serving one type of alcohol—if you're offering more, reduce the amount of each type)

Guests	Wine/Champagne	Beer	Spirits	Liqueurs	Nonalcoholic
5	3 bottles	15 bottles	1 bottle	1 bottle	5 *(if serving alcohol as well)* / 15 *(if not)*
10	5 bottles	30 bottles	2 bottles	1 bottle	10/30
20	10 bottles	60 bottles	4 bottles	2 bottles	20/60

Holiday Menus

Use these menu cards to record what you served at Christmas dinner and other seasonal gatherings. Make note of beverage pairings, ingredient substitutions or anything else you want to remember about your holiday menu.

OCCASION:

GUESTS:

FOOD:

DRINKS:

NOTES:

OCCASION:

GUESTS:

FOOD:

DRINKS:

NOTES:

OCCASION: _____

GUESTS: _____
_____
_____
_____
_____
_____

FOOD: _____
_____
_____
_____
_____
_____
_____
_____
_____
_____

DRINKS: _____
_____
_____

NOTES: _____
_____
_____
_____
_____
_____
_____
_____

OCCASION: _____

GUESTS: _____
_____
_____
_____
_____
_____

FOOD: _____
_____
_____
_____
_____
_____
_____
_____
_____
_____

DRINKS: _____
_____
_____

NOTES: _____
_____
_____
_____
_____
_____
_____
_____

Holiday Memories

FAMILY MILESTONES

What major events happened in your family this year? Births, weddings, graduations, a new home or job, or a particularly memorable vacation?

_____

_____

_____

_____

_____

_____

_____

_____

_____

_____

_____

MEMORIES OF THE FEAST

What was most memorable about the time spent around the holiday table? What things did your loved ones say or do that you want to remember? Ask your family a question—what are they most thankful for, or which dish was their favorite— and record their answers!

_____

_____

_____

_____

_____

_____

_____

_____

_____

SPECIAL PEOPLE

Whom did you see this year that you haven't seen in a while? Who came to visit, or hosted you? Who sent a particularly lovely card, or a favorite gift?

_____

_____

_____

_____

_____

ALL ABOUT THE COOKIES!

What cookies did you make this year, and which were your favorites?
Who is on your list for getting a cookie platter or box?

_____

_____

_____

_____

_____

RECIPE NOTES

What other recipes did you try this year? Any changes you want to make the next time round?

_____

_____

_____

_____

For Next Year

GIFTS & STOCKING STUFFERS

Have a great idea for a gift for next Christmas?
Make a note of it so you remember it when
Christmas-shopping season rolls around.

_____

_____

_____

_____

_____

_____

_____

_____

_____

_____

_____

_____

_____

_____

CHRISTMAS CARD LIST

Keep track of everyone who should be
on your list to get a holiday card!

_____

_____

_____

_____

_____

_____

_____

_____

_____

_____

_____

_____

_____

_____

_____

RECIPES TO TRY

If there are recipes you wanted to try but just didn't have time for, jot them down here so you can include them in future celebrations.

_____

_____

_____

_____

_____

_____

_____

_____

_____

_____

_____

_____

_____

_____

_____

DECORATION IDEAS

Don't let your brainstorms be forgotten—record your ideas for festive decor here to get a jump on next year.

_____

_____

_____

_____

_____

_____

_____

_____

_____

RESTOCK!

What did you use the last of that you'll need next December? Wrapping paper? Ribbon? Shipping boxes? Make a list and check back next fall.

_____

_____

_____

_____

_____

_____

_____

RECIPE
INDEX

This index lists every recipe in the book in alphabetical order.
Just search for the titles when you want to find your favorites.
On page 240, you'll find an index of all the special bonus content—
including tips, how-tos and a little bit of Christmas history!

P. 104

P. 53

P. 146

BONUS CONTENT